To David with
warm regards

D1206806

THE VINTAGE HOUSE

THE VINTAGE HOUSE

A Guide to Successful Renovations and Additions

MARK ALAN HEWITT and **GORDON BOCK**

W. W. Norton & Company

New York • London

Copyright © 2011 Mark Alan Hewitt and Gordon Bock

All rights reserved
Printed in Singapore
First Edition

For information about permission to reproduce selections from this book, write to Permissions, W. W. Norton & Company, Inc., 500 Fifth Avenue, New York, NY 10110

For information about special discounts for bulk purchases, please contact W. W. Norton Special Sales at specialsales@wwnorton.com or 800-233-4830.

Composition and book design by Jonathan Lippincott
Manufacturing by KHL Printing Co. Pte Ltd
Production Manager: Leeann Graham
Electronic production: Joe Lops

Library of Congress Cataloging-in-Publication Data
Hewitt, Mark A.
The vintage house : a guide to successful renovations and additions / Mark Alan Hewitt, Gordon Bock. – 1st ed.
    p. cm.
Includes bibliographical references and index.
ISBN 978-0-393-70619-2 (hardcover)
1. Dwellings–Remodeling. 2. Dwellings–Conservation and restoration. I. Bock, Gordon. II. Title. III. Title: Guide to successful renovations and additions.

TH4816.H49 2011
643'.7–dc22

                    2010034201

ISBN 13: 978-0-393-70619-2

W. W. Norton & Company, Inc., 500 Fifth Avenue, New York, N.Y. 10110
www.wwnorton.com
W. W. Norton & Company Ltd., Castle House, 75/76 Wells St., London W1T 3QT
1 2 3 4 5 6 7 8 9 0

Page 2: Tudor house, Morristown, New Jersey. (Courtesy of Mark Alan Hewitt.)
Page 6: Poolhouse in Connecticut. (Photo by Durston Saylor; courtesy of John Murray Architectects.)
Page 10: Oakley, Upperville, Virginia. (Photo by Durston Saylor.)

To our spouses, Mia and Michele,
with gratitude and love.

CONTENTS

1. CONSERVING THE VINTAGE HOUSE   11
2. HOW DO HOUSES GROW?   31
3. UNDERSTANDING WHAT YOU HAVE   55
4. NEW SPACES IN OLD PLACES   75
5. ADDITIONS THAT STAY IN TUNE   119
6. BLOWING HOT AND COLD   155
7. FACING THE NEIGHBORHOOD   175
8. OUTSTANDING OUTBUILDINGS   205
9. THE REAL DEAL   233
10. THE LONG VIEW   267

Further Reading   279
Resources for Vintage House Owners   281
Glossary   289
Notes   293
Index   297

THE VINTAGE HOUSE

1

CONSERVING THE VINTAGE HOUSE

THIS IS A BOOK ABOUT CONSERVATION—NOT THE kind commonly associated with environmental activism, but nonetheless something deeply meaningful to all who care about the quality of life in America. For centuries Americans have developed house types that fit their cultural, ethnic, and material patterns. These dwellings exist in large numbers in historic urban neighborhoods, in rural areas, in resort colonies, on estates—indeed everywhere that we have chosen to put down roots. Some of them have been preserved as landmarks, museums, or showplaces, but most merely continue to provide shelter and aesthetic pleasure to individual owners. We like to call these dwellings "vintage houses," because they have aged well and because they will continue to be valued not just as real estate but as artifacts of American culture. If you own such a house, do work on such houses, or are interested in vintage homes in general, this book is for you.

During the real estate bubble of the 1990s and 2000s, Americans spent hundreds of millions on home remodeling projects, often spurred by the desire to keep up with their striving neighbors. Harvard's Joint Center for Housing Studies estimated that in 2006 alone, $180 million went to upgrading existing houses. Roughly half of that was spent on "discretionary" improvements such as kitchen and bathroom renovations. Psychologists and economists have speculated on the reasons for these upgrades, generally attributing them to a kind of "I've earned it" sense of entitlement. And there is little question that investment potential often played a part in the motivation to improve an older home. In this book we'll discuss renovation and addition projects without regard for cost or investment potential, but with a deliberate focus on value. Our aim will be to show the intrinsic advantages of home improvement, not the ephemeral fluctuations of the housing market.[1]

11

What distinguishes a vintage house from one that is merely old? Like fine wines and antiques, vintage houses have the stamp of quality and rarity that makes them stand out from the masses of homes that have historically been constructed by real estate speculators. Many are the product of good collaborations between an owner and an architect. Many are the work of vernacular artisans. Some are the result of utopian schemes by visionary developers. All exist because someone, over an extended period of time, has cared enough to preserve something of extraordinary value and artfulness.

"Old houses" of the type that appear in many popular publications today are not necessarily distinctive enough to qualify. Unfortunately for serious preservationists, the recent "old house" craze has been abetted by TV shows and other media created to drive a market for do-it-yourself renovators and real estate mavens who trade on fixer-uppers in America's postwar suburbs. This book will not address the generic old house with little architectural pedigree, but rather quality houses from the great eras of the American home: the late Colonial-Federal period, the Victorian age, the Progressive era of the early twentieth century, and the suburban boom of the mid-twentieth century.

The United States developed its domestic traditions primarily during eras of prosperity and political fervor. Thus, during the early years of the Republic, Neoclassical houses emerged as an adjunct to the nascent democracy. The Greek Revival was our first "national" style, and the plain, durable qualities of houses in this idiom served well in both urban and rural environments. In the mid-nineteenth century a new sophistication developed in the first middle-class dwellings—the country "villas" promoted by Andrew Jackson Downing and the ubiquitous brownstone townhouses that graced most of America's industrial cities. New house types evolved from these early forms as late nineteenth- and twentieth-century suburbs grew on the outskirts of large cities, providing both stylistic and formal models still in use today. Many of the most significant innovations in house design occurred prior to the so-called Modern Movement of the early and mid-twentieth century. Nevertheless, post–World War II building produced a new form of house—the suburban tract dwelling—that had a profound impact on the way we live today. During all of these historical eras architects and builders found a ready market for excellent, innovative designs and durable materials. Many of these houses are now becoming collectable, just as their predecessors did.

The ultimate purpose of this book is to educate owners about how to undertake an addition or renovation that enhances the design and craftsmanship they recognize and appreciate in their own vintage home. Though a renovation project may prove daunting, the prospect of enhancing the treasured spaces and characteristics of your dwelling should encourage you to proceed with confidence if you have the knowledge—not just information, but understanding—required of a true connoisseur.

The authors, who have spent decades studying and renovating fine American homes, share their knowledge in

Greek Revival Houses

During the first years of the nineteenth century, when the young Republic had few symbols to legitimize the democratic spirit, builders in city and country began to use motifs from ancient Greek architecture. Though puzzling to modern eyes, the craze for Greek ornament pervaded all building types from 1810 to 1850. In houses, the temple-fronts and heavy architraves published in handbooks such as Asher Benjamin's *American Builder's Companion* (1827) found their way into the vernacular of housewrights and ordinary farmers. The recognizable details and forms of the Greek Revival house spread rapidly throughout the newly settled regions of the United States. Today thousands of well-preserved examples of this building type exist throughout the Northeastern seaboard, the Southeast, and the Midwest.

Greek Revival cottage, Old Chatham, New York. (Courtesy of Mark Alan Hewitt.)

Greek Revival house in Camden, Maine. (Courtesy of Mark Alan Hewitt.)

Donahue-Wood House, Norwich, Connecticut, 1835. (From the Library of Congress Prints & Photographs Division, HABS CONN,6-NOR,9.)

Villas and Brownstones

During the mid-nineteenth century, as railroads and canals extended commerce westward and cities began to prosper, Americans began to seek more informal forms of dwelling to go with their increasingly leisurely existence. Andrew Jackson Downing, the leading tastemaker of the age, published books extolling the virtues of country living and gardening, and even provided examples of "villas and cottages" that fit into his vision. Eclectic in their decoration and historical associations, these "picturesque" houses began to appear in urban and rural areas. Leading magazines on farming and house-building published examples for builders and owners to follow, spurring the first popular building movement spawned by the media. Styles ranged from Italianate to Rural Gothic. In America's growing cities the modest brick rowhouses of the Colonial era gave way to larger "brownstone" townhouses, complete with double parlors, kitchens, and bathrooms with modern plumbing.

George Vail House, Willow Hall, Morristown, New Jersey. (Courtesy of Mark Alan Hewitt.)

Van Liew-Suydam farmhouse, Middlebush, New Jersey. (Courtesy of the Meadows Foundation.)

Double house, 301–303 East Henry Street, Savannah, Georgia, 1890–91. (From the Library of Congress Prints & Photographs Division, HABS GA,26-SAV, 53V.)

Second Empire style house in New York. (Courtesy of Barbara Krankenhaus.)

the chapters that follow. Each is intended to open doors to information and advice that will benefit owners of homes that are historic but perhaps not destined for museum tours and preservation awards. And, while much that follows is applicable to historic preservation, the point of view here is one of sustainability—that is, how to maintain and grow old houses to fit the needs of the twenty-first century and beyond.

Indeed, our story begins with an analysis of "organic" growth patterns in traditional or vernacular dwellings. Why do such houses look "right" as they age, while many modern houses suffer from "remuddling" and defacement? When you understand some basic characteristics of traditional building, it is not hard to perceive the formal and aesthetic principles that govern the design and construction of a vintage house. Those principles are set forth in the second chapter of this book.

Following this introductory section, we take up issues of design in four chapters, complementing these with chapters on technical matters that concern every homeowner, such as how to find the right materials, including windows and other components, for a successful renovation. Our advice about design comes from our experience with American houses, and from the experience of countless colleagues who look at design and conservation the way we do. Each chapter features not only our expertise but also that of other architects and tradespeople who have spent their lives in the pursuit of excellence.

At the end of the book, we provide resources to help

Bungalows and Mail-Order Houses

Another house-building surge influenced by publications was the late nineteenth and early twentieth-century era of "houses by mail." Not only did Sears, Roebuck market stick-built kit houses that could be shipped to the site on a railcar, but competitors such as Aladdin and Radford also sold variations in stucco, brick, and even concrete to adventurous families from the new middle class. During the Progressive era a zeal for true democratic government produced not only these model suburban houses but also utopian communities with ties to the Arts and Crafts movement. Gustav

Sears house, Rumson, New Jersey. (Courtesy of Mark Alan Hewitt.)

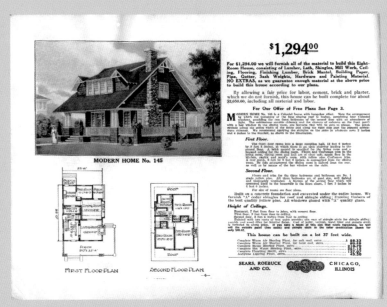

Sears "Modern Home No. 145," 1913. (Courtesy of Sears Archives.)

Stickley's magazine, *The Craftsman*, and other popular publications advocated a rustic lifestyle best exemplified in the bungalow, a low-slung, one-story cottage with an open plan and informal living spaces.

Readi-cut bungalow, sold by Aladdin. (Courtesy of Barbara Krankenhaus.)

Ranches and Levittowners

Following World War II, the GI Bill and the Federal Housing Administration offered returning veterans the opportunity to own a home with little initial cash outlay. Developers, using technologies borrowed from the military, were quick to provide affordable, mass-produced dwellings in places like Levittown, Long Island. In California and the growing Southwest, another popular form, the single-level ranch house, became the norm in new subdivisions. *Sunset Magazine* was a leading exponent of the new leisure living, which featured outdoor patios, trellised gardens, and swimming pools.

"The Rancher" model by Levitt Brothers, Bowie, Maryland, c. 1962. (From the Library of Congress Prints & Photographs Division, HABS-MD 1263.)

Ranch house by Cliff May, 1940, in West Los Angeles, California. (From Cliff May's *Western Ranch Houses by Cliff May*, Lane Press, 1958, p. 56. Used with permission.)

Levittown house. (From the Library of Congress Prints & Photographs Division, Gottscho-Schleisner, Inc., photographer, 1958.)

you find the right people to assist you with your renovation or addition, including a glossary and a list of professionals, craftspeople, and the top manufacturers of historical products for your home.

STEWARDSHIP AND VALUES

Like all objects venerated for their aesthetic and age value, houses benefit from careful stewardship and increase in value when maintained by knowledgeable owners. It is odd that houses, often our most personal, cherished possessions, do not always receive the same careful treatment that collectors give a fine violin, Chippendale highboy, or celluloid fountain pen. Most people understand that vintage musical instruments are ill served by music shops that do not recognize the unique features of the makers of a particular era. When they purchase a vintage guitar, banjo, or cello, they genereally take it to a specialist to be repaired, restored, or serviced, paying whatever price is required to get the best craftsmanship. Why don't we give our houses this kind of care and attention?

Many reasons exist for this neglect. First and foremost, our attitude toward land ownership has given property pride of place over buildings. Many homeowners look first at their "equity" in the land and are hard-pressed to find any value in the bricks and mortar. But even those who are predisposed to preserve dwellings can be caught in a financial pickle when receiving them from relatives in estate distributions. Perhaps a sibling does not see the value in the ancestral home and wishes to sell. Worse, there may be no money left in the estate to pay taxes on the property, forcing its sale. Current tax and land-use laws often stand in the way of continued family ownership of cherished homes.

Long Island once possessed the largest group of country estates in the United States, over nine hundred by one count. Built in the late nineteenth and early twentieth centuries during the great era of capitalist expansion that brought America to its dominance in world affairs, these country houses were constructed with the finest materials available. Their artful buildings and gardens represented the best American design and craftsmanship of the era. After the Great Depression decimated the wealth of most owners of these great country estates, many were sold to institutions and developers in the years after World War II. Only a fraction of these properties exist today. The expansion of the New York metropolitan area gobbled up land for Levittowns and suburban shopping malls, and Long Island was well-positioned to take advantage of new rail and highway links to the city.[2]

Another prejudice peculiar to Americans has been a desire to see "old" buildings look new again during each succeeding generation. What has been called the myth of a "useable past" has driven a lust for shiny surfaces that is much older than the aluminum/vinyl siding salesmen who inhabit the murky bottom of the home improvement market. We seem to prefer things that look brand new. That is one trait that distinguishes our attitudes toward historic preservation from those of Europeans. On the architectural side of this equation, some owners have succumbed to the outdated idea that

A Little History

As we write from our restored 1880s Queen Anne houses—Mark in New Jersey and Gordon in Maryland—our desks are piled high with catalogs for Victorian hardware, reproduction light fixtures, and museum-quality paint colors, as well as paperwork for tax incentives offered by states willing to chip in on the expense of approved work. Our neighbors understand and enjoy our houses, and our families and friends understand them too, because even though they may live in 1970s subdivisions or retirement communities, they have a sense of what vintage houses are about through magazines, movies, and myriad TV shows. Even real estate agents and local banks have added "Victorian" and "Arts and Crafts style" to their vocabularies, and when you Google "old windows" on the Internet, you're awash with information (or at least opinions) on the subject. We've both just come back from teaching college courses on old house architecture, and you've bought a book on the subject. Hard to believe, then, that we both remember when, a few short decades ago, none of this was possible.

For a field so deeply enmeshed with history, the art and science of caring for vintage houses is very young—little more than forty years old. Back in the late 1960s, the pioneering days of the historic preservation movement, restoring an old house was considered by the man on the street to be, at best, some sort of personal eccentricity or, more commonly, evidence that you couldn't afford new. But a different reality lay behind all the paint scraping and plaster patching. This was the Woodstock era, and while some brave new souls were hell-bent on fashioning the dwellings of the future—picture the geodesic domes of Buckminster Fuller or the earth houses of Paolo Soleri—another hearty breed saw the new frontier in the nineteenth-century cores of metropolitan cities. Mind you, this was still the heyday of Modernism with a capital M, and not long after two New York World's Fairs and a man on the moon. The adjective *Victorian* was a dirty word—a dark, gnarly, busy, aesthetic (if you deigned to grant it that), and something to be wiped away to make room for the atomic tomorrow.

And wipe away America did. The urban renewal programs of the mid-1960s saw demolition as the solution to housing pollution. Trouble was, in the zeal to make the world anew urban renewal took with it some perfectly viable and amazing buildings that were unlucky enough to look a little too old-fashioned at the time—never mind that they were designed by some of the giants of architecture and built with materials and labor that would never be mustered again. Pennsylvania Station in New York was the ultimate casualty for many, and finally enough people opened their eyes to see that we Americans were literally burning our cultural bridges, obliterating the architectural past of a country that had barely come of age. But back to houses.

For many folks—your authors included—among the first inklings that a Victorian house could be not only desirable but cool was through the rowhouses of San Francisco. The denizens of the Haight-Ashbury district may have turned THE ESTABLISHMENT on to new kinds of music (acid rock) and clothing (bell-bottom pants, tie-dyed shirts), but the backdrop was the mind-blowing woodwork of those rowhouses. Their Day-Glo purples and hot pinks in pulsing, psychedelic combinations may not have been what the

The historic preservation movement found early residential footing in the restoration of rowhouses in Brooklyn and San Francisco, and similar nineteenth-century cities. (Photos courtesy of Barbara Krankenhaus.)

the mainstream world was part of the zeitgeist. When it came to reviving and restoring century-old houses, it was certainly the only way to go. Through the 1970s (and 1980s) the refrain old-house lovers heard time and again at hardware stores was "They don't make that anymore," so in due course some inspired individuals began making their own—often at first for their own needs, but then as a grubstake in what was an underground economy. When no decorating store had ever heard of Victorian wallpaper, much less stocked it, a young man from Maine (Bruce Bradbury of Bradbury & Bradbury) studied patterns at museums and silk-screened the first new sheets in generations. In the Northwest a second-hand furnishings dealer (Jim Kelly of Rejuvenation) found he had a constant call for 1910s lighting fixtures and shades, so he decided to commission new parts from the decades-

original builders had in mind, but they did wake up Vietnam-era America to the immense creativity of the late nineteenth century. Images of electric decor meets Art Nouveau architecture popped up like brilliant wildflowers across the media, from magazines to record covers to postcards—and in a stroke, Victorian houses were on the path to having cachet again.

At the dawning of what the media then labeled the Counter Culture, craft and remaking civilization on a separate track from old molds of original producers. And in Park Slope in Brooklyn, New York, a local newsletter sharing hard-won information about antique buildings grew from a labor of love by its brownstone-restoring creators and editors (Clem Labine and Patricia Poore) into a national, four-color magazine, *Old-House Journal*. The movement has come a long way in a short time, but anyone who is working on a vintage house today has an easier and better job in their future because of it.

an addition to an old house must be designed in the "style of the moment" in order to reflect the fashions of current designers. Denigration of the integrity of houses as works of art and cultural treasures follows from such attitudes toward the past.

"Age value" is a cultural construct that accrues from a society's reverence for the persistence of an object over long periods of time. This kind of worthiness for preservation is slightly different from "historical value," a concern for the information that artifacts impart through their materials, methods of construction, and telltale stylistic characteristics. Thus, whereas George Washington's Mount Vernon is valuable for its age and unique qualities as an American house, a building of similar vintage may not possess the extraordinary historical significance of this homestead of an American icon. And although the authors have spent much of their careers working on genuine landmark buildings like Mount Vernon, your vintage house is a different animal that requires another level of care.

A third kind of value that is increasingly important in our resource-short world and can be attached to old homes is that of "embodied energy." Old houses, especially vintage houses, were built with the finest materials and technologies of their time, often at great expense. As people become more aware of the environmental cost of human actions, it is clear that the labor and material consumed in the making of all artifacts can

Planting Fields, the home of William R. Coe, is one of the few Long Island country houses to have escaped the development boom of the late-twentieth century. It is now a New York State park and arboretum. (Courtesy of Mark Alan Hewitt.)

be expressed in terms of energy. Scientists are now able to calculate the embodied energy in human-made things, with particular attention given to the energy consumed in making buildings. A little-known fact is that buildings create more waste and generally consume more energy than any other artifact, so it is essential to understand how many resources go into the making of a house. Vintage houses can be valued not only for their age and history, but also for the extraordinary care expended in their construction. And while it is possible to duplicate the fine craftsmanship of past eras, the energy costs of doing so are often prohibitive. This helps to account for why great houses persist while others vanish—when creative energy and fine materials come together, the results are recognized by the entire society.

So the value of a vintage house goes well beyond the price on the real estate agent's listing or the homeowner's insurance policy. That is why careful maintenance, loving attention to details, and recognition of the preciousness of materials should be prerequisites of ownership, and why this book can help you take care of your unique investment.

SUSTAINABILITY AND PRESERVATION

Preservationists like to point out that the "greenest" building is the one that is already built. Environmentalists are Johnny-come-latelie's when it comes to recognizing the importance of saving good buildings from demolition. It is nonetheless critical to understand both the advantages and the limitations of preservation as a strategy for saving energy on a global scale. The first step is a comprehension of the challenges and opportunities presented at the scale of the individual dwelling.

As Stewart Brand has pointed out in his excellent book *How Buildings Learn*, houses share with all buildings a kind of morphology (a formal pattern or type) that can be expressed in a simple diagram. The elements that make up a typical organism are very similar to the components in a typical building, and Brand calls them "shearing layers." Architects know them as skin, skeleton, and finishes, but most people can grasp the diagram (shown on page 32) of Brand's six concentric layers. We'll discuss these in more detail in the next chapter.

Building economists and real estate analysts know that expenditures on renovations and decorating far outstrip the costs of the original structure and services in a typical multifamily dwelling such as an urban cooperative high-rise. An average building will "tear itself apart" every fifty years or so in order to fit the changing requirements of its occupants and urban setting. Some proponents of novel architecture and high-tech inventions believe that this fact makes buildings older than fifty years obsolete, like old automobiles (which, after all, are built for obsolescence). Nothing could be further from the truth.

As we will show, the "bones" and many finishes in vintage houses—assuming they're left in their natural state—improve with age, especially as we lose the knowledge and capacity to reproduce the finely crafted artifacts of our ancestors. Some things become irreplaceable by virtue of obsolete materials and processes, others because the labor required to fabricate them is no longer affordable. When we recognize the uniqueness of these components, we can endeavor to conserve them. It is necessary, when evaluating any artifact worthy of preservation, to single out the unique and potentially nonreplicable elements before proceeding with any new work.

Life is rife with new discoveries and technological advances. Indeed, science and information technology have created an explosion of new potentialities in every aspect of human endeavor. The mechanical systems that control the environment and conserve energy in buildings have changed radically since the nineteenth century, when industrial innovation first transformed housing into the forms we use today. It is always appropriate to consider new building systems—plumbing, heating, electricity, telecommunications, and "smart" electronics—when renovating an older building. These are the "shearing layers" that most often wear out and need replacement in a typical dwelling, sometimes in only seven to ten years. Moreover, as regulations and standards evolve with the new sustainable economy that is contemplated by many governments, houses will be forced to change with the times.

It is essential to be conversant with both emerging technologies that will enter the mainstream and the elements in houses that can persist despite the need for renovation every few decades. A balance between employing new technologies and preserving unique characteristics can be struck, pro-

vided you are aided by professionals who keep abreast of the latest techniques in restoration and reuse. We have found that many of the common mistakes that diminish the value and character of vintage houses are the result of poor comprehension of the relationship between new technology and the historic "fabric" of older buildings, not only by well-intentioned owners but by contractors and design professionals.

In a recent address at the New Jersey State Historic Preservation Conference, the real estate economist Donovan Rypkema attacked "green design" experts for their woeful misunderstanding of the issues surrounding replacement windows in historic buildings. He correctly pointed out that properly sealed window openings, even without double glazing, contribute less to the overall thermal performance of the building envelope (a fancy way of expressing how much energy your house will lose in a typical day) than the roof, walls, and foundation. Manufacturers of window systems play on the homeowner's fear of high energy bills when touting the advantages of replacement windows, resulting in many needless renovations and the loss of priceless historic sashes and glazing, along with the fine old-growth wood that was harvested to make the windows.

Those who purchase a vintage house with a guilty conscience about "sustainability" need not worry. Preserving priceless craftsmanship and rare materials, along with the infrastructure and site construction around a typical historic house, is just about the best medicine our ailing planet can hope for as we consider our carbon footprint.

CONNOISSEURSHIP, OR THE PLEASURE OF THE CELLAR

Richard Jenrette, the multi-millionaire Wall Street financier, has made a name for himself in preservation circles for saving historic houses and bringing them back to their former glory. Although his resources were more limited in his early collecting days, he used his fine eye for great architecture to purchase and restore great houses in North America and the Caribbean more successfully than any man in recent history. When he retired, he set up the Classical American Homes Preservation Trust, a public organization that will make seven homes available for public tours. (Visit www.classical-americanhomes.org for more information.)

Like a true connoisseur, Jenrette is knowledgeable and passionate about his properties. As he said of his formida-

Ayr Mount, North Carolina. One of the houses restored by Richard Jenrette, now open to the public. (Photo by John M. Hall; courtesy of Richard Jenrette.)

ble collection: "I believe I have a role in creating beauty—at least in restoring these beautiful old houses to their former glory and preserving them as models for future generations to enjoy. Nothing pleases me more than to share these houses with sympathetic visitors who, hopefully, will be inspired to return to their home communities and follow my example."[3]

Not many of us possess the kind of wealth and time required to collect and restore historic houses as Mr. Jenrette has done. This, however, does not mean that we are not connoisseurs. Why? *The Shorter Oxford English Dictionary* provides the following definition of *connoisseur*: "A person with a thorough knowledge and critical judgment of a subject, esp. one of the fine arts; an expert in any matter of taste." Derived from the Old French for *knowledge*, the word helps to explain why people collect human-made objects—they want to know more about the subjects of their passion.

Few universities teach courses in connoisseurship, and those that do recognize that textbooks are of little use when you wish to understand subtle gradations in the quality of things like antique furniture or watches. Decades of experience with old houses has taught us that only direct engagement with the fabric of a historic building can provide the tools needed to properly care for the material at hand. So throughout this book we will recommend that owners actively engage with professionals in the restoration and renovation of their houses.

How does one acquire connoisseurship? The thorough knowledge that antiques experts exhibit comes with years of absorption and study, and is passed from one expert to another. A homeowner who immerses himself or herself in the appreciation of architecture and decoration can assimilate much knowledge without ever picking up a hammer, trowel, or bubble level. Books and magazines, and the new world of the Internet, can be the first doorways to such knowledge. In the appendixes of this volume you will find a listing of the essential texts and reference materials that will help you become a maven in the world of historic houses.

The most important factor when approaching connoisseurship is familiarity with the materials and craft traditions required in the construction of vintage houses. As we noted above, traditional building technology is often very remote from contemporary practices, and many errors occur when homeowners fail to recognize this fact. So the first lessons to learn about your home often come from a thorough study of how its materials were used historically, and why they are essential to achieving the authentic qualities you value.

For example, as simple a material as wall plaster can fool all but the best building contractors. Since gypsum wallboard became popular half a century ago, much knowledge has been lost concerning the composition of plaster and techniques of application. Traditional plasters, in use since ancient times, are composed of hydrated lime (calcium hydroxide), water, and sands or other aggregates. These wall finishes are natural and will allow moisture to move through them at a controlled rate. Modern plasters are composed of gypsum

Opposite: George F. Baker house, New York, dining room, also restored by Richard Jenrette. (Photo by John M. Hall; courtesy of Richard Jenrette.)

and aggregates, sometimes with a cement binder. They are similar to gypsum board, and do not allow moisture to penetrate the surface. Modern wallboard "compound" has a similar composition, and may contain acrylic additives or other synthetic compounds. All of these materials have their proper uses, but they should not be combined or used in layers. Old houses with lime plaster walls demand special care, yet these walls seldom get proper maintenance or restoration because of ignorance.

An informed owner or contractor can, with a little common sense, achieve a balance of economy and superior-quality construction by following traditional methods. And because houses are artifacts just like musical instruments or furniture, the patina of age and authenticity will outshine any contemporary example of "reproduction" architecture that uses contemporary techniques.

"Our dream is to live long enough to see the end of our renovation."

(*New Yorker* cartoon by Sipress, March 6, 2006. Used with permission of The Cartoon Bank, *The New Yorker*.)

FACING CHANGES IN YOUR HOME WITHOUT DESPAIR

Much as you may appreciate the unique qualities and aesthetic character of your house, you do not live in a museum. It is easy to be intimidated by the responsibilities of owning a vintage house, especially if it is in a historic district or neighborhood with many fine examples of a style or type. Historic preservation commissions can levy daunting requirements on property owners in a district. And the potential for embarrassment is there if you do not maintain your house at the standard set by competitive neighbors with deep pockets. Moreover, when you tour a major house museum and look at carefully restored rooms with authentic furnishings and decor, it may bring to mind issues you face every day, with the result that you want to run away and buy a trailer.

Owning a vintage house is not for everyone. The mere fact that a house was designed for an era without indoor plumbing or electricity can be a test for the uninitiated restorer. We have all heard stories of homeowners bringing a contractor into their prized domicile and being told that "everything" must be ripped out in order to install insulation, wiring, and a new heating system. But let's face it, most old house owners are ready for some challenges because they know the rewards will be extraordinary. How many challenges? Well, that is the important question.

Several chapters in this book address the issue of how to retrofit and restore a house for contemporary, energy-efficient living. We assume that our readers do not wish to maintain eighteenth- or nineteenth-century standards of hygiene, comfort, or food preparation. We also understand that museum-quality restoration is beyond the capacity and budget of all but the most patient and wealthy owners. That is why this book does not press you into making your house a "historic" artifact that resists all change. Change is a constant in contemporary society, and the environment must adapt to it. Your house is part of the ecology of the planet. It will change (by weathering, decay, natural disasters) whether you like it or not. The challenge is to deal positively with it.

The biggest and most daunting change faced by most homeowners is occasioned by instinctive human needs—the expansion and aging of the family. Birth, marriage, and the onset of old age are life's landmarks, and houses must morph to accommodate them. Standards for space use have changed historically in America, and many older houses were not equipped to handle the needs of the modern household. Few Americans now have live-in servants, so the ubiquitous service wing in most Victorian houses will be of no use today. Renovations of old kitchens and servants' quarters provide much-needed space for mudrooms, laundry rooms, spare bedrooms and other necessities of the contemporary household. But sometimes the house you love may just not be big enough. Expansion of a lovely Victorian may seem viable in the abstract, but making the result harmonious is not as easy as the clever *Good Housekeeping* article you read at the grocery store suggests.

People who respect the characteristics of historic houses are often loath to attempt a major expansion project. Windshield surveys of many historic neighborhoods confirm a fear that a bump-out will turn into a "remuddling," an evocative term coined by critic Lewis Mumford and popularized by *Old–House Journal* to describe the bastardization of fine old homes by uninformed owners (see www.remuddling.org). What if the project turns out badly? Can authentic historic details be created within a reasonable budget? Where can I find the craftsman and designers to make the addition a success? These questions are on the minds of many vintage house owners, virtually from the moment they take possession of their potential money pit.

Not everyone has the time and energy to pursue a high-quality rehabilitation project. The recent spate of magazines and television shows touting the virtues of do-it-yourself home renovation can engender guilt for not having the skills or gumption to undertake a potentially difficult repair in a historic house. We find that this leads to countless failed efforts, often resulting in major damage to the fabric of a good building. Overconfidence in your ability to solve problems can be as dangerous as the fear of making a mistake. Generally the best course of action is to turn to professionals with a proven record of success.

A good architect, contractor, or trade specialist can be

the answer to the technical and aesthetic challenges that face you as a vintage house owner. No professional, however, can stand in for a passionate connoisseur, especially one with intimate knowledge of his or her own habitat. Great houses come into being only as a result of the will of individuals and families to celebrate their own times and identities with a work of art. When the time comes to expand or renovate a fine house, it is equally important that the owner be an advocate for its virtues and drawbacks.

Where to start? The next two chapters will provide a strong platform for your renovation project. First, it is essential to understand the cultural and material patterns that have historically guided the growth of dwelling houses. Once these principles are taken into account, you can examine the physical condition and construction history of your house. Using this information, you can make informed decisions about repairs, upgrades, and new features. Then, with the help of professionals, you can build with the assurance that you are conserving the lasting value of your vintage house for future generations.

2

HOW DO HOUSES GROW?

LIKE ALL ORGANISMS, HUMAN BEINGS INTUITIVELY understand the process of organic growth. Cells develop and multiply, enlarging living things logically to fulfill their genetic profile. Animals and plants adapt to—and interact with—their surroundings. But when it comes to habitat, humans tend to discount the fit between their biological selves and the buildings they occupy. They expand and change houses according to rules much different than those that govern the natural world. Unlike hermit crabs, *Homo sapiens* tend to assume that they are stuck with "shells" that they have outgrown.

Preservation architects deal with change in virtually every project. Designing additions or renovations to historic houses demands knowledge of both architectural history and general principles of formal transformation. Most preservationists are aware of these principles, but for reasons that are explained below, few homeowners follow them when

considering an addition or renovation. A well intentioned but ill-informed homeowner, builder, or architect can wreak havoc with the proportions, scale, massing, and detail of a historic house merely by ignoring its intrinsic formal logic. Like introducing cancer cells into a healthy organism, bad remodeling causes irreparable damage.

Life-cycle alterations in the built environment are much akin to the sequence of creation, growth, decay, and rebirth in nature. Finding a logical pattern behind building growth is a bit like discovering the changing forms of plants and animals. The biologist and inventor Stewart Brand has demonstrated this in *How Buildings Learn*. He traces the kinds of transformation that occur when buildings are reused, expanded, or otherwise changed to fit the requirements of new technologies or users. He begins his analysis with a simple diagram.[1] Using an analogy to plant morphology, this diagram illustrates the layers in a typical building as concen-

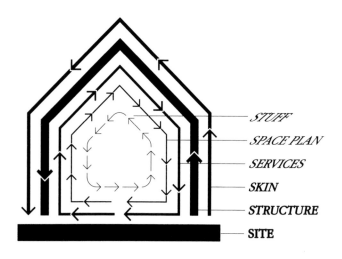

Stewart Brand's diagram of the "shearing layers" in a typical house.
(From Stewart Brand's *How Buildings Learn*, Penguin Books, 1995, p. 13.)

tric rings that start with the occupants and their "stuff." The elements that are closest to our bodies, like furniture, bedding, and appliances, are also the most transportable—hence the French word meubles. Witold Rybczynski discusses the origins of modern comfort in his book *Home: A Short History of an Idea*. He notes that only after the increased security that followed the Middle Ages were castles and manor houses equipped with furnishings that stayed with the house. Prior to that time everything required for a domicile was transported from fortified keep to fortified keep.[2] The ancient origins of our words explain the most salient aspect of our stuff—that we are apt to move it, replace it, or change it often. Paradoxically, when modern architects like Frank Lloyd Wright began

designing built-ins in most rooms, he was making them less adaptable.

Brand's second layer, though not literally one, is the spatial arrangement of the building that we call a plan. What the French call the *disposition* of functions in our homes is peculiar to cultures, families, and individuals, but it also changes when needs or standards for space use evolve over time. Some requirements in a plan are dictated by adjacencies between functions—kitchens and dining areas are best when close together. Others are the result of social norms, such as the double parlor found in many Victorian houses. No longer relevant today, in the nineteenth century these rooms were needed for formal visits. The front parlor or reception room was off the hall, serving a necessary purpose as the place where a guest waited to be seen by a member of the family. The more intimate rear parlor was reserved for family gatherings or visits by good friends. Today the living room is waning in popularity, just as formal parlors did one hundred years ago—families prefer to hang out in less formal spaces near the kitchen. A combined kitchen–dining–family entertainment room is now an essential requirement in a new house, and sometimes must be added to an older one.

We mentioned earlier that every fifty years or so a house will need an upgrade in its services—meaning the mechanical, electrical, and plumbing systems. Brand points out that although a half-century cycle is slow in relation to replacing furniture or repainting a house, the rate of change in this layer is high in relation to, say, the need to rebuild a three-

A

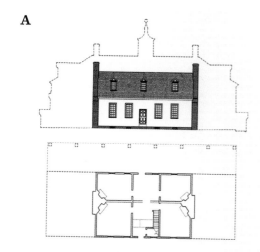

B

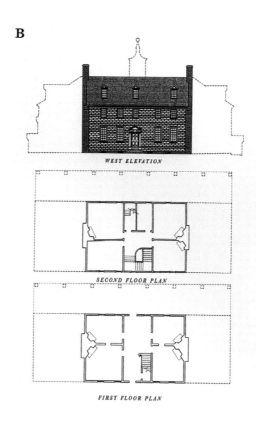

WEST ELEVATION

SECOND FLOOR PLAN

FIRST FLOOR PLAN

C

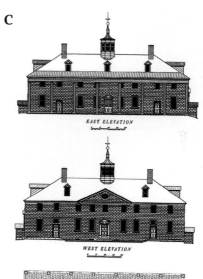

EAST ELEVATION

WEST ELEVATION

FIRST FLOOR PLAN

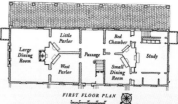

SECOND FLOOR PLAN

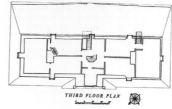

THIRD FLOOR PLAN

Building transformations, Mount Vernon. Allan Greenberg reconstructed the three major phases of renovation at George Washington's estate. "A" illustrates the house of his father as given to his brother, Lawrence, c. 1750. "B" illustrates Washington's first renovations, completed in the 1760s. "C" illustrates the familiar enlargement of Mount Vernon that we see today, from the 1790s. (Courtesy of Allan Greenberg Architect.)

foot-thick stone wall in a castle. New technologies in thermal comfort, water conservation, and wireless communication are pushing many homeowners to rethink their mechanical systems. And of course the issue of sustainable energy will cause these systems to be improved further in the coming decades.

Designing mechanical systems that fit within the skin and skeleton of a historic house can prove to be the most challenging part of a renovation or restoration project. Many homeowners fail to consider this when planning for an upgrade, and may hire contractors with little experience in the intricacies of fitting new systems into old spaces.

The results are often so destructive that good older homes lose all of their material integrity in the process. If the qualifications of designers and tradespeople are carefully weighed before going ahead, disasters can be avoided, and your house will come out better in the end.

The least malleable element in the diagram is the structure of a building. Once a large proportion of a wood frame in a historic house is compromised by rot or other deterioration, the whole building is in jeopardy. No one expects the structure of any building to fail, for if it did the occupants would be in grave danger. So building structure is not an element that requires major replacement in a typical life cycle of a century or so. Older buildings, especially wooden ones, will require repair and observation over time, but a well-maintained timber frame can last for centuries, as the stave churches of northern Europe have proven. In modern skin-and-skeleton construction, in use since the Industrial Revolution, the inner and outer skins of buildings can be replaced while the structure remains standing.

The rare cases in which structural elements are severely compromised most often occur during natural or human-made disasters such as earthquakes, hurricanes, and fires. When such events destroy portions of a building skeleton, it is often prudent to rebuild with lighter and more disaster-resistant structural systems. Occasionally large public buildings demand expensive retrofits to prevent potential damage from seismic activity, or need repairs because loading has changed over time, placing undue strain on older fabric such as stone masonry. But the most common structural changes that occur in houses are occasioned by the need to add floor space, intensify use, or simply repair damage caused by normal decay or wear.

The last layer in the diagram is the outer skin of the building. This layer takes the most punishment from the elements, and in harsh climates it can deteriorate at a relatively fast rate. For this reason the walls, windows, and roofs of houses are the most likely components to be replaced on a short repair cycle—say twenty-five years or more. Buildings with high-quality exterior materials, such as slate roofs, brick, cedar shingles, and various kinds of tile, are apt to withstand fifty to a hundred years of weathering without the need for serious repair, provided they are maintained. But many historic dwellings were not built with that kind of longevity in mind and will need attention on a regular basis. Older wooden homes require painting every five to seven years in order to maintain the weather resistance of the cladding. And despite some technological advances in finishes during the past half-century, paints will break down while shedding moisture and reflecting UV rays.

The inner, middle, and outer layers of a dwelling house are elements in a complex organism that behaves in some critical ways like a plant or animal reacting to its environment. When organisms grow and change, they tend to follow laws that are relatively consistent throughout the plant and animal kingdoms. We have found that if we apply some of the analogies above, there are some relatively straightforward principles that govern growth and changes in the houses we inhabit. Let's look at how these principles work.

FIVE PARAMETERS

Vintage houses grow in predictable patterns based on five limiting factors: the site, the skeleton, the spatial module, the roof shape, and the facade. If one understands these five limiting factors, then growing a house naturally will not be a trial. Indeed, for centuries traditional builders in Europe, Asia, South America, and Africa were able to seamlessly expand their dwellings in a natural, rather organic way. The "vernacular" governed dwelling design in most traditional societies. Rules for making houses were passed along from generation by direct interaction between parents and children. "Unselfconscious" building methods produced repeatable dwelling types that persisted for hundreds, even thousands of years. Things began to change only within the last two and a half centuries.

During the Industrial Revolution, builders began to look at houses as standardized modules that were determined by the means of production rather than the requirements of their inhabitants. The socially derived "pattern language" governing the design of European houses that had developed over centuries broke down. Mass industrial housing depersonalized the dwelling, creating the anonymous "worker" housing that dominated cities like London and Liverpool during the nineteenth century. Things got worse during the so-called Modern Movement after 1920. Rather than seeing houses as organisms, Modernists viewed them as machines that could control the natural world. The face-off between technology and the natural world began when architects acquired the means to overcome the temperature, weathering, and material limitations that had constrained buildings for centuries. The hubris of Modernists created the skyscraper, the nuclear power plant, the housing project, and numerous other building types that have fascinated and bedeviled contemporary society.

The theorist and architect Christopher Alexander studied both rationalized building systems and vernacular ones during his academic career at Harvard and Berkeley. Alexander found that mathematical, tectonic, and functional determinants of building form were far less important than cultural patterns that were developed over the course of generations rather than to meet momentary requirements. In his books, Alexander debunked many of the popular academic theories about how dwellings related to occupants. His message: The rules cannot be invented anew every decade; cultural norms are deep and longstanding.[3]

A well-designed traditional house will fit itself to the land, the climate, and its occupants as a partner with its natural habitat, not a technological combatant. Some contemporary "sustainable" dwellings have adopted the strategies of traditional builders—the Australian houses of Glenn Murcutt are a good example—in order to blend with the landscape and the climate of a particular region. Generally, though, the best examples of organic buildings—those that really fit their locale—were folk building types such as barns, modest row dwellings, Mediterranean villas, Indian wigwams, and log cabins.

Take the log cabin as an example. Log buildings have sustained life in northern Europe for centuries. The basic building form—four penlike log walls supporting a gable roof—has changed little over time. In cold climates, where humidity is low and the temperature limits rot, wood can sit on the ground for a long, long time. Log buildings don't require foundations, and their walls are single layer—the skin and the skeleton are the same. The only significant variation in building these dwellings is the method of joining the logs at the corners. In America, folk groups from Europe who migrated west carried their cultural traditions with them, including their methods of making a cabin. Some employed square corner-notching, others the V-notch, still others a primitive hollowing of the round logs to fit a perpendicular timber, known as saddle notching. No method was necessarily superior, but as with their cooking methods, Germans, Swedes, Scots-Irish, and English settlers stuck by their roots in making a home in the woods. The face of a cabin is modest to a fault: nothing but a door permits egress and protects the family from hostile humans and animals. Americans familiar with Laura Ingalls Wilder often think of the wood plank door that kept bears and Indians from invading their cabin on the Wisconsin frontier. The roof of a typical pioneer cabin was equally simple—a gable pitched enough to allow snow to fall from the eaves after a big storm.[4]

Scholars of building technology and form like to think of these simple structures as functionally determined and culturally nuanced. Like a canoe, a cabin uses readily available materials efficiently to do a job (sheltering a family from the elements) and reflects the predilections of a particular cul-

Replica of a slave cabin, built of logs, at George Washington's Mount Vernon. (Courtesy of Mark Alan Hewitt.)

tural group. Folklore maintains the pattern of construction over generations, so that the original solution or type is not lost. The fit between purpose, form, and technology is tight, virtually inevitable.

Strangely, perhaps, many buildings constructed with industrial technologies during the so-called machine age of the nineteenth and twentieth centuries do not have that same kind of inevitable correspondence between construction and end use. Though touted as logical and rational, many canonical Modernist buildings hide their true construction behind "symbolic" elements. As the architect Edward Ford has demonstrated, there is often a marked dichotomy between the professed "honesty" of construction methods in Modernist buildings and their actual technology.[5]

WHICH WAY IS NORTH? THE SITE

The earliest vernacular buildings in rural areas of the United States were placed by experienced "husbandmen" (farmers) from Europe who understood that a poorly sited building could result in the ruin of their families and the death of their animals. John Stilgoe has shown that the "common landscape" of our ancestors was the result of a complex negotiation between early European settlers, whose understanding was colored by centuries on a separate continent, and the primordial American environment that had been nurtured by native tribes for thousands of years. It took more than a century for the new inhabitants of North America to adapt their folkways to the climate, terrain, flora, hydrology, and fauna of the New World. Once they did so, an American ethos for landscape was born.[6]

The logic of siting a building to meld with the landscape and resist the ravages of climate can be appreciated by environmentalists and engineers as sustainable, but most architects and home builders trained in the twentieth century ignored the lessons of the farmers who tamed the American frontier. Suburban housing developments everywhere roll over the rural landscape with indifference to solar orientation or topography. Dolores Hayden's *Field Guide to Sprawl* makes ironic fun of the hapless "land planners" who produce these monstrous and wasteful chunks of real estate. Who would believe that the developer's term for one of these instant suburban tracts is a "Greenfield"—"a project constructed on raw land, usually agricultural."[7] About 1.2 million acres of farmland is lost each year to such developments. It is little wonder that when adding to houses in rural areas, most owners have little appreciation for how solar orientation helped to create the beautiful setting they own.

Before Americans struck out for the Great Plains during the land rush of the nineteenth century, they experienced the harsh climates of New England and the mid-Atlantic region. The lessons that early farmers learned served them well. In particular, experience taught them to respect the frigid northeasterly winds that could destroy crops, buildings, and animals during the cold months. When laying out agricultural land, barns, and houses, the husbandman looked to orient his buildings toward southern exposures whenever possible.

One of the best examples of strategic building orientation is the "big house, little house, back house, barn" pattern of northern New England farmsteads. Thomas Hubka's wonderful book on this typology shows how sophisticated vernacular siting patterns made room for the expansion of small farms over decades, even centuries, without compromising the solar orientation of individual buildings. Following a layout based on the common "four field system," farmers constructed their houses and barns facing either due south or southerly, with the front of the house toward the public road. From this they laid out three "yards" based on prevailing winds, adjacencies, and necessary relationships to crops and animals. The front yard was a formal area at the door to the street, intended only to show the public face of the family to neighbors. Next came the dooryard, the nerve center of the complex, where the ell between house and barn creates a natural locus for circulation. As its name suggests, doors open into this area from the barn, ell, big house, and little house (or kitchen), allowing the work of the farm to carry on even in bad weather. The rear barnyard, located on the back side of the barn, was reserved for animals, with a "tie up" in an adjacent area protected from the wind. By linking the buildings east–west and opening the yards on the south, the farmer ensured maximum solar gain in winter, as well as shelter from prevailing winds.[8]

When one understands the pattern of early city foundations in the American colonies, a similar logic emerges in the way buildings and yards were laid out. Boston, Charleston, New Orleans, and Philadelphia were constructed of the same design DNA as most European towns in the seventeenth and eighteenth centuries—connected row buildings with small rear gardens. As each city developed, and as original European groups melded with new cultures, particular dwelling types emerged that reflected not only a mix of people, but also the climate, flora, and fauna. One of the most distinctive of these is the famous "Charleston single house," with its

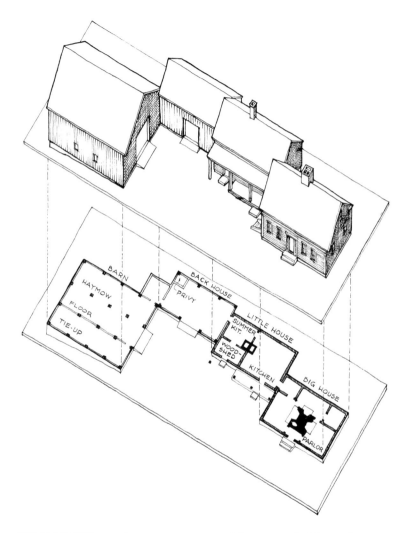

Typical building and room arrangement for connected farms in Maine. (Drawing by Thomas Hubka; from Thomas Hubka's *Big House, Little House, Back House, Barn*, University Press of New England, 2004, p. 7.)

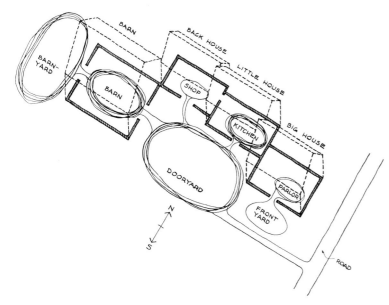

Diagram showing typical building and yard usage for connected farms in Maine. (Drawing by Thomas Hubka; Thomas Hubka's *Big House, Little House*, University Press of New England, 2004, p. 9.)

side piazza oriented to catch sea breezes. Indeed, the porch or piazza that developed in many southern cities became a signature semipublic space associated with many American dwelling types.

Rowhouse orientation along the street, inflected by stoops and porches, continued to dictate land use patterns in American cities for much of the nineteenth century. Just as in prototypical London terraces and French "places," the facades of regular row buildings provided a public datum for neighborhoods and communities throughout the United States, and they still retain their influence. That is why his-

toric preservation commissions in the oldest neighborhoods labor so assiduously to protect the character and materials of these durable buildings. When a row on an urban block loses one of its constituent facades to demolition or indifferent renovation, its sense of place is damaged, and residents feel the vacuum in their quality of life.

Dense urban neighborhoods like those in New York are not the only areas that have been threatened by hostile attitudes toward historical land use patterns. One of the greatest challenges of the past quarter-century has been guiding the redevelopment of historic railroad suburbs and exurban neighborhoods surrounding the central city. Urban renewal destroyed many fine neighborhoods in the South Bronx, Newark, Philadelphia—the list goes on. Automobile traffic created havoc in garden suburbs that were planned to handle streetcars and carriages. Many of these areas lost valuable street trees and median strips, sometimes designed by noted landscape architects. Only recently have historic suburbs such as Cleveland Heights, Short Hills, Roland Park, and Forest Hills Gardens initiated stringent controls on development and renovation to prevent such loss. Paradoxically, the most insidious agent in the destruction of these areas has not been the large developer, but rather America's "modern" land use laws that were overlaid on magnificent planned communities by engineers and attorneys bent on the standardization of urban zoning.

Thus it is not enough to be sensitive to the original landscape or streetscape around your vintage house (though that is a good first impulse); a vigilant connoisseur of architecture, urbanism, and landscape must fight for reasonable ordinances and standards in his or her community. If zoning does not permit the restoration of a stoop, carriage house, pergola, or garden, there is something wrong with local laws that officials must be informed of. And if variances or ordinance changes cannot be secured, it is prudent to organize a neighborhood association to press for these amendments or reforms. If not, a well-planned renovation can go awry.

The first rule of thumb to follow when beginning a project in a vintage house is: Understand and respect the site—not only its history, but also its organization.

BUILDING WITH THE BONES: THE SKELETON

The innermost component in a historic house is its structural system. Like a skeleton, this system not only gives strength and rigidity to the building, it governs the form.

Prior to the eighteenth century, structural systems for houses were largely limited to stone bearing walls and timber frames—readily available materials that could be mastered by vernacular artisans. These so-called monolithic structural systems, like primitive mud-brick (adobe) dwellings, log cabins, earthen or sod houses, and Native American wigwams, used one primary material as both a skeleton and an outer layer of weather protection. While practical for simple dwellings, monolithic systems did not function well in the modern city, which required cheap, multistory mass housing for large numbers of occupants. We'll talk more about these systems in Chapter 3.

The systems in use today were developed in Europe during the Industrial Revolution and in the United States, where new technologies made mass production of building materials the best alternative to traditional methods. When more complex, skin-and-skeleton systems became the norm in the twentieth century, we lost a wealth of knowledge about vernacular building materials and techniques. We also began to assume, as architects and builders, that structural parameters limiting preindustrial buildings were no longer relevant. Because of this, many historic house owners find themselves unprepared to deal with adaptations to traditional construction.

One of the most common, but misunderstood, structural systems is the braced frame or heavy timber frame. Virtually all European cultural groups settling North and South America used this framing type for houses, barns, and meeting houses. The key to understanding timber framing is to appreciate its limitations. Here we find only wood-to-wood joints (mortise and tenon connections), members supporting relatively light floor loading, and spans under 18 to 20 feet (the length of common oak timbers). A heavy timber house will follow the proportions and scale of its structural system, most often growing in modules related to the maximum length of beam spans. Openings and room dimensions relate to the rhythm and pattern of tenoned vertical studs.

Two of the essential properties of a timber frame structure are its stability and its rigidity under normal loads. The structure achieves this stability by triangulation, one of the simplest and most rigid geometric forms. Unlike modern platform or western framing, braced timber frames always require diagonal braces at the corners of the box in order to achieve rigidity. The braces create triangles that cannot move under normal loads, thus preventing the building from collapsing. Unfortunately, many contemporary carpenters and building renovators do not understand these principles. When confronted with a braced frame containing large corner diagonals, many builders cut these timbers out in order to make room for plumbing, wiring, or new structural members. This causes enormous problems, often leading to racking and walls out of plumb, and sometimes structural failure.

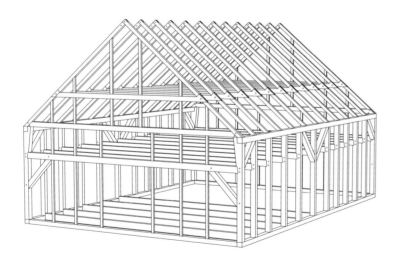

Anchor-bent framing in an eighteenth-century Dutch-American farmhouse. Wyckoff-Garretson farm, Middlebush, New Jersey.
(Drawing by Jerry A. Bruno, Jr.; courtesy of Mark Alan Hewitt Architects.)

Restoration carpenters and timber framers (many trained in New England and Pennsylvania) are sensitive to the properties of these structures and are worth hiring when one is discovered hiding under your sheetrock.

But there are not only structural reasons for following the logical pattern of the timber frame. An addition that ignores the dimensional parameters of this system, or grafts an incompatible structural system to the timber skeleton, will look out of place and out of time. Many homes that employ modern balloon framing and engineered lumber greatly expand the scale of the traditional dwelling, thereby mocking its natural proportions. Moreover, the roof pitches required for ancient timber frame houses were generally steeper than those employed in modern framing.

Another structural system with built-in constraints is the stone bearing wall. Unreinforced masonry must be thick enough to withstand both lateral and vertical forces, and walls must have internal stability created by the stone and mortar together. A stone house will not look right unless its openings are proportioned to fit the structural characteristics of the walls, and unless the coursing type fits the type of stone. The various types of stone coursing, illustrated here, range from precise, almost invisibly joined surfaces to very rustic ones. Most masonry techniques for laying stone developed over centuries in areas with abundant mineral resources, such as Egypt, Italy, Greece, and Central America.

With disuse occasioned by modern construction techniques, stone masonry declined in popularity and skilled masons became as rare as milk-wagon drivers. Because no

STONE WORK

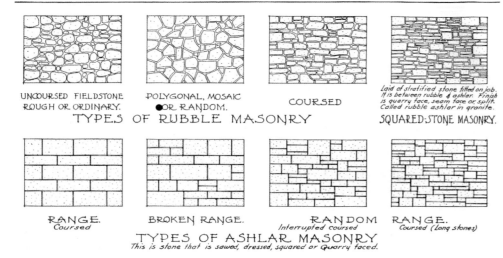

UNCOURSED FIELDSTONE ROUGH OR ORDINARY.

POLYGONAL, MOSAIC OR RANDOM.

COURSED

Laid of stratified stone fitted on job. It is between rubble & ashlar. Finish is quarry face, seam face or split. Called rubble ashlar in granite.

TYPES OF RUBBLE MASONRY

SQUARED-STONE MASONRY.

RANGE.
Coursed

BROKEN RANGE.

RANDOM
Interrupted coursed

RANGE.
Coursed (Long stones)

TYPES OF ASHLAR MASONRY
This is stone that is sawed, dressed, squared or Quarry faced.

Traditional patterns of rubble and ashlar stonework. (From *Architectural Graphic Standards, Third Edition* (1947), by C.G. Ramsey and H.R. Sleeper, New York: John Wiley & Sons, p. 43.)

one was around to pass along vernacular techniques in the building industry, many new stone veneer walls ignore traditional patterns in design and construction. They give away their false character and make poor additions to old houses. Perhaps the most egregious example of this misunderstanding occurs in the stone veneer walls that appear on virtually all upscale suburban houses in markets like the Northeast and South. When masons are hired to face a wood frame wall with thin stone veneer (often less than four inches in depth), the expectation is that they will employ what is known as uncoursed rubble patterns. Although uncoursed rubble stonework is occasionally found in the below-grade walls of traditional dwelling houses, where it will not be seen, it is almost never employed to construct true bearing walls above

ground. Why? First of all, it is less stable than coursed stone construction; second, masons were trained to cut stone in neat horizontal courses; third, rubble stonework would have seemed déclassé. Ironically, the rubble walls that were not fit for even the poorest working class dwellings prior to the late twentieth century are now found in million-dollar homes throughout America.

When adding to an early structural system, a good rule of thumb is to respect the integrity of the original materials and their limitations. Openings in traditional construction are small and should follow the dimensions of the framing or bearing materials. Width, height, and roof pitch are also telltales of historic building construction and should be followed in new additions. In short, alterations that appear to

Veneer stone in a rubble pattern, surrounded by cast stone. Non-structural and non-grammatical usage of stone has proliferated in "McMansion" developments. (Courtesy of Mark Alan Hewitt.)

follow the natural pattern of the original building will more successfully echo its character and scale.

MINDING MODULES: THE GEOMETRY

Long before industrialized housing, Airstream trailers, and other standardized shelters, vernacular builders governed the layout and design of dwellings with modules. One of the reasons that rural houses and barns look comfortable and familiar is that their builders depended on a canon of regular shapes and dimensions. Fred Kniffen, Henry Glassie, and other pioneering material culture scholars have found uncanny regularity in the patterns of folk building. In Virginia, housewrights used simple, rational rectangles to plan room layouts, while mid-Atlantic carpenters repeated standard Georgian forms in their houses.[9]

While we expect deliberate proportions in the designs of Andrea Palladio and Thomas Jefferson, more common dwellings often display an equally rigorous order based on repeating (or similar) spatial modules. In one restoration project, we encountered a striking example of modularity and scale in an 1855 miner's dwelling near Dover, New Jersey.

The Bridget Smith house was constructed by a mining company in the small village of Ferromonte, in the heart of New Jersey's iron-rich Mount Hope area. During the late eighteenth century Mahlon Dickerson opened the first large iron mine in the area, and he went on to become a New Jersey senator and governor on the heels of his extraordi-

Typical single-cell Virginia farmhouse. (Drawing by Henry Glassie; from Henry Glassie's *Folk Housing in Middle Virginia*, University of Tennessee Press, 1976, p. 43.)

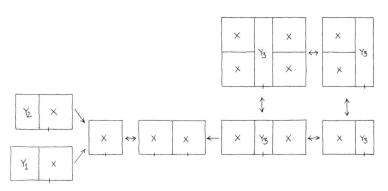

Modular patterns of "subtypes" of vernacular farm dwellings in Middle Virginia. (Drawing by Henry Glassie; from Henry Glassie's *Folk Housing in Middle Virginia*, University of Tennessee Press, 1976, p. 37)

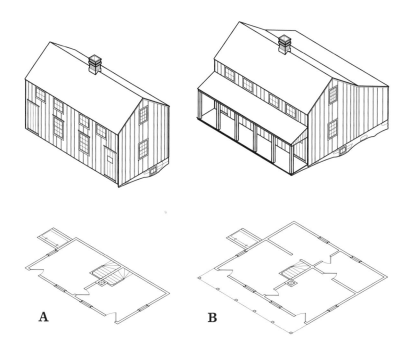

A   **B**

Belonging to a miner, this 1855 two-family dwelling in Ferromonte (Mine Hill), New Jersey is roughly a double square in its original configuration (A). After only 10 years the house got a front porch and a lean-to expansion at the rear (B). (Drawings by Jerry A. Bruno, Jr.; courtesy of Mark Alan Hewitt Architects.)

nary business success. The Morris Canal, completed in the early 1830s, made it relatively easy to transport iron products to New York or Pennsylvania. By 1855, when this small house was constructed, the area was a booming industrial center clamoring for laborers. Italian and Irish immigrants met the call and were soon living in villages around Dover and Morristown.

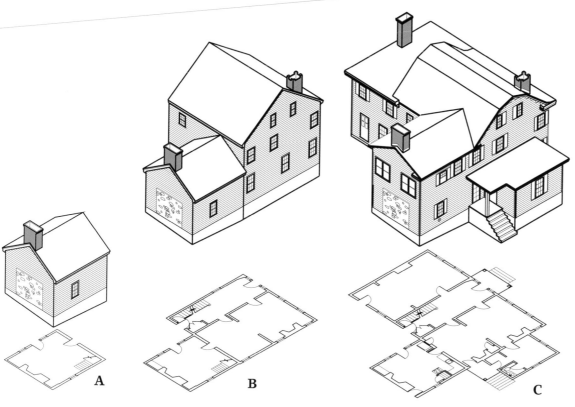

A   B   C

Modular development of the parsonage at St. Mark's Episcopal Church in Mendham, New Jersey. A small, eighteenth-century farmhouse (A) is followed by an early nineteenth-century side-hall addition (B). During the third quarter of the nineteenth century the house is enlarged significantly, with a new room and an expanded second floor (C). (Drawings by Jerry A. Bruno, Jr.; courtesy of Mark Alan Hewitt Architects.)

To house these worker families the mine companies constructed inexpensive, modular dwellings of locally available wood. Using balloon framing, the new construction method pioneered in Chicago, the builders could erect a double house in a matter of weeks. Hundreds were constructed in areas where mining flourished. The module used in these dwellings was roughly square—doubling the square produced a four-room house on two floors that could accommodate two families in cramped quarters. When the miners wanted to expand their dwellings it was a simple matter to add a lean-to at the back of the house. Our restoration of this small dwelling aptly illustrates the simple discipline of modular construction.

Modularity in houses may be tied to larger form types, such as the I-house common in America during the eighteenth and nineteenth centuries, or to dimensions related to the scale of furnishings, structural members, or even cultural and social factors. The repeating pattern of room shapes, plan dimensions, and even floor-to-floor heights is critical to its organic wholeness. If the custodians of a historic house do not understand its spatial logic, additions and renovations are bound to compromise that sense of unity.

Sometimes a historic house will morph during two or three eras, each with its own spatial logic, while maintaining an organic wholeness. This was the case at the parsonage of St. Mark's Church in Mendham, New Jersey. The Mendham house began its life as a small "Jersey Cape"—a story and a half single-cell farmhouse. When the owners outgrew the first dwelling during the early nineteenth century, they added a full two-story block to the house. At the time of the building of the Episcopal church in the 1850s the house was expanded further with a gambrel roof and a set of bedrooms on the second floor.

These are but a few of the kinds of transformations that occur in a modular expansion of dwellings. The size of room modules is directly related to the era in which a house was initially designed and built and should be carefully considered. Small eighteenth-century farmhouses can easily be dwarfed by twentieth-century additions. Early twentieth-century mansions, however, maintain a grand scale commensurate with the tastes and needs of their owners—and modern appetites for conspicuous space.

ROOF GRAMMAR: THE MASSING

If architecture is a language, as many have argued, then its rules must function as grammar. There is no better example than the discipline imposed by combinations of pitched roofs in traditional dwellings.

While framing carpenters and roofing contractors generally appreciate the challenge of creating complex pitched roofs, the grammar of roofs has escaped the purview of most architects trained in the language of Modernism, an architecture of monotonous, flat-roofed volumes. Many house additions are designed without a clue as to how traditional roofs connect to each other and shed water.

The early builders of America's houses and farm buildings employed a wonderful variety of traditional roof types. To use a more sophisticated term, these solid shapes make up the morphology (surface texture) of the house form as it grows from small massed gables into larger agglomerations of linked roof volumes. Hip, gambrel, gable, and cross-gable roofs connect according to geometric principles, creating a set of grammatical structures that cannot be ignored in additions.

This is particularly true of Victorian houses, a large stylistic group spanning most of the nineteenth century. Virginia and Lee McAllister, in their wonderful primer on American housing types, were able to draw the bewildering variety of Victorian roofs in their simple exposition of eclectic styles in the nineteenth century. Vintage house owners are well advised to purchase this book as a means of sorting out a complex subject. Those with Victorian houses will find it indispensable.[10]

Cape May, New Jersey, is one of America's most picturesque Victorian resort towns. The village is full of well-preserved cottages and villas from the mid- and late nineteenth century, many of which were converted into bed-and-breakfast hostelries twenty years ago. Inevitably the success of the resort industry led to a spate of mock Victorian houses and hotels, most designed by developers with little understanding of the subtleties of traditional architecture. The preservation commission in the town has kept a close eye on new development, especially with regard to the loss of historic buildings in the wake of development pressures.

Our office was involved in a controversial project on Washington Street, one of the town's most distinguished locales. A local builder asked to demolish a nondescript house on the block in order to construct a condominium building. His initial proposal did not meet the standards of the historic preservation commission, and he was denied permission to build. Our subsequent redesign of the condominium employed volumes and roof forms that were consonant with

the Victorian cottages on the block, leading to an approval by the commission and kudos from local residents. The variegation in scale, texture, and roof shape in this design helped to create a harmonious streetscape, a specific requirement of the town's zoning and preservation ordinances.

In a small addition to a distinguished Queen Ann house in Madison, New Jersey, we created an octagonal breakfast/family area at the rear of the house to contrast with the more square volumes of the front. The owner, who chairs the local historic preservation commission, was proud to offer his neighbors a positive example of compatible expansion to a landmark home. A nearby country house from the 1880s presented another challenge: we were asked to add a small

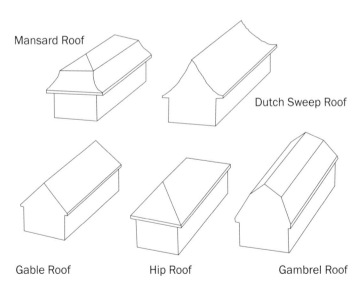

Mansard Roof

Dutch Sweep Roof

Gable Roof   Hip Roof   Gambrel Roof

Diagram of typical roof types found in American houses. (Courtesy of Mark Alan Hewitt.)

Proposed residential condominium building on Washington Street, in the heart of the Cape May historic district. In order to echo the scale, form, and character of nearby houses, the roof of the building was designed with a turret and dormers in the manner of Victorian hotels in the area. (Courtesy of Mark Alan Hewitt.)

125 Garfield, Pine Hill, a nineteenth-century house in Madison, New Jersey that was expanded in 2007. A cupola in the new breakfast room plays off of the complex roof geometries in the vintage house. (Photo by Jim Prince; courtesy of Mark Alan Hewitt Architects.)

breakfast room to the rear of a house that had already seen two alterations. In this case the porch roof shapes were critical, as they helped to create a unified composition.

As *Old–House Journal* has demonstrated in its popular "Remuddling" page, more vintage houses are ruined by insensitive roof configurations than by any other error in renovations. With a little study, both designers and owners can learn to work within the grammatical rules that govern this morphology. While we late-twentieth-century designers can't compete with folk builders, we can mind our manners in roof shape, pitch, and placement.

QUEEN ANNE VS. MARY ANNE: THE FACADE

The last, and in many respects most important, parameter governing the growth of houses is the elusive quality of *identity*. Houses have faces to present to the outside world. Their public facades often differ greatly from their private or service zones; hence the adage "Queen Anne in front, Mary Anne behind."

The character of a street front or formal facade will generally be more self-conscious than any other part of the house. Because of this, it is useful to know a little about the overall character of your neighborhood or rural context, and also a bit about the original owner or builder of your house. This information can be very useful in guiding you to an appropriate facade renovation, should one be necessary.

You may not be the first owner who decided to meddle with the facade of your home sweet home. When fashions in building and decoration change, houses often get facelifts. Though often the general design of the facade remains much the same, houses in urban areas are quite often spruced up to keep pace with neighbors. Occasionally, a facade will be almost totally restyled, as in some of New York's Upper East Side brownstones during the 1920s.

A former parsonage on Ridgedale Avenue in Madison, New Jersey got a small kitchen expansion in 2006. Some of the space is covered by a picturesque, copper-roofed turret. (Drawings by Jerry A. Bruno, Jr.; courtesy of Mark Alan Hewitt Architects.)

It is also critical to have a sense of which formal design guidelines governed the facade when it was first built, such as cornice lines, window styles, material dimensions, and lot lines, as well as the parameters that may limit your renovations today, such as ordinances, zoning, and height restrictions.

Clare Cooper Marcus discusses the psychological and social realms of domestic space in her book *House as a Mirror of Self.* Marcus is both an architect and a psychologist, and her research has opened up a new understanding of how human beings decorate their domiciles to show aspects of their persona to the outside world. Though it is clear that people personalize interior spaces with objects to reveal their inner selves, the public face of a house also shows much about its owner's aspirations—"the personal need for self-expression in the environment is present to greater or lesser degree in everyone," she writes. Her research reveals that as individuals, couples, and families move through life stages, the changes in their domiciles reflect conflicts, emotional highs and lows, growth in maturity and self satisfaction, and many other uniquely human forms of psychological development. "Unable to comprehend all that is encapsulated in the psyche, we need to place it 'out there' for us to contemplate, just as we need to view our physical body in a mirror. Thus, houses change in order to reflect very personal journeys in space, time and experience."[11]

Like Marcus, the French sociologist Philippe Boudon has researched the relationship between public symbols of self and domestic space. Seeking to understand the reaction of mass housing residents to their environment, he ventured into the experimental Modernist housing complex at Pessac and interviewed owners of small dwellings there. He found the original facades—designed by the influential architect Le Corbusier—altered beyond recognition by residents who wished only to express their individual tastes. This angered the architect, but it was a necessary step in making the complex habitable. The impulse to create a public face is the first step toward growth, and one that will enrich any dwelling. The anonymity of much Modernist architecture, and its failure to recognize a basic human desire for self-expression, has contributed to the destruction of many traditional neighbor-

ASK YOUR ARCHITECT TO CHECK THE ZONING

One of the most common issues with urban house renovations of any sort is related to zoning. Zoning laws restrict building uses, setbacks, bulk building footprints, floor area ratios, parking, height, and even some basic design elements such as stoops and porches. It is essential to understand these restrictive codes before undertaking your project. An architect experienced in renovation in your area will be conversant with the ordinances. Ask him or her about the general guidelines that you need to follow. If you are ready to proceed, your architect will visit the building department to get a formal assessment of the property and share it with you. This step is a must in all renovation projects, especially in constricted urban neighborhoods.

hoods in American cities. Architecture, particularly domestic architecture, contributes to a sense of identity in communities and cultures and ties group identity to locale.[12]

Though historians often assume a high degree of stasis when studying the houses of famous public figures, family disagreements, property transfers, and changing political ideologies often lead to major alterations in prominent houses. At the family home of New Jersey's Revolutionary-era glassmaking family, the Estells of Atlantic County, each new face represented a generation's public posture toward the changing world outside. Seeing the three faces side by side reveals the subtle ways small alterations can change the character of a house. One of the great revelations of recent res-

toration practice in the United States was the reconstruction of early fabric at Montpelier, the plantation home of James Madison. Not only did the fourth president make significant alterations to his father's modest Georgian house during the late eighteenth century, the Du Pont family nearly obliterated Madison's mansion in their early twentieth-century remodeling. Today visitors see not the Du Pont house but that of the president in his later years.

Nevertheless, carpenters and architects in the nineteenth century respected the character of old houses, and this is generally reflected in additions made to venerable family seats. Not so in the twentieth century. Because few contractors and architects appreciate the details and proportions of

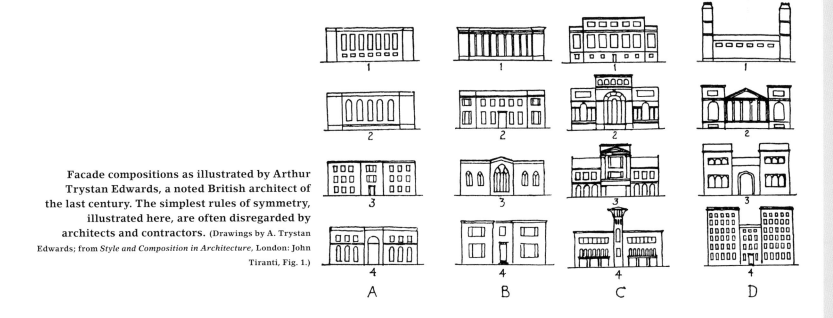

Facade compositions as illustrated by Arthur Trystan Edwards, a noted British architect of the last century. The simplest rules of symmetry, illustrated here, are often disregarded by architects and contractors. (Drawings by A. Trystan Edwards; from *Style and Composition in Architecture*, London: John Tiranti, Fig. 1.)

traditional buildings, many historic houses suffer from the architectural equivalent of botched plastic surgery. When remodeling contractors cut, chop, and cover up fine old materials and details, the damage is often difficult to undo. Architect Marianne Cusato, frustrated by what she saw in the housing industry after she designed the famous Katrina Cottage in New Orleans, produced a fine book that she hopes will ameliorate the situation. *Get Your House Right* is a very useful compendium of details and rules of thumb that any one who works on vintage houses will want to consult.[13]

Much of this book concerns proportion, scale, and the conventions of traditional design (generally informed by classical precedents). Though homeowners need not learn the intricacies of classical proportion, every owner should be aware of the importance of "regulating lines" in the design of facades. If a contractor suggests enlarging a dormer that was carefully designed by your architect with regard to scale and proportion, your answer should be no, unless the architect approves. Jonathan Hale, in his book *The Old Way of Seeing*, argues that good proportion was a fundamental concern of builders and architects prior to 1850, when these sensibilities began to be destroyed by a trend toward functionalism. Whether or not his thesis is correct, there is much to be said about the virtue of traditional proportions in relating elements in a facade—doors, windows, porches, cornices, and ornamental details. Not all architects or builders are aware of traditional systems of design, so it pays to consult a specialist.[14]

Character and identity are as profound as structure,

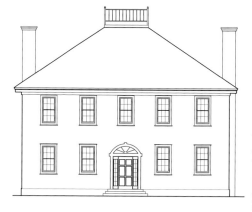

The metamorphosis of Estell Manor in Atlantic County, New Jersey is remarkable for its three "facelifts." Built in 1832 (top) by glassmaker Daniel Estell, the manor house was given a Victorian porch during the 1870s (middle). New Jersey's first female mayor, Rebecca Estell Bourgeois, remodeled her family house in the Colonial Revival style following a fire in the 1920s (bottom). (Drawing by Jerry A. Bruno, Jr.; courtesy of Mark Alan Hewitt Architects.)

space, and morphology. When designers consider the process of growth in a house and the forces that guide it, maintaining the distinctive public visage should be high on the priority list. Like the other parameters, the face of a building determines its overall aesthetic and stylistic identity. Following traditional patterns when considering interventions will ensure that the historical and architectural integrity of an old house is maintained for the pleasure of succeeding generations.

FOUR STRATEGIES FOR SUCCESSFUL EXPANSION

Knowing how houses have expanded and changed historically provides a basis for making informed decisions about how to "grow" your vintage house. As professionals, we have seen many projects go awry merely because these simple principles went unheeded. In addition to grasping the patterns that govern changes in historic houses, an architect or preservationist should also have experience with the most useful strategies for putting these ideas into practice. We have found that the most common of these fit into four categories:

1. Renovations that utilize the space in the existing footprint of the building, including the basement or attic, can result in a house that looks virtually unchanged, or they may produce subtle changes in room decor, circulation, and interior design. There are even ways to get more space by changing the roofs or adding compatible dormers, without building a full addition to the house. We discuss these in Chapter 4, "New Spaces in Old Places."

2. Various kinds of renovations that involve adding new spaces outside the footprint of the original dwelling are the most common means of getting the extra space you need. Additions are not always large and may not affect the overall character of the house very much, as long as a skillful designer is in charge. They are the topic of Chapter 5, "Additions That Stay in Tune."

3. Giving a house a "facelift" or freshening up the street facade may be desirable if the original building was modified without sensitivity to its character and context. These treatments are particularly important in rowhouses, terraces, and other locales with a collective rather than individual identity. It may also be necessary to borrow space from a house next door, creating a larger dwelling where two separate ones once stood. Chapter 7, "Facing the Neighborhood," has all the details.

4. When a vintage house is complete and aesthetically inviolable, the owner often turns to an architect for the design of compatible outbuildings such as a garage, pool pavilion, or guest cottage. In larger estates or suburban enclaves, outbuildings are often critical to establishing a coherent site plan or garden layout. Thus, when a new building is added, it must complement the existing ensemble just as if it were an addition joined to the original building. In Chapter 8, "Outstanding Outbuildings," we'll have more to say about this topic.

The central chapters in this book are arranged to present examples from each of these categories, so that an owner can evaluate the potential ways of gaining needed space in a particular place or with a building type that is well understood by designers. By presenting "best practice" examples in our analysis, we hope to impart some of the wisdom gained by our colleagues over decades of practice in particular locales.

In Chapters 4, 5, 7, and 8 you will find plans, photos, and analyses of projects from all over the United States, though concentrated on the Eastern seaboard, where the authors reside. Our intention in this presentation is to guide you through successful projects (none without flaws) as a means of preparing you for your own foray into old house renovation. While other books present examples of additions to older houses, we believe that ours is the first to offer truly noteworthy design thinking with a bias toward both sustainability and traditional, complementary idioms.

So far we've learned that the essential principles to understand when adding to an old house are the same ones that guided our ancestors in their practical endeavors to grow dwellings to meet new circumstances. As we look at examples of vintage houses that have been successfully expanded in recent years, the lessons we've outlined here will be illustrated in a host of different ways. Our next subject, however, will be one that is immediately useful to any first-time buyer of a vintage house: knowing what you've got. In the next chapter you'll find out how to get help with historical research, site analysis, deeds, structural and mechanical assessments, material conservation, and other basic matters that are not only on the minds of homeowners, but occupy a lot of time when architects first encounter an old building. Let's do some detective work.

3

UNDERSTANDING WHAT YOU HAVE

JUST AS WITH ANTIQUE FURNITURE OR CLASSIC CARS, understanding the design and condition of your vintage house is as fundamental to making improvements as caring for it. Frustrating as it may be when you're fired up to get out the hammer, nails, and shovel, the all-important first move is to literally do nothing. Taking the time to quietly study the house you already have and understand why it is shaped, formed, and detailed the ways it is (whether the results are good or not) will produce more logical, economical, and satisfying results when you set to work.

Preservationists like to call this step a conditions survey, or "building pathology." The analogy with medicine is sometimes apt, for buildings decay and have certain illnesses, such as fungal growth and water damage, that affect their general well-being over time. On the most basic level, you are looking at the house you've bought to determine its form, history, style, physical traits, and the condition of all its parts, from roof to foundation.

To make the most of the work to come, it is essential to comprehend your house not only as it appears right now but also as it has changed and grown during its entire life cycle. Garden designers and enthusiasts always encourage homeowners to "live with their garden" for a year before doing any planting. This way they can really observe what shrubs and flowers are already in place and how the garden works, noting what plants enter and leave the garden through the seasons, blooming and dying back, as well as what is missing or what could be better. The same is true of old houses. The first step is to understand your house as it was envisioned the day it came to light on the drafting board—the house's concept, including its style. The second step is to see how the concept was brought to reality in the original materials and construction—the execution. The third step is to see how the house has been altered, expanded, and upgraded, as well as how it has aged and grown over the decades. These forces have most likely left you with a building that is not exactly as it began, but they are very much what has made it the unique vintage house you treasure today.

Understanding the conceptual and material components of the house will not only make the future changes you undertake a better mechanical fit with the building—down to the level of mating old and new siding or plaster so they don't leak or crack—but will also teach you what parts work (or don't work) and why, and how you can use this information to improve on the house in your future work.

HOUSE FORMS OR TYPOLOGY

Anyone looking to expand a vintage house must have a rudimentary knowledge of historic house forms or types. Traditional forms are the building blocks—even the DNA—of a house, determining in many ways why it looks the way it does. What's more, these forms are critical to recognize because retaining them and working with them often makes addition options more readily apparent and "natural" but fighting the forms—or in the worst case, obliterating them—undermines and destroys the essential character of a vintage house—the very character that was the reason you bought the house in the first place.

Architectural historians have spent much time tracing and dissecting three hundred years of houses into their derivative parts and origins. Their work is a little like that of biologists, who name and categorize species in order to understand evolutionary patterns and other life forms. Though the nuances of this analysis may be interesting or hair-splitting, depending on your taste, what is most useful to the average vintage house owner is being able to recognize the handful of fundamental house forms and massing (proliferation of rooms or interior spaces) that are at the core of most of houses in North America.

Front Gabled, One Story—A small house or cottage typically one room deep, with the roof running perpendicular to the front entrance.

New England or Mid-Atlantic "Cape"—A one-and-a-half-story dwelling with a steeply pitched roof, generally almost square in plan.

Front Gabled, Two Story—A two-story version that is the basis of many farmhouses, especially those built in the Greek Revival style by the 1840s.

Side Gabled, Two Story—A rectangular house whose roof runs parallel to the front entrance, a form highly popular from the colonial era right into the twentieth century.

Side Gabled Saltbox—A rectangular house whose roof extends off the back to make an addition—a highly popular form for early houses in New England.

Foursquare—A cubical house with walls of equal size and typically a pyramidal roof, widely built in the early twentieth century.

I-house—A thin, two-story gabled house, typically only

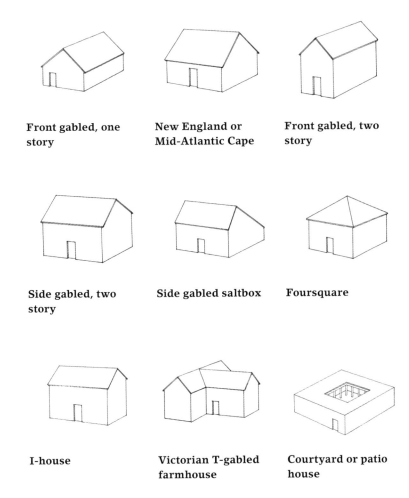

Front gabled, one story

New England or Mid-Atlantic Cape

Front gabled, two story

Side gabled, two story

Side gabled saltbox

Foursquare

I-house

Victorian T-gabled farmhouse

Courtyard or patio house

House forms or typology. (Drawings by Rob Leanna.)

one room deep, built throughout the Midwest and South during the Scots-Irish migration of the late eighteenth and nineteenth centuries.

Victorian T-gabled Farmhouse—A popular form of the mid-nineteenth century throughout the United States.

Courtyard or Patio House—The common form of Southwest house borrowed from Spanish forms, and ultimately from the Roman atrium house.

While by no means a rule, it is also useful to note that the general plan of a house is usually either symmetrical (with the front door in the center) or asymmetrical (with the front door to one side). Moreover, like music and art, most houses can generally be classed as either classical or romantic. Houses that are classical in inspiration (in the Georgian or Greek Revival styles, for example) are typically rectangular and symmetrical. Houses that are romantic in inspiration (such as Queen Anne Victorians and most English Revival houses of the early twentieth century) are irregular and asymmetrical.

TRADITIONAL ADDITION FORMS

Like basic house forms, additions, expansions, and extensions have, over generations, boiled down to some basic patterns and techniques—especially in houses from the early twentieth century and earlier. Not only are these approaches the product of empirical "research," of builders perfecting them through the laboratory of trial-and-error, but they have been repeated for generations and are time-tested ways to gain room in a traditional house. The added beauty of this history is that it helps these forms look "right" on an old house even if the addition was built last week. In many cases their geometry is basic, timeless, economical, and if not always elegant, at least reduced to its essence. Most people will recognize these basic approaches:

Lean-to or shed-roof addition

Wing and hyphen

Rear el

Unit repetition

It is closer to a rule than an exception that the majority of houses over, say, eighty years of age have very likely been added onto—perhaps even more than once. The evidence of these additions may be obvious or subtle—visible in the exte-

rior form of the house or hidden in the record of the materials used to build the addition.

STYLE

Style, from the Latin word *stilus*, is defined as a characteristic way of making things, including forms as diverse as art, music, and architecture. Styles can be associated with individual artists, schools of artisans, guilds, epochs in art, discrete cultures, or nations. When it comes to historic architecture, style refers to a fashion popular at one time, and the way a building's form, materials, and detailing were influenced to meet that fashion. When planning an addition or remodeling, it is important to understand that style can have a tremendous impact on the

Shed Roof Extension: A room with a single-pitch roof that, when it continues the roof at the back of the house, creates the traditional saltbox form.

Wing-and-Hyphen: Subordinate wings or outbuildings connected to the main house with links called hyphens; common in classical mansions.

Rear El: A secondary extension—often for a kitchen—built off the back or side of the main house and at right angles to it.

Unit Repetition: Enlarging by repeating a primary unit of construction or design, say, by "cloning" the left side of a half-cape house on the right side to make a full cape.

Traditional addition forms. (Drawings by Mark Hewitt.)

appearance of a house, or it can have little or no impact at all, because while style can have an influence on the basic house forms, it is most often regarded as something applied to a form. A famous example is the foursquare shape, which might appear in the trappings of the Colonial Revival style (set off by classical porch columns), one of the late Victorian styles (flaunting much spindlework "gingerbread" on a porch with chamfered posts), or in the Arts and Crafts vein (with tapered porch supports and conspicuous eave brackets)—or even in the Prairie mode (distinguished by a high second-story line, deep eaves, and plain, large squarish porch posts).

Few houses fit neatly into one single historic style. Many are blends of styles, or have next to no style at all. Moreover, the thrust of many additions and remodeling has been to

Historic Districts and Surveys

If you are trying to find out more about the style of your house, it is sometimes possible to consult documents filed with the town or county. But first check to see if you are in a local or National Register historic district. If so, you may be able to access the nomination forms and other data, either online or through the state historic preservation office. The basic information—date, architect and style—are often on such documents. Some historic districts or neighborhoods even publish design guidelines for homeowners. These booklets contain all sorts of useful information about the house styles, appropriate materials, research sources, and even paint colors that are peculiar to your neighborhood.

change or update the style of an old house. The glossary at the end of this book will help you get a handle on the parade of historic styles over the last two hundred years.

BUILDING SKELETONS

For over four hundred years, the vast majority of North American houses have been built out of either stone or wood. While in the Southwest adobe bricks and mud renders have been used for centuries, this ephemeral and climate-specific building material has not been adopted elsewhere. Because of the abundance of timber in U.S. forests, wood has always been the most common material for domestic building. The second step in understanding your house is to appreciate the technology used in its structure. As we noted in the last chapter, the skeleton has long been what determines building form in dwellings. Here are the most common systems:

TIMBER FRAME

With the exception of some very specific and regional construction types, the earliest houses in North America were timber-framed—that is, the supporting structure of the walls, roof, and floors is a system of heavy wood members, typically 7" to 8" square but as much as 11" in some cases. Timber framing (also called post-and-beam or post-and-girt construction) is a medieval system that came from Europe with New England, mid-Atlantic, and Virginia immigrants who laboriously hand-hewed logs into beams, posts, and girts (transverse members) cut from massive virgin-growth trees. They then connected the timbers like a Chinese puzzle using not nails, but all-wood mortise-and-tenon joints. Settlers from East Anglia (the Puritans) employed timber joints specific to that region. Those from the West Country, mainly Pennsylvania Quakers, used common forms from their home

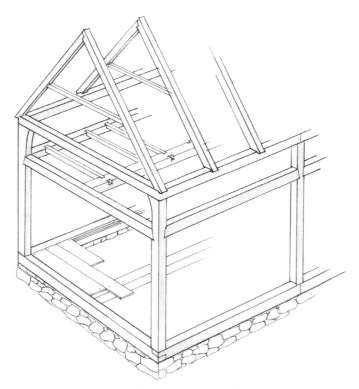

Timber Frame: Heavy, hand-hewn timbers, 8″ square and more, assembled in a self-supporting frame. Lighter lumber (not shown) fills walls and partitions but does not hold up the structure. (Drawing by Rob Leanna.)

counties. And Virginia planters, lacking rot-resistant wood, utilized bricks and timber common to medieval buildings in the south of England.

Though timber framing remained common for building barns through much of the nineteenth century, it became obsolete for houses once sawmill lumber grew plentiful after 1830. Nonetheless, many hundreds of timber frame houses are still in use in the earliest communities of New England, the mid-Atlantic region, across New York, and into Ohio. Even without looking in attics or under later siding, knowing eyes recognize these houses by features like exposed corner posts in rooms or their invariably basic, rectangular forms—the direct result of the relatively inflexible, boxy framing system.

Because timber framing relies on a skeleton—not walls—to hold up the house, it was reborn as a modern system in the 1970s for high-end, rustic-style houses with large, open cathedral ceilings and big windows. Original timber-frame buildings also share these characteristics, and for this reason they are surprisingly amenable to major repairs, by some restorers' standards, because interior partitions can be relocated or removed without affecting the structural system of the house.

BRACED FRAME

After 1800, carpenters began experimenting with framing that used lighter members—on the order of 4″ x 6″ and 4″ x 4″ for girts and post—and this system, called the braced frame, became the transition to modern styles of house construction. The major components of a braced frame house—the sills, girts, corner posts, and braces—still resemble a timber frame in that they are fairly heavy timbers connected with mortise-and-tenon joints. However, braced frame houses add diagonal braces at corners (the source of the name) that help stiffen the frame without the aid of sheathing. What really distinguishes braced frame construction, however, is that the

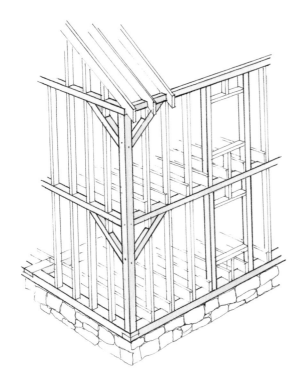

Braced Frame: An improved version of the timber frame using machine-sawn lumber (4x6s for corner posts, sills, and joists); sawn 2x4s are used for studs that still do not support walls. Angled members brace major corners and posts. (Drawing by Rob Leanna.)

wall spaces between posts are filled with lightweight sawn studs. These studs are mortised into the sills and girts, or even toe-nailed into place, and while they are spaced 16" apart they do not carry any structural load—the job still performed by the heavy frame. Braced frame houses were more efficient to construct than timber frame houses, and though this method was most popular before 1850, it pops up in rural areas into the later nineteenth century and is worth recognizing for how it supports a house.

BALLOON FRAME

The construction innovation that is almost synonymous with vintage houses is the balloon frame, a system that it is generally agreed to have been developed in Chicago around 1830. Rather than employing large, hand-hewn timbers, the balloon frame is built exclusively of light, sawmill-sawn lumber (2x4s, 2x6s, etc.), connected not with joinery but machine-made nails. Sills, corner posts, and plates at the top of the wall are built up from two or more pieces of 2x lumber. What's more, walls are built entirely of 2x4 studs that hold up the floors, roof, and all loads. While better-built balloon frame houses incorporate diagonal braces to hold the frame rigid, generally the system relies on the exterior sheathing as an important component for keeping the frame from leaning or twisting, and for this reason the sheathing is often nailed on diagonally across the walls.

The hallmark of a balloon frame house, however, is that the wall studs run continuously from the foundation to the

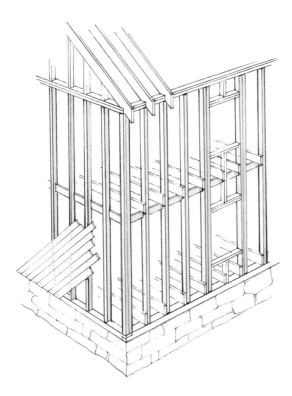

Balloon Frame: The entire frame is machine-sawn 2x4 and 2x6 lumber. Wall studs offer support and run the full height of the building. Floors are "let in" to studs later. Diagonal sheathing covering the exterior helps stabilize the frame. (Drawing by Rob Leanna.)

grew increasingly scarce, and constructing walls with uninterrupted studs tends to exacerbate building movement and shifting, it does have its advantages for repair and remodeling work. Because studs run uninterrupted from sill to eave, the bays or voids between them can make a convenient chase for running wiring, pipes, and so forth. In construction, good carpenters would add fire stops (horizontal boards between the studs) to block air movement that would produce a chimney effect in the event of a fire. Since these stops are placed at random heights, they can thwart running utilities until another path around them is discovered—sometimes by switching to another bay.

Balloon framing offered many advantages over heavier timber and braced frames. First, it was cheaper and much faster to erect a house with a balloon frame than with earlier methods—as quick and light as blowing up a balloon, according to legend. Balloon framing also reduced the need for highly skilled labor. While balloon framing allowed developers and architects to produce lesser quality buildings than timber framing—and certainly more of them—on the positive side it was a far more flexible system. For the first time, balloon framing made practical the wall jogs, bay windows, complex roofs, and creative architectural features that we associate with the innovative buildings of the Victorian era.

PLATFORM FRAME

Balloon frame construction was the standard way to build houses from the Civil War until about World War I, but shortly

eaves—a radical difference from twentieth-century framing techniques. Another characteristic feature is that second- and third-story floors are constructed after the walls are up by resting the floor joists on a horizontal board, called a ribband, that is recessed into the studs. While balloon framing became obsolete because the long lumber necessary for studs the foundation; next, the first-story walls are framed (often by tilting them into place); then the second story floor is built on top of the walls and the process repeats. Platform framing really took off after World War II and remains the standard construction method today because the platforms add stability to the frame, which, when sheathed with plywood (in common use after 1945), becomes a braced box that resists racking.

SOLID MASONRY

Most of the houses built in the twentieth century—especially since the 1920s—that appear to be stone or brick construction are actually wood-frame houses with a veneer of masonry materials. But prior to around 1910, solid masonry houses— that is, buildings whose walls are brick, stone, or concrete block for their entire thickness and are load-bearing (holding up the house)—were almost mandatory for high-end houses and even common for average houses where the materials were plentiful.

Stone, of course, is an ancient, natural building material that requires skill to extract from the earth and shape and place into a useful form. Brick has long been a distinctive and durable building material where supplies of clay are plentiful. Like stone, brick is also fireproof and therefore was mandated by law for cities by the early nineteenth century. Brick became more economical and available in the late nineteenth century with the invention of wire-cut brick produced by machine, making possible the miles of rowhouses in Eastern cities. Even when faced with another material—typically

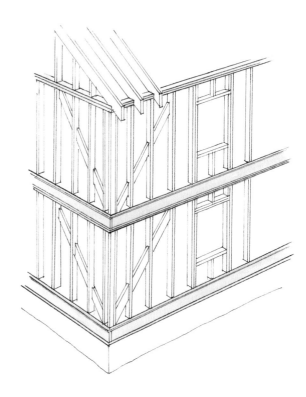

Platform Frame: The frame is all machine-sawn lumber, but wall studs only run the height of each story, where they are capped by the platform of the next floor that helps stabilize the frame. (Drawing by Rob Leanna.)

thereafter the platform frame system started to take over. Originated in the West, and therefore also called Western framing, platform framing improves on balloon framing by using shorter lumber and building each story independently, one on top of the other, like a layer cake. For example, the house begins with building the first-story floor—or platform—over

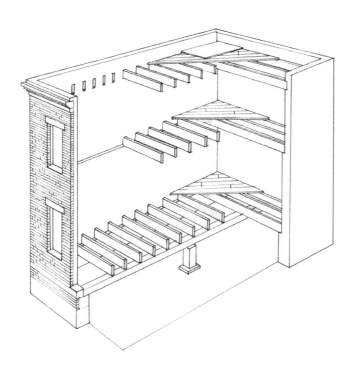

Solid Masonry: A house or rowhouse (shown here) is a shell of stone or brick, sometimes faced with a stone veneer. Floor joists and other structural members are set into pockets in the masonry walls.
(Drawing by Rob Leanna.)

brownstone or limestone—the load-bearing walls behind the veneers are invariably brick. The last late blooming of solid masonry houses came with the improved production of Portland cement in the 1890s, which spawned a new form of masonry unit: the ornamental concrete block. Hand-cast on site by tamping damp mortar into a collapsible mold, ornamental concrete block was heavily promoted by equipment producers such as Sears, Roebuck and Co.

ASSESSING MATERIALS AND CONDITIONS

One of the mantras of vintage house care is "Do not destroy good old work," advice attributed to the English designer William Morris in the 1880s. While the concept is easy enough to grasp, the key, of course, is being able to separate the good from the not-so-good.

Assessing and inventorying the form, design, and structural concept of your vintage house is only part—the high-minded theoretical part—of understanding what you have. The other useful part is looking at the materials that make up the physical structure—in terms of what they are (which can tell their own tales about the age of and changes to the building) as well as their quality and how they are performing. Professionals call this exercise a conditions assessment, and though it can take different forms depending on the age and complexity of the building, the idea is to present a snapshot of the overall status and health of the building. This assessment can help you determine what parts need to be replaced or even discarded, and what you will want to keep.

MEASURE THE BUILDING AND ITS BEHAVIOR

The primary way to begin understanding what you have is simply to document your house as it stands. Taking a series of good photographs is a logical place to start, and a fundamental step in more professional preservation activities. So is making measurements of the building. Professionals documenting significant buildings will undertake what are called measured drawings: such plans, sections, and elevations that document the current dimensions, materials, structure, and other components in a house. The Historic American Buildings Survey, which keeps standards for such drawings, suggests that the architect provide enough information that a building could be reconstructed if it were lost. Making these very detailed drawings is not practical for most old house owners; today, a good digital photo can be converted to an adequate scaled drawing using common software in an architect's office.

Measurements don't have to be comprehensive, large-scale, or done with a yardstick to be useful. One of the most valuable kinds of measurement involves noting two major changes in the condition of the building: cracks and moisture. Few houses get to be the vintage age without developing a crack or two or a sticking door or sagging window here

Vestigial House Parts

Most old houses exhibit telltale evidence of service utilities or systems that were state-of the-art when the house was built but are no longer used and frequently long forgotten. These may be in the form of quirky feature or spaces—even whole small rooms—that serve no apparent purpose in today's lifestyles. Others, especially from the late nineteenth century on, are often in the form of pipes, voids, or conduits left in the walls after the operating parts have long since been removed. Though the passage of time has often mythologized early examples of such features with fanciful purposes—such as calling any small or unusual door or space part of the Underground Railroad—more than likely the origin is far more prosaic and utilitarian. Some classic examples:

Low, rectangular hole in kitchen wall: ice/milk pass-through or
    laundry iron safe
Iron pipe in wall at eye level: gas sconce

W. R. OSTRANDER,
Manufacturer of
THE IMPROVED
Speaking Tube Whistles,
SPEAKING TUBES,
Mouth Pieces and Flexible Tubes.
Private Dwellings Fitted with Speaking Tubes and Bells in all parts the country.
19 ANN ST., NEW YORK.

When these terminals are long gone, speaking tubes are only mysterious pipes. (Courtesy of the National Archives Associates.)

Large brass pipe in wall at eye level: speaking tube
Iron pipe in ceiling center: gas chandelier
Porcelain tube in framing: early knob-and-tube electric wiring
Alcove off kitchen: breakfast nook or pantry
Floor-to-ceiling cabinet in kitchen or pantry: dumbwaiter (in row-
    houses) or California cooler (in bungalows)
Large-diameter pipe in baseboard: central (gas) vacuum cleaner

and there. Indeed, in minimal form, such age marks are to be expected and accepted. What's more, cracks that are minor and come and go with the seasons—such as in plaster walls— or never grow in width or length are generally considered stable (typically the result of initial settling) and not a concern. What is a concern is a crack that is moving and growing, especially in a load-bearing wall. Here small devices and methods called crack tell-tales or stress gauges positioned on the crack can help determine if it is, in fact, active and the symptom of a potential problem by measuring the slow movement over time.

An even more low-tech device for determining evidence of movement is an empty picture frame, or a right-angled rectangle cut out of a piece of shirt cardboard. Viewing the house through this window at various facades and angles can

immediately reveal if any parts are out of square, particularly if walls are leaning or spreading at the foundation, which can indicate structural problems.

Another class of condition-measuring tools are devices for detecting moisture. Meters that assess the amount of moisture in wood or stone by measuring the electrical current between two probes, or transmitting radio waves through the material, are widely used to evaluate patterns of moisture—for example, in a brick wall that continues to bubble off plaster. More low-tech but equally valuable are tell-tales—paperlike materials of one sort or another that will change color or shape in the presence of water—enabling the user to, say, find an elusive roof leak when placed on the attic floor.

Moisture meters are valuable diagnostic tools for "seeing" the moisture content in various materials. They help to identify high-level areas and, thereby, the sources of problems like peeling paint. (Photo courtesy of Barbara Krankenhaus.)

Crack or stress gauges are low-tech but critical tools for measuring the amount and speed of any building movement. (Photo courtesy of Barbara Krankenhaus.)

INSPECT THE SITE

Take a good look at how your house sits on its site, especially relative to the surrounding landscape and plantings.

Grading, slope, and drainage—Many vintage houses are among the original dwellings in their area, and their builders took pains to locate them on the best sites: high and dry, with good drainage and grades that fall away from the foundation. But later development—particularly repeated paving of roads—may have actually raised the surrounding grade to the point that the earth pitches water toward the house. Swales (earth depressions designed to conduct away rainwater) may have become filled in, and plants and landscaping added against the foundation may have brought the grade closer to wood parts, inviting moisture and insect problems. (Builders always maintain at least 18" of unobstructed foundation masonry above grade to prevent termites from creating mud tubes that allow them to travel from soil to wood.) Look also for evidence of ponding (rain accumulations) and water in basements.

Vegetation—Be aware of trees that have grown close to the house or limbs that overhang the roof or cause excessive shade. Nearby trees can also be the source of roots that crack and undermine foundations. Today it is common practice to surround a house in a dense nest of shrubs, but prior to about 1920 homeowners and builders wisely never did this because they knew plants invite moisture that rots buildings. Make sure any plantings leave at least three feet of free space in front of the foundation.

INSPECT THE FOUNDATION

The condition of the foundation is the leading indicator of the condition of the house, as well as important evidence of its construction quality and history. If the foundation is not sound, or is in danger of collapse, renovation will be at best expensive and at worst impossible.

Note the construction—Is the foundation simple—say rubble stone in light mortar or dry laid—or more sophisticated coursed masonry, such as stone, brick, or concrete block? Is it poured concrete walls or a concrete slab? Is there a basement? Can you tell if there are footings? A footing is the bottom-most element in a foundation, spreading the load of the wall over the soil. Many old foundations do not have them, and this is a crucial factor when excavating for additions, because it is expensive to install footings below existing stone walls, and dangerous to build against shallow stone foundation walls not built on footings.

Note the condition—Cracks, water intrusion, loose mortar, spalling, frost heaves, and rotten wood are all indicators of potential foundation problems, either from the past or still on-going.

INSPECT THE ROOF

The second most important component of any building is its roof, the first defense against water, the leading cause of damage in any building. Is it made of a durable material, such as slate or tile, or an ephemeral one, such as rubber, tin, or thatch? What is the condition of areas between the roof and the walls, such as eaves, gutters, parapets, and gable moldings?

Identify the roof type and roofing material—Vintage house roofs usually fall into one of the six or so basic forms, even when they are complex and made up of multiple subordinate shapes and form. On houses, roofing is usually asphalt shingles of one type or another, but may also be one of the time-honored materials—slate, clay tile, metal, or wood shingles—or a modern man-made material (see Chapter 9).

Consider the condition—Each roofing material has its own expected lifespan and characteristic signs of age or wear, but generally be on the lookout for signs of trouble like flaking,

No matter how durable the roofing material, moss is a sign of moisture buildup from lack of maintenance, such as trimming overhanging limbs or cleaning, that can lead to deterioration. (Photo courtesy of Barbara Krankenhaus.)

delamination, and loss of shape (slate and asphalt); cracked or missing units; moss, lichens, and other organisms indicative of high moisture (especially on wood); and rusting or corroding flashings, fasteners, and drainage system components.

INSPECT THE MASONRY

As we've noted, except in cities, houses built with stone or brick masonry began to grow increasingly less common after about 1910, but even where masonry is relegated to the foundation or areas of veneer over a wood frame, its condition is just as important to assess.

Plant growth—Attractive and romantic as they may be, vines that grow up masonry walls can damage them and should be removed, especially when excessive. Leaves prevent sun and air from reaching the wall and drying the brick or stone, and roots and anchor pads can dislodge mortar and soft brick as they grow. For this reason, never pull live vines off the building.

Water erosion—Splashback from roof runoff can erode soft brick and stones, such as some sandstones. The same effects can be the result of snow pile-up in wintertime and high-pressure spraying to remove graffiti.

Discoloration—Though usually only a cosmetic issue, water runoff from copper flashings or other metal elements can sometimes discolor light stones with objectionable green or brown stains.

Bedding plane flaking—In some older buildings, sedimentary stones were improperly installed so that their bedding planes are not horizontal (the way the stones were formed in nature) but vertical. Over years of exposure, this vertical orientation can lead to flaking away of the stone, as in the infamous "brownstone eczema" on the stone veneers of many New York and Boston rowhouses.

Mortar joint erosion—Over decades, gradual wearing away of the mortar between brick and stone masonry units is to be expected. But when the mortar becomes deteriorated and joint depth becomes pronounced (about $3/8''$, depending on joint type), moisture is more likely to penetrate and the wall is ready for repointing.

Mortar mismatch—Spalled and cracked bricks in a building from about 1890 or earlier are often the result of

Sandblasting not only removes paint, it erodes the outer, protective crust of the bricks, destroying their appearance and exposing the softer, porous interior to the elements. (Photo courtesy of Barbara Krankenhaus.)

Sedimentary stones installed perpendicular to their bedding planes expose the layers to weather that can lead to the "brownstone eczema," a condition endemic to East Coast rowhouses. (Photo courtesy of Barbara Krankenhaus.)

repointing the brickwork or making repairs with mortar that is too hard. Bricks and lime mortar used before the 1860s are much softer than later, industrially made versions—particularly modern Portland cement, which is relatively inflexible. So when the wall expands, the compressive forces cause the bricks, which are weaker than the cement, to fracture.

Blasted brick—Sandblasting brick facades to remove paint was a common practice in the 1960s and '70s until it was realized that blasting removes the protective outer "crust" of brick. This leaves an unattractive, pockmarked surface that exposes the softer, inner core to moisture penetration.

Rising damp—In locales with very high water tables, brick walls and foundations sometimes become prone to rising damp—moisture drawn by capillary action out of the ground and several feet up the masonry wall. At this point it evaporates in a "tide mark" of crystalline efflorescence that damages plaster and paint.

Veneer/cavity wall delamination—Many solid brick walls built in the nineteenth century are actually an outer and inner wall tied together around a hollow core. When water damage or poor construction causes these ties (sometimes made of metal) to break, the outer and inner walls can bulge and delaminate. The same can happen in twentieth-century houses with brick or stone veneers applied over a wood frame.

Structural cracks—Initial building settlement or ongoing foundation problems can lead to characteristic cracks in masonry walls, especially near openings such as windows.

Cracks in masonry are symptoms of building movement and often appear in characteristic patterns. Step cracks near grade, for example, may indicate a shifting foundation. (Photo courtesy of Barbara Krankenhaus.)

Identifying the crack pattern and measuring its movement can help determine its cause and severity.

Freeze/thaw damage—When a brick or soft stone wall is subjected to excessive moisture and cycles of repeated freezing and thawing, the force of the expanding ice can cause the materials to spall and flake.

Iron exfoliation—When iron or steel anchors set in stone become wet to the point that the metal rusts, the metal can flake, expand, and blow the stone apart.

Chimneys—Note the style of the chimney masonry (rubble, coursed stone, brick pattern, etc.) as well as the construction and design. Condition includes the status of the flue (lined, unlined, or parged) as well as the integrity of cap masonry and flashing where the chimney meets the roof.

INSPECT THE WOOD

Most houses in North America are overwhelmingly composed of wood, and though cellulose can last for centuries when kept dry, when subjected to moisture over a certain level it quickly succumbs to decay from wood-eating organisms. One of the best ways to get a snapshot of the condition of your house is to inspect the wood components in areas that are prone to water exposure. A simple visual inspection will reveal obvious deterioration, but probing the wood with a penknife or ice pick is a low-tech, minimally invasive way to assess conditions below the surface. Anywhere the blade penetrates the wood more that 1/4" is a possible sign of deterioration under the paint. Begin with the following basic checklist:

Contact with masonry—Examine the perimeter of the house where it rests on the foundation, both outside (along the bottom of the siding or cladding and water table trim) and in the basement, where the sill member will be evident. Outdoor areas with excessive moisture exposure, such as from rain splashback or poorly maintained gutters, may show fungal attack; more likely the problem will be wood-eating insects infesting any heavy timbers. Be especially on the lookout for termites; they build mud tubes up from the earth and across any masonry or into cracks in stone or brick to reach the wood, which they then excavate without any exterior signs. In solid masonry houses, also inspect any areas where structural members, such as floor joists, rest in pockets in walls.

Contact with ground—Generally, good builders avoided placing any wood parts in direct contact with the earth, but in early, rural, or simple buildings it was sometimes done anyway. Inspect any support posts in basements to make sure they rest on masonry footings of some kind. The same is true for any wall sills or floors. Also inspect the supports of porches and exteriors stairs, which are often built on minimal bases—perhaps nothing more than a flat rock—that may have moved or become buried.

Lintels and exposed beams—Inspect lintels—the horizontal spans over windows and doors—and also the beams that support porch roofs between posts. Look for signs of stress cracks along bottom edges and sagging, as well as deterioration.

Siding and shingles—Note whether the walls are clad

Wood cladding, such as this horizontal siding, can last for generations with proper care. However, paint failure—such as poor preparation indicated by peeling between coats—can open the door to rot. (Photo courtesy of Barbara Krankenhaus.)

with wood shingles or one of the many types of wood siding, such as vertical boards-and-battens, horizontal clapboards, or milled drop siding (German, novelty, etc.). Look for paint peeling down to wood, rusting or popped nails, rotting areas, and other signs of water problems, as well as splits, curling boards, and insect damage.

INSPECT THE WINDOWS AND DOORS

First, create a log of all the windows in the house—typically forty or more—organized by building facade (for example, south side, second floor) and the exterior doors.

Age and type—Note their design as well as the condition. Windows have characteristic muntin patterns, profiles, and construction in any era (see Chapter 10), and you should expect to find that the windows been upgraded one or more times in the past—a practice that goes back to preindustrial times. Be on the lookout for the original or oldest windows, often found in the upper stories or service spaces where the expense of new windows was deemed less important. Reserve a special comment for decorative windows, such as fanlights, ovals, or those of stained or leaded glass. Do the same for all exterior doors.

Condition—Besides noting any broken or missing glass, evaluate the condition of the glazing putty and paint and the wood muntins and sash frame. Usually the worst conditions are found along the bottoms of sashes—especially the top sash—and the windowsill. Test the window to see if it operates and note the condition of the hardware and any balance systems, such as weights and pulleys. Follow the same procedure for casement windows, both wood and steel, and accessories such as screens and storm windows.

INSPECT THE INTERIORS

Finally, take a close look inside the house to see how well the important interior structures are holding up.

Walls and ceilings—Note whether walls and ceilings are plaster or another material, such as wood paneling or beadboard, and their condition. Waviness and minor cracking in plaster is to be expected, particularly in early construction, but large bulges or soft spots—especially in ceilings—indicate a mechanical failure of the plaster or water damage.

Floors—Determine the flooring material: wood, ceramic tile, or resilient flooring such as linoleum, cork, rubber, or vinyl. Wood species for floors may be hard to determine, but can usually be recognized as being either softwoods (typically pine) or hardwoods (typically oak or maple). The cut of the flooring wood is also noteworthy, but more obvious may be board width and flooring type (wide board, strip tongue-and-groove, or parquet), and finish (varnish, paint, or bare wood). Note the condition and any serious defects (wear, water or animal damage).

Even modest vintage houses will have forty or more windows, invariably of different age, design, and condition. Making an inventory is an essential part of assessing the building. (Photo courtesy of Barbara Krankenhaus.)

OLD HOUSE CHRONOLOGIES

Once you are familiar with the materials, details, and condition of your home, a little research on its building history—what many in the preservation field call the "paper trail"—will reveal much about why it has aged as well or poorly as your discoveries have shown. As in genealogical research, the sources for building history have expanded during the digital age, so your task will not be as difficult as you imagine. And if you prefer to hire a professional, more and more specialists are emerging to help you get the data you need.

Any comprehensive building chronology should address certain fundamental questions about who designed and constructed the original house, the subsequent owners, and significant changes made over the years. If you are working on your own, try to answer these important questions:

1. When was the land purchased, and by whom? Was another house on the property prior to yours?
2. Did the original house appear in any historic atlases or on maps, such as Sanborn Fire Insurance maps (available at http://sanborn.umi.com)? How did it change when maps were updated?
3. Can you locate any biographical or genealogical data on the family of the original builder? If so, are descendents alive who might provide insights into the house?
4. Was an architect identified with the design of the original house in any publication, deed, or family record? If so, you may be able to find data on his or her career and buildings at organizations like the American Institute of Architects (www.aia.org) and the AIA Historical Directory of American Architects.
5. If no architect can be found, is the builder's name or company recorded? In the past, a new house in town was noteworthy and often written up in the local newspaper's real estate pages.
6. Are original photographs or drawings available that record the condition and design of the house immediately following its completion? (Hint: sometimes these drawings are kept in attics, closets, or basements.)

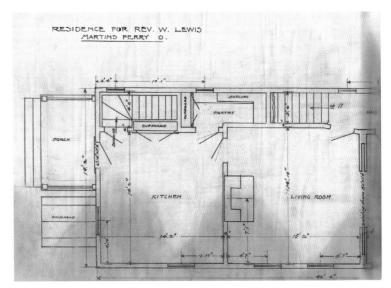

Original construction drawings, such as these linens from 1900, can be enlightening pieces of a house's historic paper trail. Though not a guaranteed find, they may be filed in the county building department or even secreted away in the house, say, in a hollow newel post. (Photo courtesy of the National Archives Associates.)

7. Did the house appear in any city directories or publications during its early years?
8. When did the property change hands during its history? Can you find deeds in the county courthouse that provide dates and ownership transfers?
9. What kinds of oral history records exist about the neighborhood? Do local history documents, such as newspapers, provide any information about the house, owners, or setting?
10. What do the previous owners know about the house? Can they share records, photos, or memories with you?

With these facts you can compare the physical evidence you've discovered with records of changes in the house. Fascinating new questions may emerge as you learn to make connections between dates, people, and construction evidence. Part of the fun of owning an old house is seeing how history unfolds in the development of an artifact, and relating your own family story to that of your predecessors.

Any or all of the survey work outlined above can be accomplished by a well-educated homeowner, but even the best prepared will not be able to make judgments about how to treat problems with historic materials and construction technology. Why? The answer should be obvious—professional education in historic building conservation is arduous and specialized, and even the best architects in general practice do not have the knowledge to attack complex issues in an old house. Specialists in the building trades will have solutions that relate only to their own areas, and may ignore problems that are interwoven with the fabric of the building. So while it is necessary to appreciate and understand the varying conditions and characteristics of your house, you should acquire that knowledge with the help of professionals. The next step in your vintage house project should be designing your expansion with an architect. In the next chapter we explore how sophisticated design can solve numerous problems in an old house, even without expanding its footprint.

4

NEW SPACES IN OLD PLACES

ANY HOUSE THAT IS MORE THAN FIFTY YEARS OLD will contain spaces and features that were created to address ways of living that are probably obsolete or irrelevant today. These include not merely the butler's pantry, summer kitchen, keeping room, root cellar, and smoking den but also more recent must-haves such as the sunken living area with lava rock fireplace. Even "modern" houses of the 1950s are equipped with gimmicks that today seem quaint, nostalgic, or silly because they are out of fashion. Think of those perforated metal screens that often separated the entry hall from the living room and you will know what we mean. If you are lucky enough to purchase a vintage house with most of its original fabric intact, you'll want to keep all of the original materials and elements *except* those that now impinge on a twenty-first-century lifestyle.

Updating a great old house is the first thing most savvy owners do, and that usually means replacing outdated plumbing, electrical, and heating systems. With rare exceptions, kitchens and bathrooms are renovated with all new appliances and fixtures, even if the decor maintains a vintage look. When those spaces are reconfigured a few walls are removed and perhaps relocated to accommodate new stuff. Occasionally a contractor does the redesign, but most often a good architect will create the new spaces with an eye toward preserving the integrity of adjoining rooms and decorative features.

If merely upgrading building systems is hard, a greater challenge occurs when families require significant new spaces for things like mudrooms, study areas or home offices, breakfast rooms, media rooms, and family and recreation rooms. Though the impulse to create bulky additions for these things is often hard to resist, it is not always necessary or prudent to add rooms when underutilized spaces are available. Good architects challenge their clients to see solutions in unexpected places and pursue novel strategies, often with results that are a delight to all who use or visit the renovated house.

One space that is increasingly common in new houses is the home office. More people are choosing to telecommute or perhaps start a home-based business. With two working parents in the family, childcare and school commitments can be a challenge. So when families look at their space needs in older houses, a home office is often on the list of must-haves.

As we pointed out in Chapter 2, it is easier to destroy the character of a dwelling with misguided interventions than to knit new rooms into the intricate patterns of vernacular building that sustained our forebears long ago. Structure, modular proportions, and characteristic room designs govern the form of all vintage houses. The elusive rules of style and grammar must also be learned and respected when approaching even a modest renovation. In this chapter we will look at ways of achieving a balanced and appropriate result when the best option is to renovate within the existing footprint of your house.

The three most common issues owners face when renovating a house within the existing envelope or footprint are the treatment of service wings, the expectations for open circulation between rooms, and the use of ancillary areas such as basements, attics, and porches. In each case, designers must analyze both the current condition of the spaces and the historic patterns that governed their use and decoration. Once owners and designers comprehend the different and often contradictory requirements posed by today's design

standards and those of the past, successful solutions can be achieved with less remorse. While trade-offs between historic and contemporary standards for comfort and space are inevitable, once expectations are adjusted it is possible to create new spaces that enhance quality and convenience without doing harm to the character of a vintage house.

SERVICE WINGS WITHOUT THE SERVANTS

Throughout the eighteenth and most of the nineteenth centuries, American households included servants to help with cooking, cleaning, laundry, and other necessary domestic labor. The spaces reserved for hired live-in help were generally meager, while in the South slave quarters were most often distant from the big house. During the mid-nineteenth century many women began to address the need for more commodious service areas in articles and books on "domestic economy." The result of these efforts was a significant improvement in the design of the working areas of houses, seen in working-, middle- and upper-class dwellings.

By the dawn of the twentieth century a technological revolution was changing the way families approached domestic chores—labor-saving machines were invented to handle virtually every aspect of household work. Upper-class houses maintained smaller domestic staffs, but lower- and middle-income families began to depend on some form of domestic appliance, if only a stove or refrigerator. Servants' wings

Seth Thomas House, exterior view, Morristown, New Jersey. Original architect, Harrie T. Lindeberg. (Photo courtesy of Mark Alan Hewitt.)

became smaller in large houses and were jettisoned in the typical suburban dwelling. Some scholars have argued persuasively that appliances were often designed to keep women busy in new kitchen and laundry areas, replacing one kind of domestic servitude with another, more insidious variety. But the result was that the service wing no longer occupied a significant portion of the typical American house.[1]

It is rare today to find an intact example of a service wing containing fixtures and cabinetry from the original house. Our occasional discovery of such vintage rooms is cause for celebration, as they often contain artifacts that help us interpret the life of the family, both upstairs and downstairs, as the adage goes. Typically, however, such spaces were renovated with new kitchens and work areas during the twentieth century. It nevertheless makes sense to study the configuration of rooms and the circulation in old service wings when considering any kind of renovation. In our experience, seldom do owners work deliberately to maximize the usefulness of former servant work areas and bedrooms. There is almost always some wiggle room in a service area that can be better configured for contemporary uses.

It is unusual for an architect to happen upon a fine house with a completely discrete and well-preserved service wing, but we were lucky enough to find one in the historic Seth Thomas house in Morristown, New Jersey, in 2006. This five-part Colonial Revival house was the work of the outstanding early twentieth-century architect Harrie T. Lindeberg (1869–1959).[2] The original owner was a third-generation tycoon of the famous Seth Thomas clock company of Hartford, Connecticut. It had recently been purchased by a young family in the area who wished to maintain its historical integrity while updating the services for their needs. Fortunately, the building and a portion of the large estate remained in excellent condition after only three owners. Our task was made easier because the large service wing on the east end of the building was in poor condition, requiring a complete renovation.

Once we understood the owner's program things fell into place very logically. The basement of the wing would be renovated to serve as exercise rooms for the family. The main floor would become a kitchen, pantry, children's cooking area, mudroom, and office for the lady of the house. A garage that had been converted into an apartment was to be restored to its original use, and a second one added to

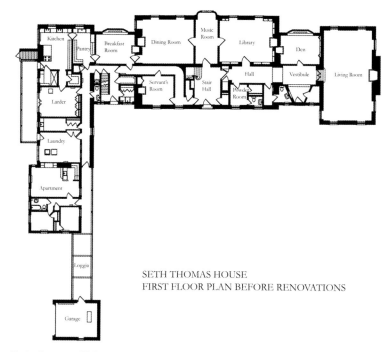

SETH THOMAS HOUSE
FIRST FLOOR PLAN BEFORE RENOVATIONS

Existing conditions plan of the Seth Thomas house, before renovations in 2006. (Photo courtesy of Mark Alan Hewitt.)

form an auto court. On the second floor the old servants' bedrooms were removed to make way for an apartment for the owner's elderly parents, who wanted a place to stay when business brought them to town.

Good architecture always provides logical clues for renovation, and Lindeberg's designs are notable for their elegance, proportion, and functional clarity. Even though it was designed during the early 1920s, this house might well have been planned for a contemporary family of means. Though large by American standards, the building was designed to flow effortlessly from room to room, and each space was only as big as it needed to be for the functions required. When we began designing the new spaces, it almost seemed as if the original architect had laid out the renovation for us in advance. Subdividing the rooms in the barlike wing was a breeze, and the circulation connected logically with the existing hallways and vestibules. We were also fortunate that the family wanted to keep the new rooms in character with the old ones, and that a sympathetic interior designer, Laurie Finn, was our collaborator on the project.

The kitchen suite of the house is an expansion of the old service area on the first floor. We included both a large pan-

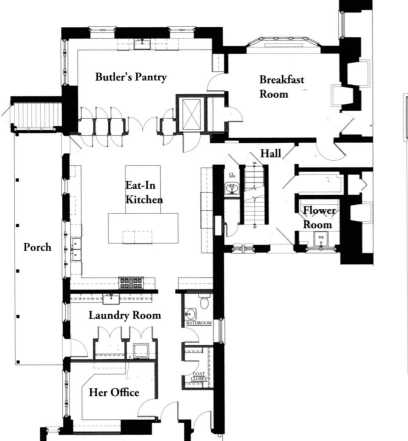
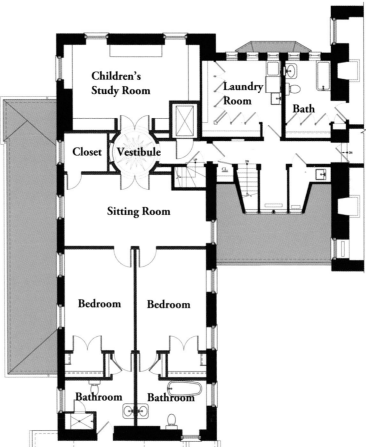

Seth Thomas House, first and second floor plans of the service wing after renovation. (Drawing by Jerry A. Bruno, Jr.; courtesy of Mark Alan Hewitt Architects.)

Seth Thomas house, new kitchen as renovated. (Design by Joan Piccone and Laurie Finn; courtesy of Mark Alan Hewitt Architects.)

try/servery, with glass-front cabinets for china, and a smaller children's cooking area. The main room is a large kitchen with central island, designed to evoke the aura of the 1920s—two kinds of finishes were employed on the cabinets to set off the center area from the side prep counters. Adjacent to the kitchen and connected to the garage, we fashioned a mudroom for athletic children (and parents) and a personal space for mom to do her important work.

Directly adjacent to the kitchen wing was a courtyard formerly used for deliveries and service vehicles. The family, working with landscape architect John Charles Smith, identified this area as a potential outdoor living room that could be used for informal meals, barbecues, and relaxation in good weather. Using a few low stone walls and plantings, Smith framed a delightful patio that is now a focal point of family life in the spring, summer, and fall. Subsequently connected to an outdoor pool terrace, the ensemble is screened from the formal gardens that were part of the historic landscape. In this way the character of the place remains much the same as it did in the 1920s.

Upstairs the family had requirements based on the integration of the younger and older generations into the life of the house. For visits from the owner's elderly parents we designed separate apartment that would allow privacy but also occasional interaction with their grandchildren. We created a vestibule near the old back staircase to mark their domain, but placed a children's homework room nearby so that younger family members could look in on their grandparents from time to time. Both suites were tailored to par-

Seth Thomas House, new family dining terrace created in the old service yard. (Courtesy of Mark Alan Hewitt Architects.)

ticular needs, but maintained the overall character of the interiors—classic but not too formal.

John Milner has been restoring historic houses in the Philadelphia area for over forty years. He began his career as an architect with the National Park Service, and went on to teach historic preservation at the University of Pennsylvania, training dozens of young architects. There is little he hasn't seen. When asked to update Sogno Mio, a 1915 house on Philadelphia's Main Line, originally built by the outstanding campus architect, Charles Z. Klauder, he and his staff took up the challenge with relish.

"Sogno Mio" translates from the Italian as "My Dream."

Few homes have had such a colorful history revolving around fine art and music. The original owner, John Frederick Braun, had it built to house one of the most impressive collections of American art of its day. Braun was a manufacturer, concert singer, art collector, and a patron of music and art. He married the former Edith Evans, a pianist, in 1920. Braun was president of the Philadelphia Art Alliance, served on the boards of the Philadelphia Orchestra and the Presser Foundation, and was a member of the Philadelphia Museum of Art.

John Milner Architects converted a compact service wing (to the right in the photo) at Sogno Mio into a beautiful space for family living with convenient access to a pool terrace. The renovation required not only research into the home's original design but the demolition of some ill-advised later additions. (Photo by Tom Crane Photography; courtesy of John Milner Architects.)

Like many classical houses, this Mediterranean style gem had a clear and very generous circulation system based on symmetry and balance. What it did not have was space for informal family living or enough upstairs bedrooms. Milner recognized that its compact service wing, located to the left of the main entrance, could provide the needed amenities. Unfortunately, a previous addition had engulfed the old wing, and part of the original terrace had been destroyed in the process. The owners were reluctant to demolish it, but Milner convinced them that the result would bring back the spirit of the Klauder design. "We wanted to respect the art and craftsmanship that went into the original house, to honor the work," said the owner, a leading mural artist who admired the classical details and spaces.

On the first floor the architect's interventions were minimal but brilliantly effective. The existing kitchen was expanded to create a dining area, and an old breakfast room was converted to a family/media space. Because the large transverse hall was the nerve center of the house, the architects recognized the need for an inviting connection to it from the newly renovated wing—this was provided by creating a "family room hall" with French doors where there had previously been only a wall. The resulting space was much more than a mere corridor, functioning instead as a gateway to the new center of the house, the family/kitchen wing. Existing classical details in the main hall were maintained and extended, but the overall effect was not stiff or formal as in the old house, but light and airy.

The old kitchen from 1915 was modernized and outfitted for family use. The architects designed a skylight to illuminate the new island, brightening a space that was formerly dim and constricted. (Photo by Tom Crane Photography; courtesy of John Milner Architects.)

The large stair hall facing the garden terrace originally came to a dead end at the old breakfast room. After renovation, the space was opened up to invite visitors into the new family/kitchen wing. The hall serves as a gallery for the work of its owner, one of America's most esteemed mural artists. She and her husband have four children, so the room also serves as a living space. (Photo by Tom Crane Photography; courtesy of John Milner Architects.)

New bathrooms in vintage houses are often a compromise: new showers and larger sinks can overwhelm the charm of the old rooms. In this master bath Milner balanced modern and traditional elements—a glass door shower and a paneled soaking tub—to exquisite effect. The owner served as her own interior designer. (Photo by Tom Crane Photography; courtesy of John Milner Architects.)

The second floor required major rearrangement, as the existing servant rooms were small. The new design created two suites—one for guests and one for children—that balanced the generous spaces in the old master bedroom wing. Because two large chimneys needed accommodation, some of the bathroom planning required squeezing and some compromises. Indeed, it was the owner's request for private baths in every room that challenged the designers most—each bedroom retained its necessary storage spaces in a new arrangement. Moreover, the master suite gained an elegant dressing room and a distinctive bathroom that captured the spirit of an Italian villa, Klauder's original inspiration for the house.

Accustomed to working in the tight spaces of eighteenth-century Pennsylvania farmhouses, Milner and the contractor, Cherokee Construction, were well-prepared for this unique project. Moreover, they understood the particular modules that were commonly used in planning classical houses during the early twentieth century, and repeated them in the new spaces they created both upstairs and downstairs. As a result, nothing appears out of scale or proportion with the original spaces and details. Not surprisingly, John Milner Architects have produced some of the finest new classical houses in America.

WHEN THE FLOW ISN'T FLOWING

One of the most common problems that old house owners face when considering a renovation is the configuration of historic circulation systems, especially hallways and staircases. Since the advent of modern open planning in the early twentieth century, families have grown accustomed to circulation with few boundaries between spaces. Pre-twentieth-century houses were generally planned to strictly segregate male and female domains, servants and family members, and the social realms of formal and informal contact between family members and guests. In addition, rooms were designed as contained formal spaces with highly defined codes of surface decoration and prescribed arrangements of objects. Thus, although breaking the boundaries between rooms has become an accepted strategy in contemporary house planning, in many historic houses the removal of a wall or enlargement of an opening between rooms will result in a terrible breach of grammar and formal coherence. Such design faux pas are signs that the architect, owner, or

Seattle bungalow, historic photo. (Courtesy of the Johnson Partnership, Larry E. Johnson, Principal.)

Leschi addition renovation by the Johnson Partnership. (Photo by Howard Miller; courtesy of the Johnson Partnership, Larry E. Johnson, Principal.)

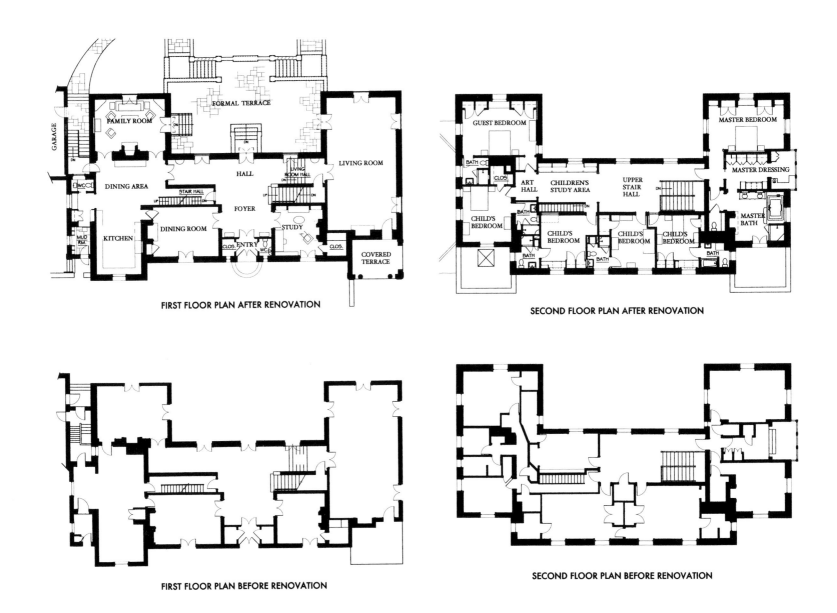

FIRST FLOOR PLAN AFTER RENOVATION

SECOND FLOOR PLAN AFTER RENOVATION

FIRST FLOOR PLAN BEFORE RENOVATION

SECOND FLOOR PLAN BEFORE RENOVATION

Sogno Mio, first and second floor plans before and after renovation. The service wing is on the left side of the house. (Courtesy of John Milner Architects.)

Plans of the Leschi addition before (left) and after (right) renovation. (Courtesy of the Johnson Partnership, Larry E. Johnson, Principal.)

contractor has misunderstood the formal and stylistic rules that govern the layout of the dwelling.

The tension between contemporary expectations for space use and circulation and those of our ancestors can be frustrating for vintage house owners, but needn't prevent families from modifying houses to improve the flow between interior and exterior areas, upper and lower floors, or formal and service zones. Indeed, the *transitions* between living areas in a house, facilitated by circulation paths, are critical in the design of any modern dwelling. Sometimes the connection between outdoor and indoor spaces is altered by changes in the configuration or design of the surrounding site. Perhaps

Leschi kitchen before (left) and after (right) renovation by the Johnson Partnership. (Photo by Howard Miller; courtesy of the Johnson Partnership, Larry E. Johnson, Principal.)

a former garden must be used for auto circulation, making it necessary for a formerly open interior with windows to become more private. Conversely, service areas in the rear of the house that once faced a perfunctory court may now be required to open to a new enclosed garden.

Then there is the problem of stairways that may be obsolete, or begin and end in the wrong places, or no longer function well in their current location. Architects learn early in school that stairs are difficult to design, especially when their placement does not reinforce a logical circulation system. Evaluating the efficacy of existing stairways can present a challenging puzzle that some designers fail to solve.

Often an owner poses the question of how to fix persistent problem with flow in an old house that seems congested and cramped. If stair halls and staircases are interfering with the natural circulation, for whatever reason, family members will become irritated by the resulting impediments to their daily routines. One of the most common causes of vertical circulation problems is the relocation of an entrance from the front to the auto side of an old house. If there is no service or second staircase, tortured rerouting of circulation through formal rooms can result. And if a second stair is too small or badly configured, location near a kitchen or mudroom will not solve the problem.

The hall of the Leschi house now allows circulation from both side-to-side and front-to-back, improving the flow. (Courtesy of the Johnson Partnership, Larry E. Johnson, Principal.)

Bustle Back Dormers

There's nothing new about adding a dormer to the back of a gable-roofed house—indeed, the rear is often the favored facade for finding more room because it doesn't tamper with the street-side appearance. However, when the "dormer" extends the full width of the house and right to the outside walls, it not only stretches the concept of of a dormer but obliterates any hint of the original roof line. Invariably, the urge to maximize space—especially for 1990s-style mega-master bathrooms—also cranks up the rear wall, giving the new dormer roof a much shallower pitch than the front roof. Seen from the side, this mismatch in slopes can give the house a conspicuous humped derriere that, to some eyes, resembles a bustle—a frame worn by Victorian women to support the back of a skirt.

Indeed, the relationship between formal and service areas in an older house is very often at odds with the needs of contemporary families. As we've seen, the strict segregation between servants and masters in Anglo-American houses created highly specific room arrangements that can bedevil modern residents in these dwellings. In extreme cases it is sometimes necessary to move kitchens, pantries, and dining areas to the opposite side of a house when a former service wing does not connect well with new garages, entrances, or stairways. More often, when the disused service wing is converted to new uses, a modification in the interior circulation will be required to fuse the new and old together.

Larry Johnson and Howard Miller of the Johnson Partnership, a Seattle architecture firm noted for its historic preservation work, are well aware of the importance of maintaining a sense of orderly flow in houses. In one of their most subtle remodeling projects, they turned a worn and tattered historic bungalow into an Arts and Crafts gem with a few subtle strokes. Assessing the difference between the ground floor plan before and after the renovation takes a bit of scrutiny—how did moving just one wall make such a profound difference? (See p. 87.)

Classic bungalows, of which Seattle's Henry Wilson was a leading purveyor, work on the basis of a simple theme taken to endless variation. Start with a low-pitched roof, drape it on a simple rectangular plan, add a porch and a stone foundation, and you're done. At the turn of the twentieth century

The dining room was improved with the addition of a built-in Arts & Crafts style server. (Courtesy of the Johnson Partnership, Larry E. Johnson, Principal.)

solution appear out of nowhere. As a feng shui expert might put it, this house had blockages in its ch'i nearly everywhere. Though the entry hall was elegantly trimmed with oak in the best Arts and Crafts manner, there was no clear distinction between doors to a back bedroom and the tiny kitchen in the space. Moreover, the staircase was nearly invisible, making access to both the basement and the bedroom floor a mystery.

The simple scheme devised by the architects worked wonders with the stair hall and took care of the blocked circulation. By nudging the lower landing of the stair into the room, the designers gave the second floor more prominence in the circulation. By hiding the guest bedroom door, the kitchen door took on its proper central place in the hall. Even the dining room was improved when the architects converted a pass-through into a serving cabinet. In the best sense, this renovation brought out the essential nature of the bungalow, allowing it to fully realize its potential.

bungalows offered inexpensive, rustic shelter to folks who liked an outdoor feeling—hence the large porches on front and rear. Despite their lack of pretension, bungalows maintained a distinction between service areas and living areas. Kitchens and bathrooms were squirreled away in corners and behind small doors and were not readily accessible.

The family wanted their renovated bungalow to flow logically from front to back, and had in mind a kitchen that would become a focal point, not an afterthought. Their back yard wasn't roomy enough for a large addition, but their architect had one or two tricks up his sleeve that made a

When the Boston architect Jim Righter first saw the dwelling that would become the Long House in Mattapoisett, Massachusetts, he was challenged by the narrow site. An original Greek Revival house stood close to the street in a common orientation, but previous renovations had added a boxcarlike ell to the rear of the building that created a poor functional layout and impossible circulation from front to back. Moreover, the house seemed catawampus in relation to the side garden, and his clients were avid plant lovers who wanted to spend time outdoors.

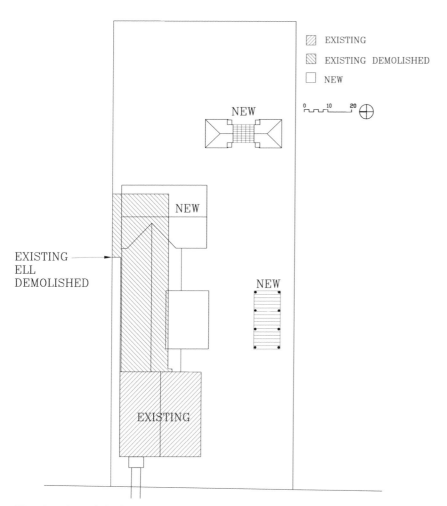

The site plan of the Long House shows how Albert, Righter & Tittmann Architects handled a long, narrow lot. The demolished service wing of the original Greek Revival cottage became a template for a new wing of bedrooms and a kitchen/dining area. (Courtesy of Albert, Righter & Tittmann Architects.)

Right: The plan of the Long House. The architects created a circulation spine on the north side of the site, allowing the new rooms to open out onto a new garden and dining terrace. (Courtesy of Albert, Righter & Tittmann Architects.)

Recognizing that circulation would drive the design of this renovation, Righter developed a clever plan that balanced the house with the garden as yin and yang. In order to solve a problem with a faulty foundation, the house was picked up while a new concrete foundation was constructed. Once this was done the new ell could be seamlessly attached to the older wing in an A-B-A arrangement. The old wing was renovated to preserve the large main-floor room, but its stair hall was rebuilt to create a continuous circulation spine running the entire 83-foot length of the site. The logic of this configuration is clear when one considers the requirements of a modern family—outdoor living and dining, continuity between kitchen and family areas, private and public zones at opposite ends of the site, and informal, open spaces in the new portions of the house. A brilliant feature of the renovated, yet vintage, Greek Revival gem is the striking gable of the street facade, with its side entrance—a subtle totem for what lies behind. Once one crosses the threshold, the view down the surprising axial hallway runs almost one hundred feet if the master bedroom door is open. It's definitely not your grandpa's kind of stair hall.

Indeed, the Long House functions as one continuous

A problematic foundation below the existing cottage needed complete replacement. The solution was to lift the house on massive steel girders (needles) and build under it (left). Once replaced, it regained its Greek Revival elegance (above). (Courtesy of Albert, Righter & Tittmann Architects.)

The hallway of the Long House is a dramatic space, quite unexpected after entering the front door. All major rooms connect to it. (Courtesy of Albert, Righter & Tittmann Architects.)

open room that is permeable from both the "service" and the garden side. Instead of the claustrophobic effect of small, interconnected rooms that had been a feature of the old building, Righter was able to strike a balance between visually open spaces and privacy by simply clearing an axis along the left side of the site. A former professor at Yale, he knew the power of extending the perceived size of a room by creating visual connections between spaces and by varying the heights of ceilings from room to room.

The resulting string of spaces, each opening to a portion of the new garden, is sublime. The center section of the house—the B of the A-B-A design—contains a combined kitchen, mudroom, and dining room filled with light from an adjacent outdoor eating area. Muted colors and funky furniture give the space a charming pastoral feeling. At the rear of the site the master bedroom rises as a foil to the "temple" on the street side. Adjacent to it is a small pavilion that serves a similar formal role, terminating a new garden axis created by a gate at the street.

The bedroom has a vaulted ceiling and formal furniture arrangement that make it a kind of temple for sleeping. Built-in bookshelves and transom windows create two lower zones that reduce the apparent scale to human proportions. The pavilion next door provides a small private garden space for reading, meditation, and communion with the outdoors. In sum, the Long House is deceptive in its apparent size and scope. Though visitors may think they are in an entirely new building, virtually all of the renovated spaces are within the old footprint. The open feeling created by extending vistas

A terrace off the kitchen/breakfast area is perfect for entertaining or informal leisure. (Courtesy of Albert, Righter & Tittmann Architects.)

Powering Up Powder Rooms

Hard to believe that well into the 1940s the typical house was built with just one bathroom—the eponymous, compact, "five-foot bath" trio of wall-hung wash basin, toilet, and enclosed tub. In fact, indoor bathrooms weren't even mandatory until the 1920s. What this means is that while time has inevitably improved most original bathroom installations, today's vintage house owner may still want to add a half-bath or powder room on the first floor—or any floor—to keep up with modern lifestyles.

The catch in creating a half-bath within an existing floor plan is not so much the mechanics of running new plumbing and wiring (an experienced contractor can do almost anything), but finding sufficient space without short-changing another room. The secret, if there is one, is to think small.

Designers have been searching for the optimum volumes of living spaces for over a century and, in the case of bathrooms, they boil down to the distances necessary to maneuver around a toilet and between features like walls and wash basins. These minimum clearances—generally, 12" to 15" from the fixture's center to either side, and 18" to 21" from the front forward—form the basis of building codes in most parts of the country. When viewed with the toilet as the most critical fixture, these dimensions also become the basic formula for a viable powder room. So the trick to a petite powder room is making these dimensions work, and some creative thinking and problem-solving fixtures can help.

For example, one idea is to position the toilet in a corner, rather than perpendicular to a wall—an installation that, under the right conditions, can buy critical inches of clearance at the front and sides. Since the tank on a standard toilet is what obstructs a corner installation (unless you resort to half-burying it in the stud space), a good way to open up options is to look beyond toilets with conventional tanks:

High-tank or institutional-style toilets

Victorian-style high-tank toilets sold as reproductions locate the tank high on the wall, and their plumbing usually allows for mounting to one side, which may make a corner installation work. So too may commercial toilets that have no tank because they flush with a siphon jet. (Note that these units require a 1" minimum water supply).

Corner-tank toilets

Thanks to at least one manufacturer (Eljer), vintage house owners can take advantage of a commode specifically designed for corner installations—that is, one with a triangular tank.

Concealed-tank toilets

Europeans have long put a premium on bathroom equipment that is efficient and space-saving—think single-handle faucets—as well as elegant and hygienic. Concealed tanks are more common overseas than on this continent, in part because all they expose is a wall-hung bowl, but the 6" or so they save by burying the tank in the stud space can be the real advantage when it comes to old-house powder rooms. Concealed-tank toilets are not a panacea—they usually require building a 6"-deep stud wall, and the units are pricey—but they add the benefit of being easy to clean under the wall-hung bowl.

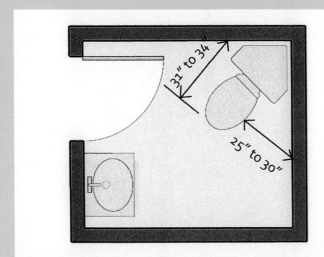

In most communities, codes require a minimum clearance of 18"
to 21" from the front of the bowl to the nearest obstruction, and
a minimum of 16" at either side. Placing the toilet in a corner—
say, with a corner tank unit—can often provide clearance that is
otherwise hard to find. (Drawing by Mark Alan Hewitt.)

Low-profile toilets

Those American-made units do minimize the tank by dropping
it down close to the bowl. This frees up wall space above the
toilet for cabinets or just more open area.

Of course, a wash basin is essential for any powder room,
and fortunately these are commonly available in corner models
and wall-hung designs (which require no space-hungry cabinetry). Whatever fixtures you choose, be sure to have them
on hand before the plumber arrives to avoid costly errors in
measurement while putting together the close-fitting pieces of
your new powder room.

The master bedroom in the Long House is analogous to the old
cottage, but turned 90 degrees to allow for south light. It's a temple
for sleeping and reading. (Courtesy of Albert, Righter & Tittmann Architects.)

and heights creates the impression of freshness and moder-
nity within a historic envelope.

From the street, neighbors are hard pressed to tell
whether there was any renovation at all. In some neighborhoods that is as it should be. A discreet intervention such as
this one attends mainly to the private realm that nurtures
a family. The public face of the house may or may not tele-
graph what occurred when new owners chose to freshen
things up. Indeed, part of the charm of the Long House
is the surprise of crossing the threshold in 1820 and find-

The garden at the Long House has its own small dining pavilion on the east side. (Courtesy of Albert, Righter & Tittmann Architects.)

ing yourself in 2010, like the Connecticut Yankee in King Arthur's Court.

UPSTAIRS AND DOWN

One of the delights of owning a pre-1920 house in America is the discovery of underused attics and basements. Folks who grew up in the "Leave it to Beaver" split-levels, capes, and ranches of postwar America never saw these nether reaches of domesticity because builders had done away with them in their drive for economy and efficiency in construction. When William Levitt erected his little GI-bill houses on Long Island in a matter of days, he had no time for anything but a slab on grade and a little roof insulation.[3] Eichler homes in California had a different selling point—they were not just inexpensive and functional, they were also jet-age modern. Flat, abstract planes and open plans signified a rejection of the past and a view to the future.

There are many advantages to spaces beneath and above the living areas in a house. One is that things like HVAC systems, electrical lines, and plumbing can be concealed in areas that are both accessible and out of sight. Another is that vertical circulation is often already available from other floors. A third is that renovation costs for finishing do not include foundations—among the most expensive elements of construction. Finally, areas above and below the main floors are seldom fully utilized and offer an inexpensive means of expansion.

There are also drawbacks to finishing a basement or attic. Both are exposed to the elements more directly than main floors—the attic to rainfall and ice, the basement to ground water, insects, and earth forces. We have found that many owners seem unaware of the potential costs of waterproofing exposed areas—it is in fact impossible to water*proof* any part of a house, merely to prevent the transmission of water in liquid form through substances like wood, stone, or concrete. We'll cover some of the issues with water in later chapters. Attics can be drafty and basements damp, and it is difficult to make them fully comfortable without some costly extra effort—digging to install sump pumps or foundation drains, installing extra insulation, and so forth.

Occasionally a client will ask us to create a basement under a portion of the house that has only a crawl space, thinking that any area below the footprint of a building will be easily excavated for added space. This is seldom the case. Older houses were often built on shallow foundations constructed of fieldstone, lacking spread footings to distribute loads to the ground. Modern foundations are usually reinforced against lateral earth forces and are placed at least two feet below the frost line on ample footings of reinforced concrete. In order to create a full basement where none exists, the upper walls must be supported, the existing foundations pinned against lateral earth forces, and new excavation done by hand—a labor-intensive process that can break a budget.

Those issues notwithstanding, reclaiming upper and lower floors for living space is a proven strategy that adds value to any vintage house. Clever designers make the most

Allan Greenberg's addition to an eighteenth-century house in Guilford, Connecticut was one of the first compatible classical renovations created by a modernist architect. Most of the new space is below a box dormer on the second floor. (Courtesy of Allan Greenberg Architect.)

of every square inch of area in an old house, so it is worth listening to their suggestions on how to get the most out of your cellar or attic. Here are two examples of how they work their magic.

When Allan Greenberg came to the United States from South Africa in the mid-1960s, he had a foreigner's appreciation for American buildings grounded in solid tutelage from English architects. But he was a quick study, and he soon came to admire the order and clarity of form in early American houses, so much so that he purchased an eighteenth-century house in Guilford, Connecticut. Following his student years at Yale, he had an opportunity to work on a modest renovation of a house like his own. Instead of looking at the common precedents at the time, he chose to adhere closely to the rules that eighteenth-century house carpenters had used in building the original building. The owner, a single woman, needed additional space for a bedroom and studio on the upper floor. Greenberg's solution was to create a box dormer on the top floor with a prominent Palladian window in the studio space. Working with very little, the architect created what he has called "the first classical building in America by a modernist architect."

A similar, though more elaborate, transformation in Mendham, New Jersey, was the brainchild of architect Nick Cusano just a few years ago. This quaint village is blessed with a

Nick Cusano found space in a little used attic when designing this renovation on Main Street in Mendham, New Jersey. (Courtesy of Cusano Associates.)

tree-lined main street that might well be a Norman Rockwell painting. Maintaining one's house in the historic district is a matter of pride, so when Cusano's clients purchased their modest and sadly neglected Victorian house they needed the services of a savvy architect from the neighborhood.

Though the original dwelling had some charm and met the space requirements of the growing family, Cusano recognized that there was room for improvement, especially above the eave line. Moreover, the street front of the house was no longer the main entrance, and a mudroom was required to access the auto court at the rear of the large property. Rather than accepting the attic areas as originally conceived, he recognized that with a few skillful framing changes he could create marvelous spaces for children's rooms and play areas while also making the building into a Queen Anne gem.

In order to make room for a kitchen expansion and better circulation in the rear of the house, Cusano took off the existing roof and flat facade, turning the gable to form a T-shape and gaining even more area on the second floor. He also made a more emphatic stair hall by adding a small dormer above the run from first to second floors. Perhaps most important, he

The front and side of the house before renovation. (Courtesy of Cusano Associates.)

Right: First-, second-, and third-floor plans of the Mendham addition, before (below) and after (above) renovation. (Courtesy of Cusano Associates.)

The side of the house had a small family room addition that offered new space above. (Courtesy of Cusano Associates.)

Rear of house before and after renovation. (Courtesy of Cusano Associates.)

removed the unsightly vinyl siding and replaced it with sympathetic shingles in contrasting patterns for each floor. A more authentic color scheme enhanced the effect of the shingle patterns by distinguishing upper from lower levels. What was a virtual eyesore on a pretty street is now one of the most distinctive residences in Mendham.

REVERSE MAKEOVERS

Occasionally a fine vintage residence falls into disrepair, obscuring the finishes that made it distinctive in its time. Or an unsympathetic owner messes with the best features of the house, leaving it scarred. When this happens it may be prudent to consider a "reverse makeover" to bring the building out of its coma. Reclaiming spaces and features that made a house distinctive isn't necessarily restoration, especially when lifestyle requirements dictate the need for new uses in an old envelope.

When William F. Stern, of the firm Stern and Bucek, was hired to upgrade the Frame/Harper house in Houston, he found a 1960 masterpiece by Harwood Taylor beneath years of grime and ill-conceived renovations. Houston is the home of dozens of Mid-Century Modern houses that once graced the covers of magazines extolling the virtues of elegant, space-age living just around the corner from NASA's headquarters. This superb house is one of the best, according to Stern.

Bringing the building back from the brink of ruin was a tough challenge, but the new owners had the patience and funds to make it happen. There were also period photos and complete working drawings to guide the architects in the

The Frame/Harper House in Houston was designed by Harwood Taylor of Neuhaus & Taylor in 1960. It had fallen into disrepair when Stern & Bucek began their renovation in the early 2000s. (Photo by Hester & Hardaway; courtesy of Stern & Bucek Architects.)

A

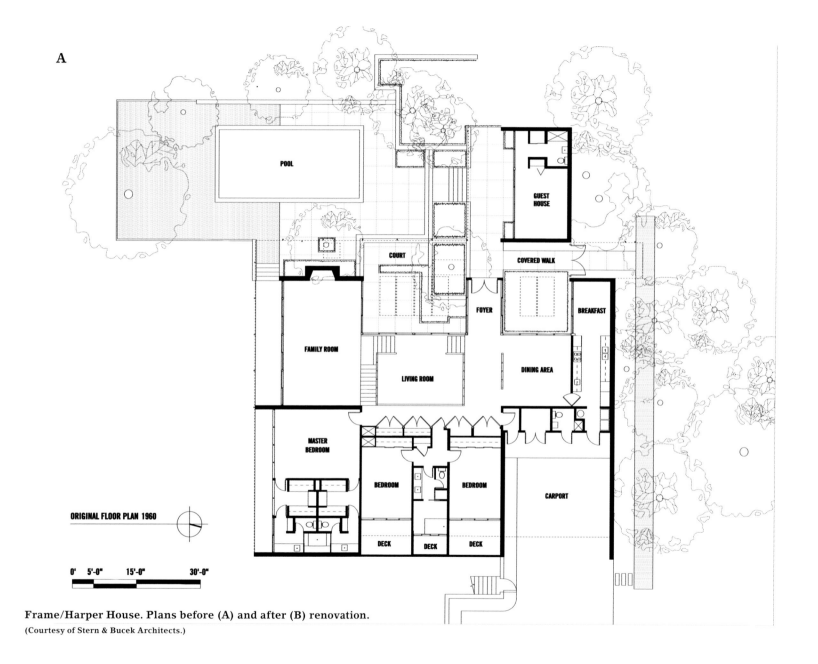

POOL

GUEST HOUSE

COURT

COVERED WALK

FOYER

BREAKFAST

FAMILY ROOM

LIVING ROOM

DINING AREA

MASTER BEDROOM

BEDROOM

BEDROOM

CARPORT

DECK

DECK

DECK

ORIGINAL FLOOR PLAN 1960

0'   5'-0"   15'-0"   30'-0"

Frame/Harper House. Plans before (A) and after (B) renovation.

(Courtesy of Stern & Bucek Architects.)

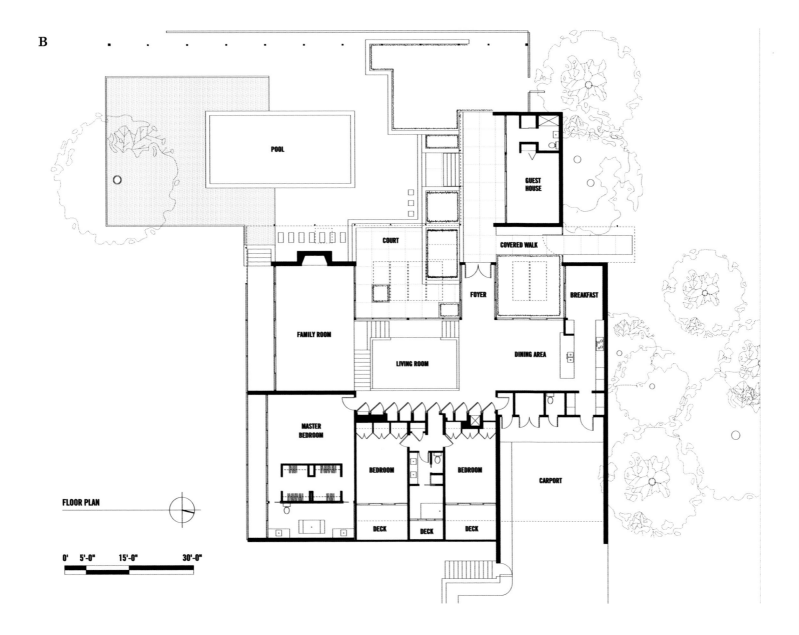

POOL

GUEST
HOUSE

COURT

COVERED WALK

FOYER

BREAKFAST

FAMILY ROOM

LIVING ROOM

DINING AREA

MASTER
BEDROOM

BEDROOM

BEDROOM

CARPORT

DECK

DECK

DECK

FLOOR PLAN

0'   5'-0"   15'-0"   30'-0"

painstaking process of reclaiming details, colors and finishes. Stern and Bucek had recently completed the restoration of Philip Johnson's De Menil house from the same period and were very familiar with the style. Still, with all the authentic elements in place, the owners needed a few amenities that weren't essential to a 1960s family. Finding space for these was a matter of using nooks and crannies in the building that no longer served their original function. In addition, the subtle interplay between indoor and outdoor living areas had been lost over the years, so work was required with the landscape.

One of the brilliant conceits of this house was its open-plan living area—a multilevel suite of rooms facing the gardens and pool terrace that was virtually all glass-enclosed.

Taylor's interpretation of the Miesian courtyard villa used masonry walls on the street side for privacy while opening the living areas to light and air on the southeast with glass. The original dining area connected to a tiny eat-in kitchen that had vanished in subsequent renovations. A less sensitive architect might have expanded the kitchen, using a portion of the raised dining room to gain space for food preparation. Recognizing that spatial continuity was essential to the flow of the house, Stern designed a galley kitchen/breakfast area that fit within the old space while also significantly enhancing the functions available to the owners. Cabinets and appliances were rearranged, and a small space formerly used as a garage entrance was redesigned to serve as a pantry with additional cabinets for storage. And the handsome

The entry terrace of the Frame/Harper House was transformed with a series of terrace and landscape interventions. (Photo by Hester & Hardaway; courtesy of Stern & Bucek Architects.)

The pool terrace was covered with a wood deck and extended to provide additional space for outdoor entertaining. (Photo by Hester & Hardaway; courtesy of Stern & Bucek Architects.)

Following renovation the south elevation regained its elegant layering of columns, screens, and window walls. (Photo by Hester & Hardaway; courtesy of Stern & Bucek Architects.)

The interiors of the family room (above) and living room (below) were furnished with Mid-Century Modern pieces. (Photo by Hester & Hardaway; courtesy of Stern & Bucek Architects.)

new breakfast area was given a new garden court, significantly improving light and views.

Stern and Bucek made another subtle improvement in the living spaces by changing the circulation between the family room and the pool terrace to recapture a feature of the original design that had been lost—a cedar deck that maintained the pool coping level at the ground plane. Not merely a restoration, the new design gave the owners additional deck space for a grill and seating near the pool and added new planting that would not obscure pool views from the interior of the living or dining rooms. Perhaps most important, the architects removed years of paint from the beautiful brick exterior walls and restored authentic roof and window details. The elegant aluminum window-walls of the original house were not salvageable, but new double-glazed windows were fabricated to maintain their configuration and design as closely as possible. Now the building is insulated against the harsh Houston climate, protecting the owners' investment and keeping energy bills low.

The new owners wanted to restore not only the architecture but also the period interiors of the house. Stern and Bucek assisted with interior finishes and furniture selections, recommending classic Knoll designs by Eero Saarinen and Charles and Rae Eames to complement the dining and breakfast spaces. While the lighting was improved with low-voltage area lamps in the ceiling, the architects also used wonderful period fixtures by Isamu Noguchi and other designers to accent key furniture groupings. The Frame/Harper house has won local design awards for both preservation and interiors.

It is a superb example of what can be done to bring a vintage house back to its former glory while also adding necessary amenities and energy-saving technology.

The story of the "Gothic House" in Glen Ridge, New Jersey, is far more complex than that Houston success story. Architects Mark Wright and Karin Robinson were faced with a dysfunctional construction site when they arrived several years ago to help a homeowner revive her historic gem.

Following a disastrous fire in 2004, the owners began to rebuild the house with the aid of a well-regarded local contractor, who quickly found that the construction issues were intractable and that the project had to be completely rethought. At his urging the owners brought new architects aboard and charged them with redesigning the project and getting construction started again within six weeks.

Before fire gutted the interior, more than a century of improvised alterations and additions had scrambled the plan and destroyed many historic features. The first thing the architects did was to research the history of the building, discovering that it had been built between 1890 and 1894 in a very unusual Gothic style. An early photograph from the local library showed that the building was roughly square in plan and had a modest porch at the front entry, below an octagonal bay. The overall design was quite different from the typical Gothic Villa of the mid-nineteenth century, and the house had intriguing details, such as window-head moldings inspired by medieval stone church architecture. Previous

Gothic House, Glen Ridge, New Jersey, photo dated October 1, 1899. (Photo by Nathan Russell, Sr.; courtesy of the Glen Ridge Public Library.)

owners had largely stripped the exterior of its Gothic details. Porch additions were in tune with the original style, and these escaped major damage in the fire. The building is in a historic district, and the local commission urged the owners to preserve as many historic elements as possible in their renovation.

As foundations had already been poured and some framing begun before work stopped, the architects accepted the enlarged footprint and general program. But the plan had no coherent circulation system or internal structure—conceptual and practical deficits that had led the contractor into difficulties. Several key design breakthroughs solved the big

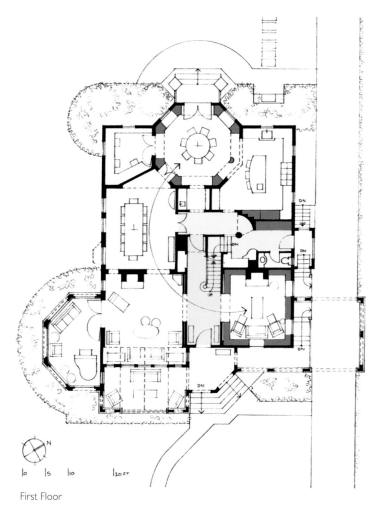

First Floor

Plans of the Gothic House as renovated by Wright & Robinson Architects. (Courtesy of Wright & Robinson Architects, © 2009.)

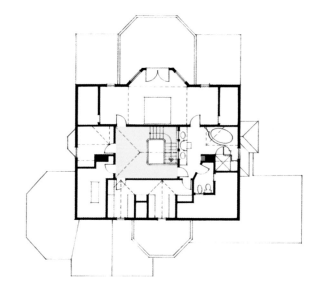

Attic

Second Floor

problems. First, the staircase was reconfigured and centered under a large conservatory skylight, giving the dark house a luminous core. Second, the roof plan was rationalized, reshaped, and restructured. Third, the principal ground floor rooms were linked with generous openings into an informal enfilade, improving the house as a setting for parties. Astonishingly, the architects were able to design the new plan while the house was in the midst of construction, minimizing extra costs. A trusting, collegial relationship with the contractor was essential, as many details had to be worked out in sketch form during construction.

The first and second floors now have new siding milled and painted to match the original (discovered beneath stucco

Street view of the Gothic House. The architects restored the distinctive front porch that had been enclosed, and added space in the attic, while maintaining the historic facade more or less as it was originally designed. (Courtesy of Wright & Robinson Architects, © 2009.)

Details such as the alternating shingles, window hoods, and leaded glass were critical to the success of the Gothic House renovation.
(Courtesy of Wright & Robinson Architects, © 2009.)

The interior remained basically unchanged; however, this distinctive staircase was inserted to tie the floors together. (Courtesy of Wright & Robinson Architects, © 2009.)

added in the 1920s), plus new trim and windows that are perfectly in keeping with the original 1890s design. Some windows were shifted, regrouped, or had their proportions adjusted. Notwithstanding these changes, the first floor facing the street looks much the same as it did before the fire. Modifications to the rear were more pronounced owing to the new third-floor master suite and the requirements of other bedrooms. Walkout terraces on the second and third floors give most bedrooms direct access to outdoor space. The balcony railings are scroll-cut wide boards to increase privacy while reinforcing the Gothic idiom, and the texture of the shingles follows the ragged coursing originally used on the attic level—a common method of articulating the facades of Queen Anne houses. Since the front of the house already had three porches, no similar spaces grace the rear. The owners preferred to admit as much sunlight as possible into the kitchen and new octagonal breakfast room, and didn't want overhangs that blocked the sun.

The bold and idiosyncratic massing of the enlarged house echoes that of the original 1890s dwelling but makes no attempt to replicate its design in toto. To have done so would have entailed the wasteful destruction of much sound, if unsympathetic, twentieth-century work. A slavish recreation of original features, such as would be appropriate in the restoration of a museum house, would have made it impossible to bring coherence and order to a chaotic and compromised structure. If the designers and owners respect both the spirit and the style of the original, a house can grow as naturally as any vernacular building even as its energy performance and durability are improved. The architects' philosophy of maintaining the traditions inherent in buildings from various eras, rather than deliberately creating disjunctive additions, continues a practice respected in most cultures but discarded by Modernists. Our increasingly pluralistic view allows us to move beyond the wrongheaded strictures of twentieth-century avant-garde theories and into the new world of sustainability.

Increasingly, the imperatives of the twenty-first century will call upon architects to look at older buildings as reusable vessels, often requiring the conversion of a nonresidential type for family living. While this book does not address this issue in detail, one example of a makeover will demonstrate what may be a coming trend.

Hiland Hall Turner Associates were asked to look at a carriage house/garage on an estate property in the Somerset Hills of New Jersey five years ago. The question posed by their client: Can you convert this into a house? It was a considerable challenge, but the architects accepted it. The results prove that occasionally an outbuilding can move to center stage (more on this in Chapter 8).

Project designer Edwin Heinle was inspired by the robust Tudor details already in the building and decided that very little needed changing on the exterior. He worked his magic inside, beginning with the volume of the old garage itself. Opening up the roof with new heavy timber structural rafters, he added dormers to gain more light in the space and installed a second floor using long-span girders. Below this new bedroom level he maintained the open feeling of the garage with an unbroken kitchen, dining, and living area.

The warm materials of the original building—brick, oak timbers, and stone—were made a theme for the interior work. New brick and stone fireplaces occupy the center of each gable wall, one for a stove, another for a hearth. A large fireplace provides a focal point for the master bedroom on the second floor. In the same room, the architects exposed old rafters and timber trusses to add an antique flavor to the decor. Some existing finishes, like the paneling in the dining room and the white subway tile in the kitchen, were maintained and cleaned. Indeed, the new decorative elements, such as the white paneling and ceiling in the main room, are quite minimal and entirely in tune with older finishes. It is remarkable how such fresh and lively interiors could be created from a utilitarian space like a garage.

Additions to the exterior were explicitly created to enhance living functions, and to go virtually unnoticed. The chimneys are more prominent, and a small bay at one end gable extends bedroom space. Otherwise, only the dormers are new, yet they look as if they were always part of the design. The architects paid careful attention to 1920s details at the eaves and dormers, and above the stone piers. The craftsmanship is superb, particularly in the new cedar-

The Carriage House in the Somerset Hills region of New Jersey is a conversion of a former outbuilding into a residence. Hiland Hall Turner Architects maintained the character of the original building with subtle interventions on the exterior: new French doors were inserted into the garage bays, while a new dormer allowed space for a second floor bedroom. (Photo by William Psolka; courtesy of Hiland Hall Turner Architects.)

shingle roof; without it, the most prominent element on the exterior would detract from other fine details. As Heinle stewarded the project through construction, he made certain that such details were carried out perfectly. Like all the examples we've described, this renovation succeeds because its architects and owners profoundly appreciated the essential qualities of the original building. Each design decision was consistent with their intention to enhance the intrinsic character of the building, not add extraneous elements.

Felicity in its themes, materials, and style ensured a successful result.

Understanding the patterns and principles that guided the designers and builders of old houses is essential when working within the tight constraints of an original footprint. It is even more important when a family or household is pushed to add to the footprint, whether on a small or large scale.

The dining room of the Carriage House was once part of the chauffeur's apartment. (Photo by William Psolka; courtesy of Hiland Hall Turner Architects.)

117

Achieving an artful addition to a vintage house is perhaps the most difficult and elusive challenge that architects and owners confront in expansion projects. In the next chapter, we suggest that such challenges can be met with the same fundamental guidelines we've outlined above. Just remember the five parameters we outlined in Chapter 2: site, skeleton, spatial module, roof shape, and facade.

Above: The entire second floor was added in the roof space above the garages, including this bedroom and fireplace. (Photo by William Psolka; courtesy of Hiland Hall Turner Architects.)

Left: The open plan of the main floor integrates a kitchen, dining, and living areas. (Photo by William Psolka; courtesy of Hiland Hall Turner Architects.)

5

ADDITIONS THAT STAY IN TUNE

VIRTUALLY ALL PRIMITIVE SOCIETIES MAINTAIN social order via myths and stories connecting present-day families with their ancestors. This connection between the present and the past is vital to the preservation of group cohesion and individual identity. The modern concept of "patrimony" is taken from this basic relationship of living humans to the thousands of generations who precede them. In most societies prior to the modern era, buildings were considered part of the cultural heritage or patrimony that preserved this relationship. Not only did they preserve cherished symbols by repeating design motifs, they often replicated spatial patterns over many generations, and retained sites that had become sacred or cherished for even longer.

In contemporary society we confront change in virtually every aspect of our lives. Contrary to the popular adage, change is not always good. Although touted as necessary for progress, political advancement, and technological innovation, many kinds of upheaval and shifting norms cause deep psychological and even physical pain in humans. David Lowenthal has analyzed these negative aspects of change in the historical built environment, pointing to the modern historic preservation movement as a tonic for the shock of the new.[1] He cautions us neither to worship the past nor to denigrate it when contemplating the conservation of historic artifacts. All contemporary attempts at preservation actually alter the object in some way, if only by reframing its interpretation. Other writers have also underlined the alienating reality of a world that is destroyed and rebuilt every twenty-five years. James Howard Kunstler calls this "the geography of nowhere."[2] The numbing monoculture of contemporary buildings, highways, and cities fosters a life of monotony and secular nihilism that is pervasive throughout the developed world. Humans are increasingly disconnected from the places they knew as children, a condition that is relatively new when we consider that we have been on the planet for thirty thousand years. The past is indeed, as Lowenthal says, "a foreign country."

Yet despite our distance from historic places and events, we require some connection to our ancestors. Humans form profound associations with the places where they grow up, raise families, and grow old. When a cherished family home or former domicile is torn down to make way for a new one, families experience a deep sense of loss. Likewise, when unsympathetic changes occur in neighborhoods or individual buildings, both individuals and groups experience a loss, an emptiness that cannot be easily healed. This is one reason why the Congress for the New Urbanism, a progressive group of planners, designers, and social thinkers, calls for "an architecture of place" where new neighborhoods are linked to existing cities or landscapes. Taking a long view of growth, these theorists resist the Modernist dictum that all "new" architecture should reject the past in favor of current trends in design.

When it comes to additions to historic houses, nearly a century of thinking about preservation versus change has resulted in a conundrum that bedevils contemporary attempts to blend the new with the old. The current National Parks Service policy on additions to government-owned buildings suggests that additions "harmonize" with the historic materials, proportions, and scale of the original building, but also distinguish themselves as products "of their own time." That this position is more often than not oxymoronic does not bother the bureaucrats. Seldom are contemporary additions in harmony with historic buildings, especially ones that garner awards for avant-garde architects. A recent book on old house additions makes a distinction between this attitude, appropriate for bona fide landmark houses that are protected by preservation laws, and other historic houses, which needn't create obvious distinctions between old and new elements.[3] Indeed, the practicing architect or preservation contractor lives constantly with this double standard. Most homeowners want additions that maintain the style and materials of their existing house, yet when Mark Twain's Hartford house is changed to accommodate rest rooms, they must be unmistakably "contemporary."

What happens when, in thirty years or so, the addition that was thought to be contemporary begins to age and look simply dated, ungainly, or wrong? To use a musical analogy, it is out of tune with the rest of the building and can't be tweaked to eliminate its dissonance. To the architects and owners in this book, and to the authors, the double standard will not answer the fundamental question of how to create additions that stay in tune over decades, even centuries, just like the houses we admire when we visit places that have achieved a harmony of design, materials, and local traditions. Think of a historic town that is a popular tourist destination and consider whether its architectural character is maintained over decades, even centuries. The island residents of Corfu, the fishermen of the Cinque Terre in Italy, and the merchants of Fez, Morocco, never argue over whether or not to retain the forms and materials of their ancestral buildings, and would not think of overturning them for a passing fashion. Nor would the residents of Edgartown, on Martha's Vineyard, the Vieux Carré in New Orleans, Old Santa Fe in New Mexico, or the Battery in Charleston. Why do so many Americans feel the impulse to change styles when adding to their valued houses?

One of the answers to this question is cultural. Americans have consistently demonstrated a bias toward things that maintain their usefulness over time. This bias has pushed our society toward things that are new—the newer the thing, the better it works (or so we think). Respect for old things, including old people, has not been high on the list of values that Americans hold dear. In Japan, venerable artists, craft workers, and writers are given the status of cultural landmarks or icons, even receiving government support in some instances. In Italy and Greece, destruction or damage to ancient monuments is a punishable offense, because these artifacts are the basis of a booming tourist economy as well as national pride. Not so in the United States, where old buildings have seldom been given pride of place in any realm. Even old sports stadiums, the scene of acts of heroism more revered than all other endeavors, are torn down routinely to make room for "new-old" ballparks that can accommodate thousands in luxury boxes and deluxe seating.

Such deep-seated biases are hard to change overnight, and preservationists have been chipping away at them for decades with little success. American tourists look quizzically at ruins in European countries when they are left to decay naturally, wondering why the government has been slow to polish them up and give them the shiny "new" look that

our landmarks often have. The "anti-scrape" philosophy first articulated by John Ruskin has deep roots in England and France, discouraging "restoration" that attempts to remove the patina of age. You will be hard pressed to find American monuments in the kind of grimy, unkempt state that many Europeans tolerate, or worse, expect! We scrape and scrub to get rid of any sign of aging. If there were a Botox for buildings, we'd use it.

Americans also have a fondness for technology and science. After all, we sent a rocket to the moon and invented the digital computer. Once we began to notice that the decaying landmarks of the founding fathers, such as Mount Vernon, were looking ragged and untidy, scientists started the quest for beauty creams that would stem the aging process in buildings. The U.S. building industry now has dozens of miracle materials—such as PVC "wood" moldings and "slate" made of old tires—that promise eternal youth. As we noted in Chapter 1, a preference for technological wizardry is older than Thomas Edison in this country, and won't let go in the construction industry. There will always be a better way to build, and Americans look at old ways with suspicion. We'll look more closely at these attitudes in Chapter 9.

Yet there are ways to get the advantages of new technology while maintaining venerable vernacular building practices. This usually means spending a lot of money to make every contemporary transplant invisible. Not many homeowners can afford to do what museums do to hide the services. That is only one reason why staying close to the design, technology, and materials of your vintage house will pay off in the long run. Adding to a vintage house in a manner respectful of its original form, materials, and style is an art not often mastered today. Yet somehow our predecessors in the twentieth century confronted these dilemmas and often devised persuasive solutions that maintained the continuity of past and present.

OLD MASTERS

On New York's Upper East Side, visitors to Carl Schurtz Park walk by a handsome house every day without much noticing its virtues. Most people know that it is one of New York's most important residences. Gracie Mansion is the official residence of the mayor, and also sees its fair share of gala events during a typical year. What few people realize is that the mayor would not be able to entertain in his historic East River digs were it not for an addition that more than doubled the size of the house in 1966.

When Archibald Gracie built his country retreat on the river in 1798 he could not have dreamed that it would remain on its site until 1923, when it was purchased by the city of New York to serve as a museum. The delicate porches and wood details were hardly fit for grand entertaining during the 1920s. By 1934 it had deteriorated badly enough to require a thorough restoration under Robert Moses. Modernized for residential use, the house became the home of Mayor Fiorello LaGuardia in 1941, hastening its renown among Manhattanites. By the time Mayor Robert Wagner and his family

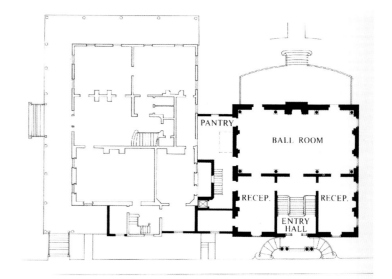

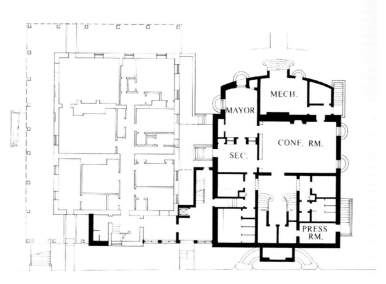

Basement and first floor plans of the Susan B. Wagner Wing, Gracie Mansion. Mott B. Schmidt's addition of 1966 expanded the house to accommodate mayoral offices and press rooms. (From Mark Hewitt's *The Architecture of Mott B. Schmidt*, Rizzoli, 1991. Used with permission.)

Elevation of the Susan B. Wagner Wing. The old house is to the left. (From Mark Hewitt's *The Architecture of Mott B. Schmidt,* Rizzoli, 1991. Used with permission.)

began their tenure in the early 1960s, it was again showing signs of wear and tear.

The Wagners hired a team of designers to create a new wing for the house that would allow them to inhabit the old mansion in privacy while also admitting the press and the mayor's staff into a more public wing on a daily basis. Mott B. Schmidt was the architect who masterminded the Susan B. Wagner wing, and he took some criticism from modernists for not producing a "contemporary" design. Rather than electing to contrast with the style of the original house, Schmidt chose to echo its details and general proportions without overtly copying anything. In fact, he studied the precedents used by Gracie's original builder so that he could create spaces that were modern and yet had all the detail and elegance of the Federal period.[4]

Gracie Mansion is but one example of successful twen-

tieth-century additions to venerable old houses that should be better known to architects and homeowners alike. The few books that treat additions to historic buildings from the last century are rigidly biased toward what are called "disjunctive" relationships between the old and the new. Architects such as Schmidt, Edwin Lutyens, and Duncan Lee were ostracized by critics because they did not choose to ignore the style, materials, and proportions of the houses they were updating for modern living.

Gracie Mansion's new wing is patently different, and more modern, than its eighteenth-century neighbor, but both buildings are made of the same DNA. Schmidt understood that the addition would have to respect not only the scale and proportions of the earlier house but also all of the nuances of Federal-style decoration that Gracie's craftsmen knew implicitly. He thus made every double-hung window

123

Photo of the Susan B. Wagner Wing, showing integration of the new wing with the existing mansion. Though criticized at the time of its construction, it is now a beloved and well-used part of the mayor's residence. (Courtesy of Mark Alan Hewitt.)

with stiles and rails comparable to the old sash, and maintained the slim muntin profiles that distinguish Federal-era windows. His elegant cornices and pilasters in the ballroom were inspired by the work of Robert Adam, the British architect who set the standards for decoration in the early nineteenth century, when Gracie was building his country retreat. The new wing at Gracie abides by all of the parameters we outlined in Chapter 2—indeed it is exemplary in every way.

The same is true of the many additions and expansions to English country houses designed by the great early twentieth-century architect Edwin L. Lutyens (1869–1944). As a young architect in Surrey, Lutyens studied the vernacular buildings of the countryside in much the same way that Ralph Vaughan Williams, his contemporary, studied the folksongs of England and Scotland as inspiration for new musical compositions. Lutyens's first commissions were for small houses or alterations to existing country houses. Though he later went on to design major buildings such as the Viceroy's House in New Delhi, he cut his teeth on domestic work before World War I.

English country houses are intimately tied to their county of origin, and most are characterized by the use of local materials. They are both culture- and place-specific, a fact understood by both Lutyens and his aristocratic clients. So, when altering the rustic island compound at Lambay off the coast of Ireland for Cecil Baring, the architect used local stone laid in patterns found only in this remote spot. His 1905–1912 renovation and additions to the castle/fort built between 1575 and 1595 began with an understanding of the unique site. When he was finished the new elements appeared to have grown from the rocky soil as organically as the flora.

In his biography of the architect, Christopher Hussey wrote that "the old building, like the whole island, takes its color from the sea, bright colors washed out by ages of storm and bleaching sun," and that Lutyens designed the new walls so that mortar would cover the stone in the way that old gray harle dappled the feldspar and sandstone. "Thus all the buildings are much the same colour as the rosemary that flowers below them, and the sea of a misty day."[5] The resonance of material, scale, and form gives the ensemble a timeless qual-

Lambay Castle, Ireland. Plans of the 1905–12 additions by Edwin L. Lutyens. The blue lines indicate the original castle. (After Lutyens; courtesy of Mark Alan Hewitt.)

Top right: View of the old castle and west forecourt, showing a bit of the addition over the wall at left. (Courtesy of Country Life Archives.)

Bottom right: View of Lutyens's joint between the old castle and the new wing, from the north court. (Courtesy of Country Life Archives.)

ity, so that no modern eye can discern the difference between 1912 construction and that of medieval times.

Another of Lutyens's masterpieces of integration was Folly Farm, a house that he remodeled not once but twice. His first expansion, for H. H. Cochrane in 1905–1906, was a significant new building attached to a small half-timbered cottage. The old building was transformed into a kitchen and service wing for the H-shaped main block, somewhat formal in appearance. The central space in the new wing was a grand, double-story hall decorated in black, white, and red woodwork. Once finished, the architect never dreamed of having to touch the house again.

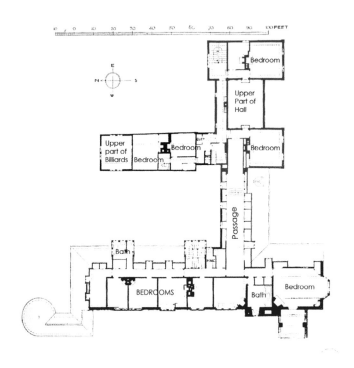

First floor

Second floor

Folly Farm, Sullingstead, England. Plans of enlargements in 1906 and in 1912 by Lutyens. Original house, blue; 1906 addition, purple; 1912 addition, red. After Lutyens. (Courtesy of Mark Alan Hewitt.)

The 1906 wing, on the left, is formal and symmetrical, as oriented to the gardens. The 1912 wing defers to the 1906 addition; it is lower, appearing to be an appendage to the earlier house. (Courtesy of Country Life Archives.)

He was surprised to receive a request from mine-owner Zachary Merton, whose German wife was a friend of his own spouse, to create a second enlargement of Folly Farm in 1912. The Mertons had recently purchased the house from Cochrane and found it too small—a larger dining room, kitchen, servants' wing, and seven new bedrooms would be required for their large family. Lutyens's challenge was to add to his own symmetrical block in such a way as neither to upstage it nor render the old farm buildings obsolete. He met it with characteristic wit and bravado.

In order to keep the new wing in its subservient role, the architect placed it on a lower level than the main house and gave it a large "cowshed" roof with very low eaves. The L-shaped mass frames a charming "tank" garden with a loggia of arched brick buttresses that are like nothing in the canon of British building. Nevertheless, the new wing has a rustic, agricultural character that complements both the "Wrenaissance" 1906 house and its medieval predecessors.[6] Though commentators in the Edwardian era found the resulting combination of forms charming but in direct contrast to one another, today's audience appreciates the architect's sensitivity to melding old, new, and newer so seamlessly as to draw no adverse reaction whatsoever. Lutyens used the same gifts of marrying the modern with the ancient at Lindisfarne Castle, Abbey House, Great Dixter, and a number of lesser country house commissions during his long career.

The loggia and tank court, virtually all roof, are minimal and very modern. Lutyens's ingenious composition, inflecting toward the earlier house, inspired many later architects. (Courtesy of Country Life Archives.)

Thus in the twentieth century a number of highly successful and aesthetically distinctive residential additions were designed in styles that respected the scale, materials, and details of original vintage houses, whether fifty years old or four hundred. You may be surprised to learn that today we are fortunate to have an equally wide range of creative additions and renovations, created within the past ten years, that use the same intelligent strategies as those of Schmidt and Lutyens. Unfortunately, in the United States we see little of this work in architectural publications because of the overwhelming bias toward contrasting Modernist work, and the disdain of many critics. This book is the first to publish many of these designs, which illustrate the principles and best practices that we outlined in Chapters 2 and 3. Let's look at a few.

BUMPS AND EXTRUSIONS

Our survey of the best in contemporary additions to vintage houses begins with interventions that are often so subtle as to pass unnoticed. We like to call these "bump-outs," because it often seems that the skin of the existing house has simply swelled out in one or two locations to accept new functions. Modest and relatively inexpensive, a small addition can sometimes provide the needed space with little or no major construction.

Anne Fairfax and Richard Sammons have designed some of the most elegant and critically acclaimed traditional houses in America during the past twenty years. Both studied at the University of Virginia, where they learned architectural history and were able to study the work of Thomas Jefferson and other American classical architects. But after setting up practice in New York City, both were able to enrich their knowledge by direct experience with historic houses, such as one in Quogue, New York, on Long Island's south shore—a Cape Cod cottage that had served as a modest fisherman's house for most of its life. Its owners came to the firm in 2004

Fairfax & Sammons designed this subtle addition to a shingled cottage in Quogue, New York using many of the principles outlined in Chapter 2. The key to the composition is the roof massing, which echoes the vernacular design of the original cottage. (Courtesy of Fairfax & Sammons Architecture.)

The well-lit kitchen is the result of banks of windows in the addition that do not clash with the vernacular windows of the old house. (Courtesy of Fairfax & Sammons Architecture.)

The dining room retains the rustic character of the early "saltbox" dwelling. (Courtesy of Fairfax & Sammons Architecture.)

wanting an expansion that would not alter the rustic character of the building. Tired of cooking in a room the size of a closet and wiping their boots on the living room rug, they simply needed a new kitchen and mudroom.

The simple mass of the shingled cottage was nearly perfect in itself, so the architects recognized that any large addition would ruin its prismatic lines. But the house was very dark (cozy in the summer but dusky in winter), and the kitchen provided an opportunity to offer a light, airy space as a tonic to some of the old rooms. The final design was based on formal patterns that a vernacular builder would have understood implicitly, but that few contemporary architects would have dared to build: a classic lean-to such as might

have existed in seventeenth-century New England (where most early Long Islanders came from).

By simply extending the steeply pitched roof on the seashore side to mimic an existing lean-to, and wrapping the porchlike volume around the side of the house, the architects were able to gain enough space for a comfortable, light-filled kitchen. By painting most of the interior white, they maximized the available light in the new areas. The exterior of the addition was treated as a bank of "ganged" double-hung windows with a single door to the exterior. While there is little question that this portion of the house is not part of the original, its similarity in size (modularity) and shape maintains continuity with the rest of the shingled volume. It has

A dormer adds precious space in an upstairs bedroom. (Courtesy of Fairfax & Sammons Architecture.)

The strong lines of the old house remain in the remodeled one, the result of subtle interventions by the architects. (Courtesy of Fairfax & Sammons Architecture.)

virtually no effect on the massing of the house from most angles.

Two subtle but effective additional pieces rounded out the renovation: an upstairs box dormer and a square pergola on the seacoast side of the house. The dormer increases the apparent size of an upstairs bedroom considerably, while bringing in southeast light in the morning. The covered portion of an existing terrace appears to be a natural extension of the void in the house created by the two small projections on the south side. The architects placed it approximately twenty-five feet to the south in order to create a virtual courtyard for dining and entertaining in the evening hours. During the heat of the day, the table can be moved into a shady area under the pergola, which features wisteria and other climbing plants. Like many Long Island shore houses, this cottage lies on an exposed, windy plain with good beach views and privacy from neighbors. The architects enhanced its drama by leaving most of the site unplanted—underlining the imperative of their modest, elegant gestures. Sometimes a simple solution proves to be more effective than a complex one.

When the assistant dean of Columbia's respected historic preservation program came to Mark Alan Hewitt Architects with a "little project" to improve her Queen Anne house in Madison, New Jersey, we were somewhat intimidated. After all, she had just published the authoritative book on Queen Anne houses in America—what could we possibly design that would not mar the beauty of her late 1880s gem in the midst of a historic district known for its painted Victorians? The historic Goldsmith-Spencer house was on Maple Avenue, the heart of the district.

Fortunately, we had designed similar additions for Victorian houses in recent years and had a few solutions to suggest that made minimal alterations to the house. The plan and room arrangements in this house were ubiquitous in late nineteenth-century pattern book plans. Our previous additions had utilized what we call "extruding" a portion of the main block of the house to gain additional space. We tried a very small bump-out that was met with little enthusiasm. When the client insisted that she wanted more space than first contemplated, we found a solution more in keeping with past successes. Why not extend the two-story volume of her existing house ten feet to the west?

Extruding had several advantages over building a more discrete wing on the back of the house. Cost was a significant factor—the new foundation was minimal. The contractors were able to continue shingle and trim details that were on the old building without elaborate detail drawings. A half-timber pattern used on the front of the house could serve as inspiration for one on the back gable. Most important, rooms and circulation on both the first and second floors attached seamlessly to the new master bedroom and family room in the addition. The only drawback, unknown at the time of the schematic design, was that a foundation wall under the existing wing was built without mortar and would need reconstruction. After a few anxious days, the project was back on track, owing mainly to the skills of our Irish-born contractor.

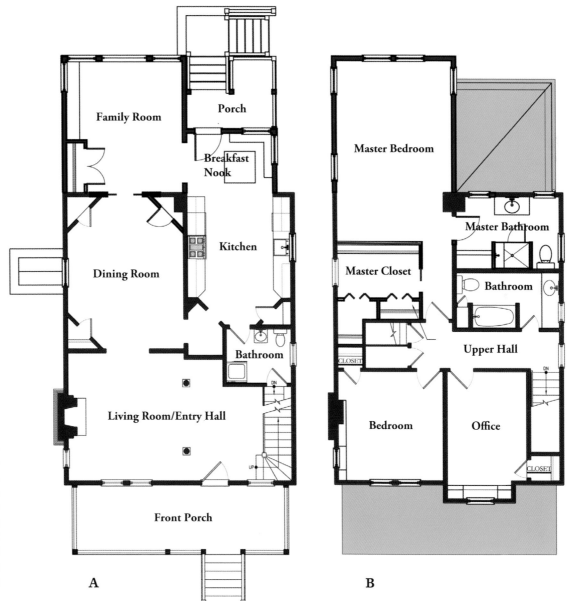

In the addition to the Goldsmith-Spencer house in Madison, New Jersey, Mark Alan Hewitt Architects simply "extruded" a gable volume toward the back of the old house. Lower plan (A) and upper plan (B). (Courtesy of Mark Alan Hewitt Architects.)

A

Family Room

Porch

Breakfast Nook

Kitchen

Dining Room

Bathroom

Living Room/Entry Hall

Front Porch

B

Master Bedroom

Master Bathroom

Master Closet

Bathroom

Upper Hall

Bedroom

Office

CLOSET

CLOSET

As the framing took shape, everyone was able to assess the quality of the new spaces in relation to the old.

The client and her husband were immediately pleased with the views from the expansive master bedroom, but were surprised by some of the other advantages to the expansion on the first floor. As we noted in the Long House

A photo of the street front shows the textures, massing, and colors of the house—critical elements in the historic district that were retained in the addition. (Courtesy of Mark Alan Hewitt Architects.)

The new elevation of the rear retains some motifs from the front, but uses them in different ways to create similitude. All of the roofs are matched in pitch and in eave details. (Courtesy of Mark Alan Hewitt Architects.)

in the last chapter, spaces connected on axis (enfilade) borrow a sense of depth and scale from each other, appearing larger than their actual dimensions. This is the case with the family room in the house—the light from its wraparound windows and its connection with an existing formal dining room make the space seem vast and airy. Moreover, the cou-

The new wing offers more light to the back of the house, while maintaining the Victorian flavor of the original. (Courtesy of Mark Alan Hewitt Architects.)

Left: Details of the new back porch are similar, but not identical, to those of the front. (Courtesy of Mark Alan Hewitt Architects.)

ple realized that their clogged circulation patterns would be solved by the new loop around the existing kitchen and dining rooms. Perhaps most important, our new entry porch dealt with the three levels between the driveway, back yard, and first floor—access from auto to mudroom was vastly improved.

In this project, simplicity was again critical to success. Following the patterns established by the original architect/builder, we were able to create an extension that is perfectly consistent with the language and form of the historic house. Room modules, roof shapes, historic details, and an intelligent site plan were the key. Was the addition too obviously a "copy" of the original house? The client didn't think so. In order to give clues to future owners about the date of our work, we were careful to alter the details of the new rear porch to delineate the difference from the large front verandah. Recognizing that the work was exemplary, the local American Institute of Architects Design

Jury gave this project a gold medal in 2009. Our client was pleased with both the award and her new family room.

The Philadelphia Chapter of the AIA found the modest Radnor addition designed by Voith & Mactavish Architects

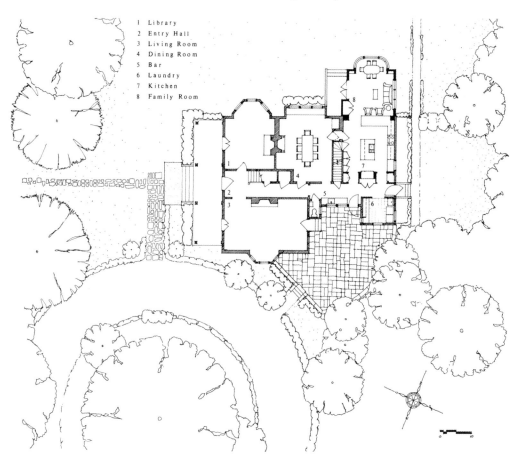

1 Library
2 Entry Hall
3 Living Room
4 Dining Room
5 Bar
6 Laundry
7 Kitchen
8 Family Room

Voith & Mactavish Architects planned their addition to a historic Main Line house from the site inward. The new kitchen and breakfast room are at the upper right. (Courtesy of Voith & Mactavish Architects LLP.)

impressive enough for an Honor Award, just one of many that the firm has garnered over twenty-plus years of practice. In this project they made the most of a relatively small addition, not only rationalizing an unsightly rear facade but also providing just enough additional space for a kitchen/ breakfast area. As a family house, the 1870 stucco residence provided plenty of space for bedrooms and living and dining rooms, but the "service" side was underdeveloped. Cooking in a small kitchen designed for Victorian servants was frustrating at best.

"Our clients wanted to open the kitchen on both sides, build a family/breakfast room addition, and reinforce the connection to the rest of the house and garden," says partner Cameron Mactavish. He notes that the house had a garden setting that was beautiful but not exploited to enhance the experience of viewing the exterior from the major rooms. When considering their addition the architects were intent on bringing the outdoors inside with big glass openings, but the style of the house did not permit window walls. Their solution was to study bay window designs common during the late nineteenth century and modify them to suit the twentieth. Another inspiration was the characteristic "jerkinhead" or "nun's hat" roof on the existing house—a hip roof style that was popular during the late nineteenth century in English cottages and their American offspring. Sometimes repeating a quirky design motif can spoil the original, but in this case the one-story addition offered a smaller-scale version of the main roof, as if to suggest a generational lineage.

The rear of the house before the renovation (top)—a flat, characterless facade that wasn't meant to be seen. The rear of the house after the addition of a small projection with a "jerkinhead" roof (bottom). (Courtesy of Voith & Mactavish Architects LLP.)

Circulation through the original house, as is typical in late Victorian plans, was awkward once the servants weren't around to use the butler's pantry and back stairs. Though the main stair hall extended to the original back of the house, auto circulation had reoriented the site perpendicular to this axis, making the original side entrance a primary access to the kitchen and laundry room. The architects used the side door to create a new axis connecting the old hall with the new kitchen and family room. The original front porch now faces an expansive lawn, but is no longer the public face of the house for visitors. This "flipping" of formal and service zones is very common in old house renovations, but is seldom handled with the creativity displayed in this design. A comprehensive garden design strategy was in place during the schematic design process, ensuring a coordinated result.

This addition was designed in 1990, before the ubiquitous "great rooms" and kitchen/family room monstrosities common in McMansion developments became a fad. When a society changes its expectations for space usage, as Americans did in the 1980s, it is futile to argue over the merits of the change. The formal rooms that Ma and Pa cherished are now relics—many dining rooms and living rooms col-

Above and opposite: Views of the new kitchen and dining space show how much can be gained with just a small "bump out" if the planning is skillful. (Courtesy of Voith & Mactavish Architects LLP.)

lect dust waiting for the old folks at Thanksgiving. Families live in the informal rooms formerly reserved for eating and food preparation. The kitchen is often the social locus of the house. It is now very common to see additions to fine historic houses with combined kitchen/family/breakfast areas, generally as an el to the back of the house.

Voith and Mactavish were not only ahead of the curve in this project, they also created a new room that is more beautiful, more functional, and more interesting than most designed during the past twenty years. As it unfolds from the hall, the new room does not yield its secrets all at once. A clever change in ceiling height and color distinguishes the new family room/breakfast space from the more neutral kitchen. The light entering the bay window is modulated by both wall colors and the "boxes" that catch it: a curved bay window and a segmental eyebrow high in the gable. The kitchen, a middle-ground space, is experienced both as a discrete room and as a volume attached to two other rooms, owing to the openings in thick walls that separate the three. Many designs make the mistake of removing old walls to create entirely open rooms that traverse old and new realms, mocking the order created by the original builders. This one gets it just right.

Last but not least, the Radnor addition made an ugly duckling into a swan—the former rear

The circulation system of the house was vastly improved with the addition of this small vestibule, on axis with the main stair hall. (Courtesy of Voith & Mactavish Architects LLP.)

The rear of the house at dusk shows how much more light flows in and out with the new addition and French doors to the garden. (Courtesy of Voith & Mactavish Architects LLP.)

facade went from an afterthought to a garden attraction. The oblique photograph of the rear shows how effectively the projecting bay and roofed volume turns the corner, while giving scale and coherence to what was once a service area. Although the bay window sounds a distinct and differ-ent note from anything in the 1870 house, its location under the nun's hat maintains a consistent tonality with the original building. As in a Charles Ives composition, the marching band passes by while a church organ plays a familiar hymn. Once the moment is over we remember that we're in church.

WINGS THAT STAY GROUNDED

Milton Grenfell is a talented Washington, DC, architect who spent the first two decades of his career in Charlotte, North Carolina. Many of his early commissions came from homeowners who had outgrown their fine old southern houses. "I made my reputation in Charlotte doing new wings for old houses," he remembers. During the 1980s and 1990s he was busy remodeling some of the best early twentieth-century "eclectic" homes in North Carolina. Appropriately, one of his projects will introduce the problem of adding a significant (meaning large) wing to a vintage house without overwhelming the original.

The original 1926 house, near Greensboro, was designed by William Lamdin in the French Provincial style popular throughout the United States in the 1920s and 1930s. The ear-

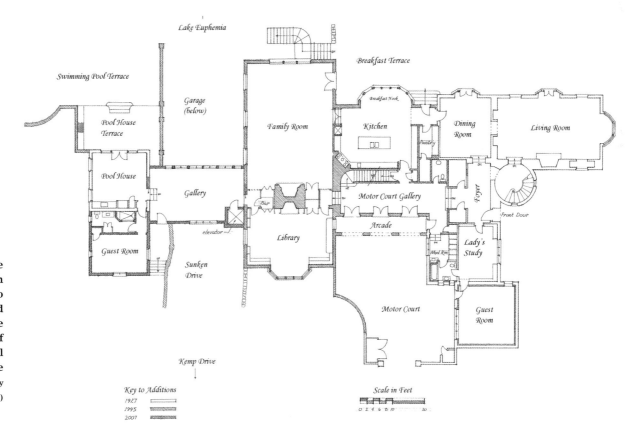

This French Norman house near Greensboro, North Carolina received two additions, both designed by Milton Grenfell. The plans show the growth of the house from a small cottage to an extensive country estate. (Plan courtesy of Grenfell Architecture.)

Lake Euphemia

Breakfast Terrace

Swimming Pool Terrace

Garage (below)

Pool House Terrace

Breakfast Nook

Family Room

Kitchen

Dining Room

Living Room

Pool House

Pantry

Gallery

Motor Court Gallery

Foyer

Bar

elevator

Guest Room

Library

Arcade

Front Door

Lady's Study

Mud Rm

Sunken Drive

Motor Court

Guest Room

Kemp Drive

Key to Additions
1927
1995
2007

Scale in Feet
0 2 4 6 8 10   20

The main facade of the house from the lawn. The two-story addition is on the right. (Courtesy of Grenfell Architecture.)

liest, and most influential, estate to find inspiration in French country houses was the Arthur Newbold house in Laverock, Pennsylvania (1919–1925). Its architect, Arthur Meigs, had just returned from France in 1919 when a wealthy Philadelphia stockbroker approached him with the idea of creating a farm retreat about half an hour from the city. Using his sketchbooks, photos, and memories of the French countryside, the architect created a rustic stone and brick house that quickly caught the fancy of Americans after it was in *Country Life in America* in the early 1920s. Surprisingly, the work was actually a renovation and addition to a colonial revival house from 1913.

Grenfell's clients had a whitewashed brick house with a turret very like that of the Newbold farmhouse. The owners needed a good deal more space than was provided in the three-bedroom cottage, and they came to the architect in 1994 with an ambitious program for additions and landscape improvements. In less skilled hands the renovation might well have left little of the original house intact.

Grenfell quickly surmised that his addition would be most successful if he approached the design as a site planning problem first, and then studied the resulting new massing in relation to the roof shapes already in the original cottage. He also recognized that no single piece of the new program could occupy a module larger than anything in the 1930s house. As a student of traditional architecture, he had no illusions about beating the original architect at his own game, but rather accepted the old building on its own terms.

Since the house was on a sloped site and the best views were on the downhill side, Grenfell hid most of the new pieces on the uphill corner of the site. The original gardens looked out on a private lake, so these were simply restored. The design began with a simple kitchen addition and a long gallery extending from a small entry foyer. This link connected the old house to a three-story wing containing bedrooms, a living room, and a library. The new three-story wing is considerably taller than the original living room wing, but its placement slightly uphill, with connections gradually stepping up with the slope, gives the ensemble an air of inevitability that is rare in American expansions. Moreover, the intimate courtyard that occupies the space between the 1920s block and the new sections adds another dimension—the outdoors—to the ensemble.

That first addition project was completed in 1996. In 2007 the owners went back to Grenfell for a second expan-

The terrace facing the lake incorporates both new and old wings in a unified composition.
(Courtesy of Grenfell Architecture.)

sion that added even more to the original house. In order to link the pool to the main house and make better use of the small pool pavilion, the architect designed a bridge gallery over the driveway. The bridge continued a wonderful game room for pool, giving the architect a chance to use a vaulted timber ceiling. The little pool house got an additional guest bedroom. When all was said and done the house was tripled in square footage without appearing significantly larger on its site. The new enclosed terrace and the old walled garden communicate beautifully by following a common vocabulary. Views from the broad lawn give no hint that the house was not constructed in one campaign.

A second addition led to this car port and billiard room, using the lower grades at the rear to hide the new program areas. (Courtesy of Grenfell Architecture.)

It is almost trivial to point out that Grenfell and his design team studied the materials and details assiduously, and that the old and new sections are virtually seamless. For without the overall site and massing strategies, the details would not have mattered. This addition, though composed of two rather large "wings," does not betray its age, and it certainly looks like nothing in the neighborhood constructed during the last decade of the twentieth century. Future owners will delight in the spaces, details, and design touches of both Mr. Lamdin and his partner, Milton Grenfell, who believed in the architecture of place, and his responsibility to history as a continuum.

The billiard room is designed to harmonize with the décor of the main house. (Courtesy of Grenfell Architecture.)

Sometimes maintaining the continuum of building in a specific place is more than just an attitude chosen by an owner or an architect. As we'll see in Chapter 7, historic districts in urban areas preserve their character with restrictions on what can be built, including how additions affect the look of a house. This is not often the case outside our major cities. But when architect John Murray began his work on a house in a 1920s enclave near Greenwich, Connecticut, he had the same kind of constraints that follow him when he builds in New York City.

The enclave was designed by Olmsted Brothers, the successor firm to Frederick Law Olmsted, known as the father of American landscape architecture. Planned in 1925, this verdant, parklike development was a precursor to many of today's exclusive gated communities. During the 1920s developers laid out subdivisions in many U.S. exurban areas along thematic lines in hopes of attracting wealthy homebuyers. Richmond's Winsor Farms, Baltimore's Roland Park, Chestnut Hill's French Village, and Houston's River Oaks are but a few of these exclusive conclaves. In the Greenwich area, this planned development stands out as a successful attempt at bringing Tudor and Cotswold influences to the design of a planned domestic landscape.

Because the Main House was designed to set the thematic character of the place, Murray's team approached the original building with a sense of reverence when a new owner hired them in 1998 to design an expansion. The gray stucco cottage was a well-balanced composition of steeply pitched slate roofs and crossing gables, offering no obvious clues for an extension strategy. One of the driving forces for the design was the necessity for a four-car garage that could be subsumed within the service wing of the house. Though the main block had ample bedrooms, including a master suite, it did not have guest rooms or areas for family recreation.

In a typical 1920s American Tudor house, a clear hierarchy exists between the main block, containing family living functions and formal rooms, and the service wing, a lower and more modest piece containing cooking, laundry, pantry, storage, and automobile maintenance areas. Murray faced

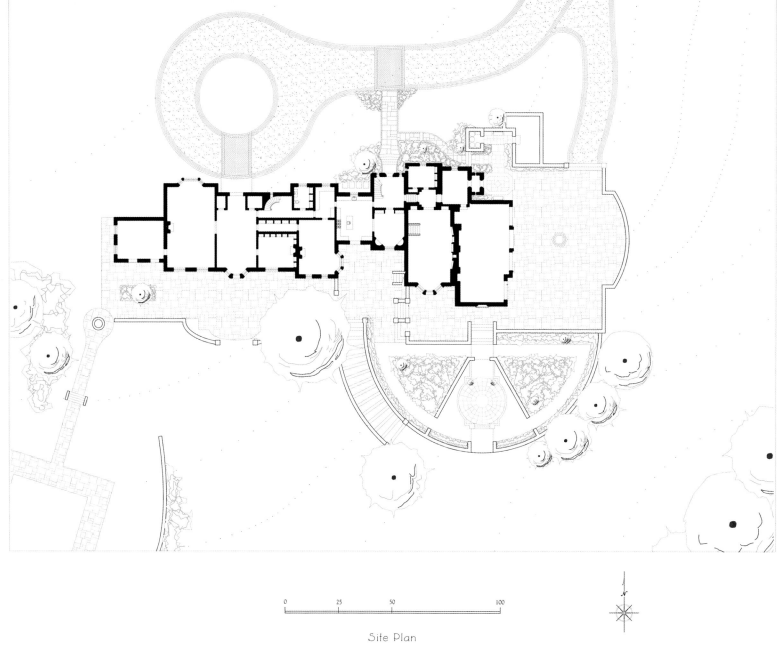

Plan of the addition by John Murray Architects of a Cotswold-style house in Greenwich, Connecticut. The old wing is to the left of the foyer.
(Courtesy of John B. Murray Architect, LLC.)

The addition, to the left, is similar in form but suppressed in scale so that the main house reads as the dominant mass. (Photo by Durston Saylor; courtesy of John B. Murray Architect, LLC.)

the prospect of replacing the outdated service wing with one that offered the same functions in a family-oriented arrangement. A new kitchen was placed in a link between the new and old wings. In order to rationalize the formal entry sequence with the new garage, the architect designed a second stair hall off the kitchen and breakfast room that could be used by the family on a daily basis. The old, grand hall would remain for use during formal affairs only. Off the new hall were a large game room and billiard room for family use, while the old library was redesigned in a more

The distinctive entry pavilion features custom stone carving inspired by Tudor architecture, and executed by an English master mason. (Photo by Durston Saylor; courtesy of John B. Murray Architect, LLC.)

The foyer inside is also inspired by Tudor-era decoration, with its wooden ceiling and stone window surrounds. (Photo by Durston Saylor; courtesy of John B. Murray Architect, LLC.)

From the garden, the ensemble appears entirely unified, as if built in consecutive campaigns typical of medieval English houses. (Photo by Durston Saylor; courtesy of John B. Murray Architect, LLC.)

informal manner. All of the new rooms were planned to complement the decor of the original house, with rich limed woodwork and stone accents.

In this addition the biggest challenge was devising a roof configuration and massing strategy that would not overwhelm the modest main cottage but could be seen as a natural extension of the original house. When looking at the front elevation, it is clear that the extension is subservient to the main wing, but less obvious that it was designed eighty years after. The architects handle both massing and detail with remarkable deftness, so that there is no obvious break between 1925 construction and the recent renovations. The new entry portico and hall are particularly successful. Simon

Verity, an English master mason, created the beautiful limestone doorways. The thick walls and traditional casement windows add an antique flavor to the room, while the light-stained oak ceiling provides warmth and scale.

Here it is important to note that successful massing and roof design without appropriate materials and details would not have resulted in the same superb resonance between old and new sections of the house. We employ the musical analogy deliberately here, for this addition will remain completely in tune, in the same key, as its original "movement" or wing. Of the five cardinal principles outlined in Chapter 2, the architects have employed a sound site strategy, similar massing modules, roofs, and facade motifs in this subtle and highly sophisticated work. While most homeowners clearly do not have the wherewithal for such elaborate and expensive architecture or decoration, the lessons offered in this case study could apply to any project.

Even something as modest as a farmhouse in a rural setting can become the inspiration for subtle transformations when additions are required. At Littlepond, a country residence in north central New Jersey, Philip Kennedy-Grant added wings on the north, east, and south sides of a smaller dwelling to take advantage of spectacular views toward open fields and forests. For this architect, the site is always a powerful generator of cues and design ideas.

As we noted in Chapter 2, farmsteads are carefully planned to take advantage of prevailing winds and solar orientation, but also must be located in order to provide access to fields. In the case of this farm site, the road access was on the northwest corner of the site, and the original dwelling was oriented east–west, with an ell on the south. The new owners wished to use the house year-round, but had no desire to spoil the rural character of the site. They maintained small pond on the southwest side, while also renovating a pool near the house.

A large part of the challenge in this renovation was rationalizing the circulation and massing of a house that had already seen two additions. Once the site strategy was set, the architect went about the business of connecting the disparate parts of the plan and re-roofing the building to provide coherence to the exterior. The two major additions were designed to maximize views and exposure to the key site features. A large family room was built on the east side to

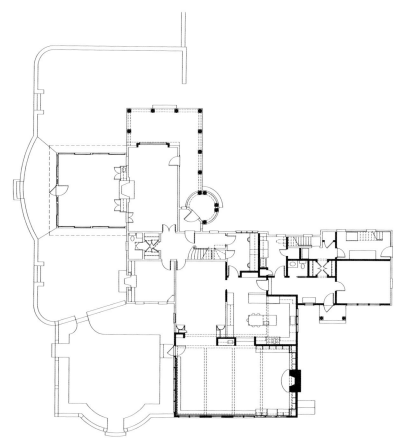

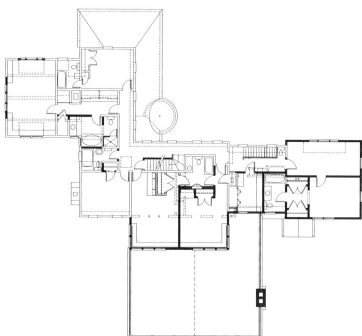

In the plans of the house it is evident that the architect studied each new space in relation to both the outdoors and the circulation system in the original house. The result is a seamless integration of old and new, and a logical flow from one room to the next. (The new walls are in black.) (Courtesy of Kennedy-Grant.)

Philip S. Kennedy-Grant transformed a mundane Colonial Revival farmhouse (top) into a more rustic shingled retreat near Bedminster, New Jersey (bottom). (Photo by Durston Saylor; courtesy of Kennedy-Grant.)

The outdoor theme is continued in the river stone fireplace in the new family room. Warm wood textures extend the metaphor. (Photo by Durston Saylor; courtesy of Kennedy-Grant.)

The large banks of double hung windows flood the room with morning light. (Photo by Durston Saylor; courtesy of Kennedy-Grant.)

The landscape around the house retains its rural character, while the additions resonate with the rustic quality of the site. (Photo by Durston Saylor; courtesy of Kennedy-Grant.)

connect directly to an existing dining room and new kitchen. In order to define and ventilate a closed-in living room, Kennedy-Grant added two porch rooms to the south and west sides of the space, while also providing a large view window directly in line with the pond and road. In essence, his strategy was to "wrap" the farmhouse in new spaces in order to create a more open plan. The main circulation through the building was maintained in a north–south corridor system that uses the existing main stair hall as a focal point.

The most impressive space in the new house is the new family room. With its rustic stone fireplace and warm timber ceiling, it set the tone for the entire renovation. The exterior was also changed from clapboard to shingle cladding, suggesting a hunting lodge more than a farm. The owners loved living outdoors, so screened porches were a plus, in particular off the living room. From nearly any angle the house appears unified but informal. It does not pretend to be a building conceived and built in one campaign, but rather lets each wing and room assert its individual character. One quirky element, necessary for marking the front entrance, is a small circular bulge at the corner of the porch in the entry court. Because the old front hall no longer faced a doorway to the exterior, the architect provided a vestibule to reorient visitors toward it.

Like the previous examples, Littlepond succeeds through a variety of intelligent strategies pursued as a result of good architect–client collaboration. Its more complex assemblage of new and old spaces might have been unacceptable to some owners desiring a smooth and tidy "new" look for an old house. Instead, this team elected to allow the new service wing, front porch, family room, and bedroom dormers to dictate their own forms as "organic" additions to the old house. Every space and roof shape relates sympathetically to the pattern established in the farmhouse. The architect understood the structure (timber frame), modular dimensions, and vernacular features of the original well enough to "grow" the house in a natural way. And, although the house is full of comforts and up-to-date technology, it remains securely in the realm of the simple farmstead. In many rural areas now experiencing growth, a nod to the farmer and his contribution is a welcome gesture, even if the pastures are empty of cows. In this way the architecture upholds the essence of place, while also providing new shelter for future generations.

In the next chapter we shift gears to address a problem already encountered in some of the case study projects: how to convert an outdated and inefficient heating and cooling system into something befitting a twenty-first-century sustainable ethos, without either going bankrupt or accepting drafty rooms. Whether you are blowing air or pumping water through ancient pipes, you'll want to read ahead to get some good ideas about sensitive retrofits for your antique systems.

6

BLOWING HOT AND COLD

COMFORT IN HOUSES—THAT IS, THE CONTROLLED indoor environment we now expect from central heating, cooling, and ventilation systems—is a relatively recent idea. For over two hundred years, the primary sources of heat in North American houses were open fireplaces contained in a single, central chimney stack, as in early New England houses, or in large, multivented chimneys during the Federal era. Messy and highly inefficient, these large, open fireplaces were basically the same as those used in medieval times. When compared with today's totally automatic heating systems that warm every room without any need to stoke fires or haul ashes, or air conditioning that pulls cool air from sweltering summers at the flick of a switch, comfort has certainly come a long way.

Few people would do without the invisible convenience of today's comfort equipment no matter what the age of their home, but when it comes to adding or expanding these systems in vintage houses, achieving the invisible part can seem as impossible as chasing a rainbow. Though modern heating and cooling pipes and boxes are neither part of the architecture of vintage houses nor historical materials in their own right (two of the central concerns of this book), without care they have a tendency to invade and undercut both elements—even in the most meticulous restoration or addition and often with monstrous results.

Fortunately, the chances of success are much better if you keep such interventions to a minimum. First, work with an understanding of how your house is built and look into ways you can extend the use of systems that are already there. Second, if facing new systems, chose those that are best adapted—even specifically designed—for the construction of your vintage house, and understand that some of the latest energy-efficient and sustainable technologies are space-thrifty and therefore retrofit-friendly as well. The following common scenarios are just an outline of the options you can consider without compromising the integrity of your vintage house.

EXPANDING AND IMPROVING HYDRONIC HEATING SYSTEMS

When it comes to vintage houses, extending or altering a relatively recent central heating system—forced air, electric or hot-water baseboards, or even the new radiant hose systems—is generally not a daunting task. While changes still take time and money, from a technical perspective all these systems are still actively manufactured and used for new construction, and every heating contractor worthy of the name is familiar with them. Moreover, there are many books, videos, and websites to lend help. The challenge for vintage house owners is dealing with the heating systems that are as old as their buildings—steam and hot water, collectively called hydronic systems. It's also working around the most visible parts of these systems, which vintage house owners invariably go to great lengths to keep—the radiators.

Adding one or more rooms of heating is not a do-it-yourself job—in part because one of the first tasks is to determine if your existing steam or hot water boiler has the capacity to handle the increased load. To find out, it's best to ask an experienced heating contractor to perform an up-to-date heat-load calculation for the new space and compare it with the boiler's rating plate. Then you will know whether or not you need to upgrade your boiler to a larger unit or even install a completely new and independent system.

While it's technically possible to add more radiators to a boiler that can handle them, in reality it's not that easy—especially for old steam systems, which are notoriously tricky to keep balanced for even heat. Changing the status quo involves not only tampering with pipes, fittings, and equipment that might have been in place for eighty to a hundred years, but also finding a contractor who knows how to work with the pipe pitches, volumes, and dynamics of a technology that was all but obsolete before he was

American manufacturers ceased producing ornamental cast-iron radiators decades ago, but new versions, such as the Classic Radiator by Burnham (www.usboiler.burnham.com), are now being imported for steam or hot water. (Courtesy of Burnham by U.S. Boiler Company.)

born. But in fact tying into an existing system may not even be necessary. If all you need is an additional radiator or two (or the equivalent)—say for an expanded kitchen or modest new bedroom—consider the following approaches that avoid intervening with the main system while adding the convenience of having the new heating devices on a separately controlled zone. If your dream is to squeeze more comfort from the equipment you already have, some clever—even middle-tech—accessories can help make it a reality.

ADDING A HOT-WATER ZONE TO A STEAM SYSTEM

A steam boiler is basically like a teakettle: a vessel partially full of water that, when heated to over 212 degrees, produces steam that can be drawn off above the water line to heat radiators. But given the right boiler and an experienced contractor, the boiler can also become a source of hot water. To do this, the contractor taps the boiler below the waterline—adding two openings to access the reservoir of hot water, not the steam—and from there runs a circuit of piping to heat the new radiator or two with hot water. The new circuit work also typically needs an electric circulator pump (to move the hot water through the radiators), a thermostat, aquastat, and control relay (to control the circulating pump and boiler burner), and flow-control valves (to control the hot water in the supply and return lines). The contractor must have the skills and experience to tap the boiler correctly (to permit best circulation across the boiler) and add a bypass line across the supply

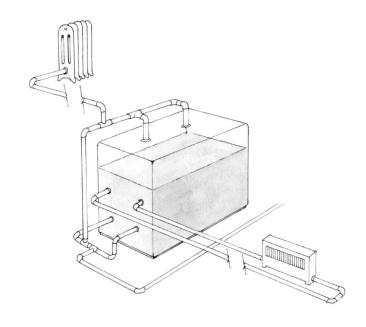

A steam boiler is also a source of hot water. To add a loop for a hot-water radiator, tap the boiler below the waterline and add accessories, such as a circulating pump. (Drawing by Rob Leanna.)

and return lines of the new hot-water circuit (to avoid having the hot water flash to steam when the circulator shuts off).

Tapping the boiler and adding a hot-water zone in this way takes skill and time. And it won't work for a radiant heating installation (because the boiler water is not clean enough for radiant hoses) unless a heat exchanger is added to the loop. But if the boiler has the capacity to accept the new load, this method has the advantages of using the existing system without disturbing it, while gaining a new, independently controlled zone.

Mad About Rads

Before you let anyone tell you your vintage radiators are just scrap iron, consider this. A century ago central steam and hot-water heating was a new, high-tech, growth industry and therefore pretty suave to have in a house. What's more, the sexiest part of the system—believe it or not—was the radiators. Rather than being considered space-hungry necessary evils, as they were by the 1950s, these cast-iron behemoths were exciting evidence of advances in comfort, and therefore something not to hide but to flaunt.

The first widely used radiators from the 1870s to the late 1890s were the tube type—a collection of wrought-iron pipes vertically set in a stand with feet and a top—many of which are still at work in historic buildings. Alternative designs, such as beefy cylinders with cast fins, tried to set the standard in another direction, but by 1895 manufacturers had settled on the column radiator familiar to us today. Radiators for steam systems were cast with large interior cavities so that steam and condensate could bypass each other easily. Since these columns were large on the outside too, manufacturers made the most of the ample surface area by casting the sections in decorative shapes—sometimes using historical motifs—and covering the columns in raised ornament. Several manufacturers vied for market share in the new industry, and each tried to outdo the other with the creativity of its designs. There once were models ranging from Greek to Rococo, as well as specialty shape and uses, like the plate- and muffin-warmer radiator for dining rooms and pantries.

The taste for ornamental radiators was already fading by the Roaring Twenties, and with the onset of the Great Depression in the 1930s, radiators turned more streamlined, with smooth, inconspicuous surfaces. The growing use of hot-water heating made large columns unnecessary, so manufacturers shifted to

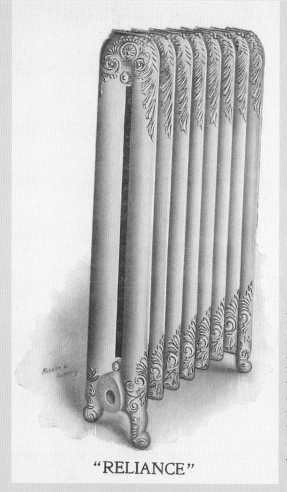

"RELIANCE"

The Reliance Model from Pierce, Butler, & Pierce Manufacturers is typical of the two-column ornamental radiator common until about 1915. (Courtesy of National Archives Associates.)

multiple thin columns—like the trend-setting Corto—that produced more surface area and, not coincidentally, were easier to conceal in cabinets and enclosures. Radiator minimalization continued through the post–World War II era, producing the wall-set radiators of the 1960s, until by the 1990s there were no longer any cast-iron radiators being manufactured in America.

The irony is that as the appeal of restoring vintage houses has grown since the 1960s, so has the cachet of radiators, because they are both practical for incorporating into an existing system and historically appropriate—not to mention the fun of having warm and working antiques. The upshot is that the used radiator market is hot, and some vintage-house lovers search for months for the right "rad" among a few specialized suppliers. Prices are measured in dollars per foot of column, times the number of columns. For large or exotic radiators, the numbers can be enough to make you gasp—and that's without shipping several hundred pounds of heavy metal. So before you assume that old heating system parts are worth little except perhaps as anchors, be aware that one man's cast-iron radiator might be another's golden treasure.

Once little more than scrap iron, the value of vintage radiators as architectural antiques has grown steadily over the last 20 years—especially for decorative or oddball designs. (Courtesy of Barbara Krankenhaus.)

The Quest for Comfort

It took one of America's founding fathers, Benjamin Franklin, to truly think outside of the fireplace box. In 1747 Franklin literally moved the fire out of the hearth and into a cast-iron container closer to the center of the room for better heat distribution, giving birth to the famous Franklin stove. In short order, Count Rumford (aka Benjamin Thompson)—a slippery military man who played several sides of the American Revolution—made scientific improvements in fireplace design during the 1790s. Rumford is best remembered today as the inventor of the Thermos bottle and the coffee percolator, but he also radically improved the hearth by creating the smoke shelf, which solved the problem of downdrafts blowing soot and smoke into the room. Even more revolutionary, however, was the way he reconfigured the firebox to be shallower, with aggressively angled walls that used less fuel while directing more of the fire's radiant heat into the room—the eponymous Rumford fireplace. Thomas Jefferson used Rumford fireplaces at Monticello, his Charlottesville home.

By the 1840s cast-iron heating stoves were common in the United States, but what really helped improve heating was the increased availability of a more efficient fuel than wood: coal. From there the next step was to build a large coal-firepot or furnace in the basement and direct the air it warmed upstairs through an octopus-like system of ducts and registers in floors. Because mechanical fans or blowers were unavailable without electricity, the air circulated through natural convection—the tendency of less dense warm air to rise. These early gravity warm-air systems started to appear in advanced houses by the

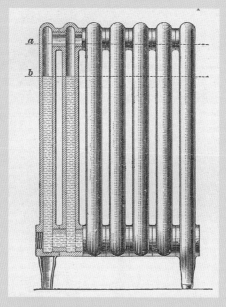

Hot water radiators are connected across the columns at both bottom and top to allow water to circulate in and out. (Courtesy of the National Archives Associates.)

1850s and were actively promoted by the new wave of domestic publications, such as the books by America's first "house maven," Andrew Jackson Downing.

Around the same time, early engineers were trying to heat buildings with steam boilers—already widely at work powering stationary engines, watercraft, and locomotives. The first successful system, devised in 1854 by New Englander Stephen Gold, used a small, low-pressure, wrought-iron boiler equipped with novel safety devices that dramatically reduced the potential for explosions, common in the era. But what really made the system practical was Gold's patented invention: a pair of iron plates hung on a wall, known as a "mattress" radiator. Steam had its advantages for heating large buildings or in cities (where an offsite source could supply district steam), but in the early days it was difficult to manage and always potentially dangerous, since the system needed pressure. Sometime between 1875 and 1885, an alternative system began taking hold in the form of gravity hot-water heating. Though tricky to install because they needed a closed loop of large-diameter piping between boiler and radiators, gravity hot-water heating systems ran at only 180 degrees and atmosphere pressure, making them easier and safer to maintain than steam and, by the late 1890s, the system of choice for heating large houses.

Along with forced-air heating (the blower-driven descendant of gravity warm air), steam and hot-water heating systems have become integral parts of the houses they serve, and they continue to provide comfort for today's households in their original as well as modern forms. What's more, as these systems evolved they've had a subtle but dramatic influence not only on homeowner lifestyles but also on the design of houses themselves. Central heating—especially with radiators that distributed heat more evenly through the house than gravity air—reduced the need to treat rooms as cells linked by a central hall that had to be closed off with doors to conserve heat from individual fireplaces or stoves. By the 1880s this new freedom from fireplaces allowed the flow between interior spaces to evolve into what we now call the open floor plan.

In the same way, in the 1950s central air conditioning started to render unnecessary the architectural features traditionally essential for making hot, humid climates tolerable: deep porches and eaves that provided shade from sun (what we now call passive solar cooling), tall windows on the ground floor for air circulation, and rooftop cupolas over a central stairway to encourage chimney-effect airflow up through the house. In the broadest view, air conditioning also made it attractive to build houses in parts of the United States that were formerly left to a hearty few, such as Florida or the desert states of the West, thereby precipitating, in the years after 1960, a population shift to the south for the first time in our nation's history.

By 1929, radiators were moving from decorative objects of display to ones that were best hidden inside a wall or partition, such the Herman Nelson Invisible Radiator. (Courtesy of National Archives Associates.)

From the People Who Brought You
Noblesse Oblige

While their starving countrymen were seething with upheaval in the streets of eighteenth-century Paris, according to one historian, the French courts of Louis XIV and XV were seeding a cushy revolution of their own before events flushed them from Versailles to the guillotine. The idle aristocracy, it seems, were obsessed with new amenities like commodes (the first indoor toilets), vented fireboxes, easy chairs, sofas, luxury upholstery, and more comfortable clothing. The social historian Joan DeJean has shown that French women like the Marquise de Montespan and the Marquise de Pompadour (mistresses of the Sun King) pressed for advances in interior design and dress that, DeJean suggests, created the standards for comfort we have come to regard as contemporary. While doing so, they and their bourgeois friends spurred architects to invent some of the things we now take for granted as essential to a civilized life, like central heating. In 1713 Nicolas Gauger, a physicist, published the first modern treatise on the design of convection heating—*Le Méchanique du feu.* In it he explained why conventional fireboxes were inefficient, drafty, and ultimately bad for one's health. He also devised the first systems of ducted heating since Roman times.[1] If that sounds a little like déjà vu, remember what Steve Martin said: "Those French have a different word for everything!"

ADDING A RADIANT HEATING ZONE TO A HOT-WATER SYSTEM

Suppose your vintage house has a working hot-water heating system, and you're remodeling a bathroom or kitchen with a tile floor that would make a nice installation for radiant heating. It's very possible that you can efficiently add a subzone of radiant tubing to the existing system if there is a hot water supply and return near the space—the taps for a removed radiator, for instance, or even a length of copper fintube baseboard. Since radiant heating carries water no hotter than 120 degrees F (to prevent damaging materials or scalding feet) but hot-water radiators run at about 180 degrees F, the radiant loop has to be plumbed in such a way that the water temperature is lowered. The heating contractor will do this by installing a mixing valve that reintroduces some of the cooler water from the radiant zone, along with a circulator pump to propel the water. This installation does not create its own zone—that is, it is still controlled by the main thermostat—but it is much simpler and less expensive than, say, running piping or radiant hose all the way back to the boiler.

USING THE BOILER'S HOT WATER HEATER ACCESSORY

If your heating system boiler is built so it can also supply hot water for bathroom and kitchen use, and you already have a separate hot-water heater, you may be able to use the boiler's hot water jacket to supply a radiant heating loop for a new bathroom or kitchen installation. Such an installation may also require accessories, such as circulator and a mixing valve but a good heating contractor will be the one who can tell.

ADDING A KICKSPACE HEATER

An often overlooked device that can solve problems in many vintage house projects is a kickspace heater. So called because they are only 4" high and therefore able to fit under cabinets where they exhaust out the kick- or toespace, these heaters are designed to make up for radiators or baseboard heating that have been sacrificed to free up wall space—a common

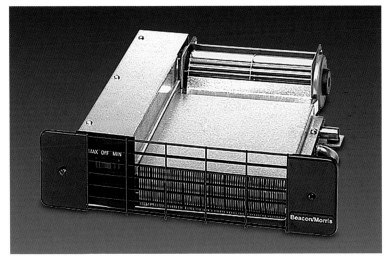

One of the original kickspace heaters is the Twin-Flo (Beacon/Morris is the originator; www.beacon-morris.com) that fits in the 4" void under cabinets or in other confined spaces. Electricity powers a cage fan that circulates warm air. (Courtesy of Mestek.)

trade-off in kitchen remodeling projects. Kickspace heaters have other advantages, though, when you think outside the "kitchen box." For example, they are equally adaptable to bathroom cabinets and can also fit under stair risers, windows, or in foyers where space for other radiation is unobtainable but heat is welcome.

Mechanically, a kickspace heater is similar to the heater in a car in that it incorporates a heat exchanger coil fed hot water by hoses with an electric fan to circulate the heat. Depending on the system in the house, these heaters can be tied into existing lines or set up as a separate zone. Not surprisingly, some manufactures also offer kickspace-type heaters that are totally electric.

ADDING OUTDOOR RESET CONTROLS

If you have hot-water heating and a system with the right boiler and components, you might be able to eliminate your old thermostat in favor of an outdoor reset control. Rather than being controlled by the temperature in one room, these devices also monitor the outdoor temperature, and then adjust the temperature of the system water accordingly. In other words, the colder it is outside, the higher the water temperature; warmer outside, colder water. Because the circulator runs continuously with these devices, they maintain a perfect level of indoor temperature. Outdoor reset controls may also help overcome the short-cycling and "Ferris-wheel" effect endemic to older hot-water systems in large houses: because the system has a large volume of water to heat up,

163

Parlez-Vous Parlor Heater?

The winter of 1902 was one for the books. On top of the cold weather, a bitter strike by miners in the Northeast dragged on for months, cutting the supply of anthracite coal—the prime heating fuel for city dwellers—to a trickle. To add insult to injury, what coal could be had jumped in price from $5 to $30 a ton, putting it beyond the reach of thousands who risked freezing in their homes. The double whammy made everyone sit up and take notice—particularly gas companies.

Well-established in many eastern cites since the 1850s, central gas companies were enjoying what seemed to be an ever-growing industry by the 1880s, expanding along with urban commerce to supply a new and vital market: street and indoor lighting. Though various primitive appliances had been devised for cooking or heating with gas—especially in England—most people felt the fuel was too expensive to be used as anything but an illuminant. The picture started to shift, however, with the turn of the century. By 1900, a new, upstart technology—electricity—was taking a noticeable bite out of the gas-lighting business, especially in cities, so the gas companies fought back. The first volley was an improved lighting fixture called the Welsbach mantle, followed shortly by a parade of new household conveniences—from gas vacuum cleaners and gas water purifiers to gas laundry irons—all designed with the hope of reclaiming lost lighting customers.

For gas companies, the troubled winter of '02 couldn't have been better. They played into homeowners' fears of another coalless winter by promoting gas-fired decorative heaters as a practical alternative. Sometimes called parlor heaters, these were typically ersatz fireplace fuels of various ilks—fake logs, coals, or jets in historical grates—installed in specially made shallow (and usually flueless) hearths. Parlor heaters could be used to back up the main furnace or boiler on very cold days, or just to take the chill off a room without firing up the central system. Designs varied over their three decades of popularity, but fell into two basic types: reflector heaters (using heat from gas burned directly in luminous flames, reflected into the room via a silvered backing) and incandescent heaters (using fire clay elements heated to incandescence by gas).

The granddaddy of today's fireplace inserts, parlor heaters were shallow, decorative gas space heaters, such as this metal log version, marketed to back up the main, coal-fired system. (Courtesy of Barbara Krankenhaus.)

Gas-fired parlor heaters started to die out in the 1930s along with the wane of coal and the rise of electric heating. But thousands still stand—picture-frame mantels and all—in row-house dining rooms or suburban parlors and libraries. While they are usually beyond recommissioning because they are not in compliance with modern fire codes or safety regulations (fake logs, fake ashes, and even hearth lining may contain asbestos), they offer a pleasing precedent for a twenty-first-century artificial fireplace—or simply an attractive feature on which to display a potted plant and pair of candles.

a conventional thermostat is already telling it to shut down about the time the hot water is just reaching the farthest radiators from the boiler.

ADDING THERMOSTATIC RADIATOR VALVES

One of the banes of steam-heat systems is their tendency to have one or two radiators that overheat. Before you think about tinkering with the pipes or the boiler, try installing a thermostatic valve on one or two of the radiators. These devices take the place of the conventional air vents that are attached halfway up on one end of the radiator. Simple enough to be installed by a homeowner—you simply unscrew the air vent and screw in the thermostatic valve—they are totally self-contained and need no wiring. You preset the desired temperature, and when the room reaches that level the valve shuts, preventing any more steam from entering the radiator (because the valve won't let any more air out). Thermostatic valves can be used on as few or as many radiators as necessary. The only caveat is not to install one in the same room with the main thermostat.

THE AIRCON CONUNDRUM

Of all the mechanical services that have added comfort to houses in the twentieth century, air conditioning may well be the most confusing for vintage houses owners. Though residential air conditioning—in the form of window units—was perfected by the late 1920s, central air in houses was rare until the post–World War II building boom, and therefore has no precedent in the vast majority of buildings we would define as historic by the fifty-year standard. The problem this presents for adding a system is not so much one of clashing with history as it is tapping into ingenuity. Unless the house is already fitted with a system of ducts for forced-air heating (which, with adaptation, can also deliver cool air), finding a way to retrofit air conditioning without being radically invasive—that is, cutting open walls and stealing space in ceilings and corners—is tricky, to say the least.

Part of the reason that adding air conditioning to a vintage house is complex is that it involves a decision tree of several choices before you come to the point of choosing a system, deciding on an installation, or breaking out the hammers and saws. The following breakdown of system types and approaches can help you climb that tree.

Once you have determined the amount of capacity you need to keep your vintage house cool, the next decision is the type of system—a choice governed principally by the way the equipment delivers air and how well it will work in your building. These system types fall into three basic categories:

CONVENTIONAL DUCTS

The type of central air system that most people are familiar with, and that has been in use the longest, is one that delivers the cooled air through large ducts of either rectangular sheet metal or, more commonly today, flexible tubes about

Adding conventional air conditioning requires running cooling lines between the condenser outdoors and the evaporator, often in the attic—a task where uncreative installers do little more to conceal lines than wrap them in downspout. (Courtesy of Barbara Krankenhaus.)

10" in diameter made of fiberglass or other materials that also insulate the duct. In these systems, the heat-shedding equipment—the compressor and condenser coil—are sited outdoors and connect to an evaporator coil, located in an attic or crawlspace, via a pair of coolant-filled lines and an electrical control cable. It is the evaporator—sometimes called the air handler—that connects to the ducts and pushes cooled air to the rooms.

Most conventional duct system components are typically not that difficult to site in and around a vintage house and, because the systems have been made for a long time by major manufacturers, they're generally not as expensive as more specialized systems. The catch—and therefore the real cost—is in installing the ductwork. Since the ducts of conventional systems are designed to be installed in the naked framing of new construction, they can generally be run in the unobstructed space of an unfinished attic to serve the bedrooms or other living spaces below. Reaching lower floors, however, is more difficult, and typically requires the cost and sacrifice of space involved in opening walls and boxing in room corners or the backs of closets (common ways to hide ducts running vertically between floors) or ceiling soffits (where ducts have no other way to run horizontally across the house).

Where practical, a better approach takes advantage of the foundation—to-eave stud bays of balloon framing which, when unblocked by firestops, can make a chase for invisibly running lines up a three-story wall. (Courtesy of Barbara Krankenhaus.)

MINI-DUCT (AKA HIGH-VELOCITY) SYSTEMS

By the 1980s, the difficulty of running conventional air conditioning ducts in finished houses led two companies

The visible evidence of a mini-duct system in a room is not a large conventional register, but a small round port, here in the floor. (Courtesy of Unico.)

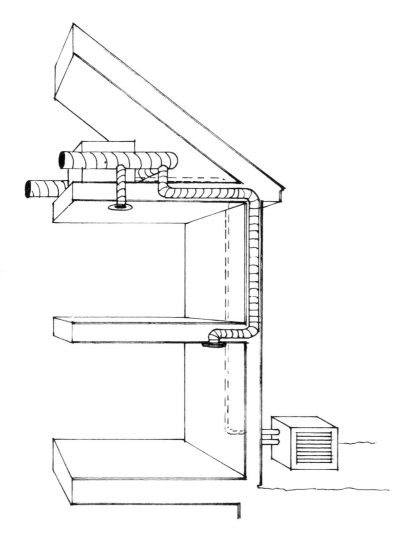

Mini-duct or high-velocity air conditioning units are proprietary systems that also take advantage of stud wall voids. In this case, the ducts are small enough in diameter to snake within the 4″ void and run from equipment to living space. (Drawing Rob Leanna.)

The flexible ducts of a mini-duct or high-velocity air conditioning system fit within a 4″ wall void but can also be run in the open across framing. (Courtesy of Unico.)

Mini-duct air conditioning is specifically designed to deal with the unconventional construction of antique houses, such as the solid masonry of the historic Van Sykel Inn in New Jersey. (Courtesy of Unico.)

The air handler for the Unico system, for example, is typically located in an attic, and is modular for assembling into tight spaces. (Courtesy of Unico.)

to come to market with an innovative alternative: systems that use miniature ducts. Only 4" in diameter, these mini-ducts were designed not only to be small enough to snake through the voids between wall studs and floor joists, but also to have much smaller, more inconspicuous round outlets than conventional rectangular registers. In the engineering world, however, you don't get something for nothing. In order to deliver the same amount of cooling as conventional ducts with a reduced cross-sectional area, the system delivers it at a greater speed—hence the often-used label *high-velocity system*.

Mini-duct systems overcome many of the problems inherent in retrofitting a vintage house with central air—

in fact they are an almost ideal match with balloon-frame buildings, with their long stud bays. Even so, these systems do come with some caveats. First of all, the mechanical equipment—the compressor and evaporator—is more specialized than conventional systems, and therefore tends to be more expensive. Second, much of the success of the system depends on the skill of the installer. For example, the outlets of mini-duct systems are often best placed in the corners of rooms (a departure from conventional systems) so that they are less likely to stream high-velocity cold air on chairs or work areas where people will be sitting. Also, the small-diameter ducts are not as forgiving as large-diameter ducts when it comes to bends and angles (which can induce noise and reduce efficiency), though a good installer will be up to this challenge.

DUCTLESS (SPLIT) SYSTEMS

Suppose your vintage house is one where neither mini-duct systems nor conventional systems seem to be workable. That is often the situation in timber-frame houses, where wall voids are irregular and blocked by heavy timbers, and it certainly holds true for solid-masonry brick or stone houses where the walls have no workable voids at all. Fortunately, the air conditioning industry has a potential solution—a third equipment type often called a ductless or split system. Though uncommon in the United States until recently, these systems have been popular overseas for decades (particularly in the Far East) where wood and stud-wall buildings are rare and tile and masonry predominate. Basically, split-system air conditioners are akin to window-mount air conditioners except that rather than having the compressor and evaporator in the same box, the units are separated and connected only by the coolant and control lines. This allows the evaporator "head" to be mounted on the outside wall of a room, while the larger, noisier compressor is located outdoors in an out-of-the-way spot. The rest of the installation involves boring a hole through the wall behind the evaporator and running the lines to the compressor.

Split systems are not as inconspicuous in the room as a mini-duct port or a conventional register—the evaporator heads stick out about 6" from the wall—but they are far less obtrusive than a window unit and much more flexible to position. Many manufacturers make models in which several evaporators are served by a single compressor. Though these systems are generally more expensive than conventional ducted systems, they do have the added advantage of being able to provide heat as well as cooling. For the vintage house where no other system is practical, they can be a welcome way to beat the warm weather.

THE GEOTHERMAL ALTERNATIVE

The place where earth-friendly heating and cooling technology, space-saving efficiency, and vintage house sensitivity all come together is literally in the ground. Geothermal heating—once the stuff of science fiction and house-of-the-future

Simple Ideas Help a Lot

When choosing a site for the compressor box, look beyond ease of installation or street-side aesthetics. While it may be nice to hide the box in the shadow of a building feature or shrub, make sure you don't block air flow that can impede the condenser's ability to discharge heat. In the same way, you're also better off not planting it where it will get large amounts of direct sun that will make its heat-exchange job harder; consider instead the shady side of the building.

prototypes—has in recent years moved beyond the echelons of large mansions and high-technophiles (who could afford the upfront costs and realize the savings over time) to average-sized houses. What's more, the appeal of geothermal extends beyond cost savings and energy independence to some real advantages for old houses in certain cases.

Geothermal is an umbrella term for a variety of technologies that collect the earth's natural heat using liquid-filled pipes and then transport it to a building where it is released indoors. Surprisingly, the concept is far from new.

Direct geothermal systems have been in use since the late 1890s in geologically active areas such as the vicinity of Yellowstone Park in the United States or in Iceland—places where there are already hot springs and geysers. Here, naturally hot water—sometimes close to the boiling point (212 degrees F)—is piped from hot springs, wells, or underground pools directly into houses and radiators, sometimes blocks away. While direct-system heating is all but free, it's not perfect; the pipes can become clogged with deposits from the mineral-rich water. The biggest drawback, though,

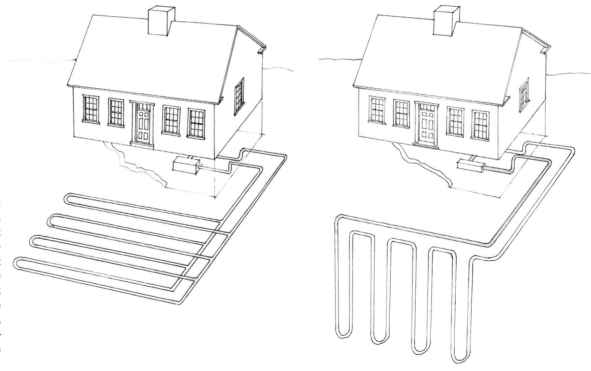

Left: Where land is ample, the most practical geothermal installation is often a horizontal ground loop—typically a circuit of pipe buried in six-foot deep trenches. Right: Where the lot is tight or difficult to work, the alternative is often vertical ground loops—one or more vertical shafts connected by a daisy chain of piping. (Drawings by Robert Leanna.)

is that suitable naturally occurring hot springs are few and far between.

What makes modern geothermal systems different from direct systems is that they take advantage of the earth's temperature below the frost line, which is about 50 degrees Fahrenheit and available almost everywhere. A refrigerant loop similar to a central air conditioner or a heat pump moves heat between two devices: the indoor device is the evaporator that heats the rooms; the outdoor device is the condenser that collects heat from the environment—or, for cooling, rejects heat into the environment. The difference is that the environment a geothermal system uses is not the atmosphere, but the earth.

Depending on the size and condition of the house's site, a geothermal system will connect to the earth in one of two basic kinds of loops. In horizontal ground loops—the easiest option where space is ample—the contractor excavates trenches about six feet deep and buries plastic pipe to make a circuit. Usually the pipe is laid back and forth in parallel lines resembling a toaster element, but if the area is limited the pipe can also be planted in coils. Where space is tight—say, in an urban lot—or where rocky soil makes trenching

How Much Air Conditioning Do You Need?

Before you can look for equipment that is properly sized for your house, you need to know how much cooling your house will need. Cooling capacity is measured in BTUs (British Thermal Units) or tons of cooling (12,000 BTUs equaling one ton), and the house's cooling needs—the load analysis—is determined by a contractor. Using a manual or computer software, the contractor calculates the load by taking into account the house's surface area on exterior walls, amount of insulation, window glazing, air infiltration, and other details of its construction. Because vintage houses are typically underinsulated by new construction standards (and the windows tend to be leaky), they are not going to be as predictable as the same size average house, so it is important not to guesstimate but do an actual load analysis.

The other important number to consider when shopping for equipment is the efficiency rating or SEER (Seasonal Energy Efficiency Ratio). While most people assume the purpose of air conditioning is to lower the ambient temperature in the house, one of its main contributions to comfort is lowering the humidity. Though keeping humidity low may make the house feel more comfortable at a higher temperate, and not make the compressor work as hard, this benefit can be undercut by the air leaks endemic to older houses, which bring in moisture. What this means for vintage houses is that it may be most cost-effective to consider premium air-conditioning products with a SEER of 15 or above, units that are likely to have better humidity controls and adjustable speed blowers. Also, in humid locales like Florida and Texas, the added efficiency of units with an even high SEER will be even more cost-effective over a long cooling season than lower-rated units—despite the higher up-front costs.

difficult, the alternative is to go down with vertical ground loops. The contractor sinks a number of vertical holes in the earth using conventional well-drilling equipment, inserts a single loop of pipe in each hole, and backfills or grouts the hole; later each hole loop is connected to the next loop in a daisy chain to make a circuit. Sites blessed with plenty of water can take a different tack. If there's a nearby lake or pond, the installation can skip any trenches and simply submerge the pipe coils in the water body as if it were a horizontal ground loop. Locations with abundant groundwater may also shift from a conventional vertical ground loop to an open loop system. Here, water is pumped directly from a well, the heat is extracted, and then the water is returned to the earth via another well—the reason the system is an open loop.

ENVIRONMENTAL AND ECONOMIC ADVANTAGES

What has put geothermal systems on the radar of many homeowners today is the rising cost of energy. Since geothermal systems rely on the earth's energy—which is both free and renewable—they have far lower operating costs than conventional systems fed by fossil fuels or a straight diet of electricity. They are also very efficient—between 50 and 70 percent more efficient than traditional heating systems—because they are stingy on what electricity they do use, and it is easier to extract heat from the earth at 50

degrees than, say, air at 30 degrees. Even better, geothermal systems can operate in reverse—that is, they can become air conditioners by removing heat from the house in summer and transporting it into the earth.

Probably the biggest limitation to geothermal is the up-front cost. Sinking numerous wells can be expensive—especially if the soil is not cooperative or the performance is not ideal. For this reason, among the earliest adopters of residential geothermal were the builders of large houses. While these owners might also be enamored of technology like satellite television and home theaters, there was more to experimenting with geothermal than a soft spot for mechanical wizardry. Such owners not only had the pocketbook to foot the up-front costs, they also had the most to gain in the form of a payback for heating several thousand square feet of living space.

Like any vintage house project, a geothermal installation benefits from thorough homework and planning. Site surveys, for example, are a very good idea, even to the point of sinking a test well. The nature of the surrounding soil has a big impact on the performance of the well; water and sandy soils have good heat transfer; rocky soils are less effective. But with good planning and an eye on the long-range benefits, geothermal is becoming an increasingly attractive option for vintage houses of all sorts—from urban buildings to country getaways—with every passing heating and cooling season.

The subject of our next chapter is one not often addressed in books on old houses: the importance of community identity in urban house facades. Americans are familiar with individual houses as the norm, but when looking for houses in dense urban areas, the object is not to pick a house that stands out but one that blends into the fabric of an established neighborhood. When it comes time to restore, renovate, or expand, a few different rules apply.

7

FACING THE NEIGHBORHOOD

OST HOMEOWNERS BELIEVE THAT THEIR houses present a face like their own to the outside world. Especially in the United States, where the detached single-family dwelling is a part of the myth of self-fulfillment at the core of society, one's house carries an identity that may be personal, ethnic, class-conscious, place-specific, or simply American. Borrowing their property-conscious culture from the English, Americans have from the beginning looked to ownership of a manor house on a green country parcel as the highest form of fulfillment. As Walt Whitman wrote, "A man is not a whole and complete man until he *owns* a house and the ground it stands on." Even the ubiquitous lawn in the front yard is an expression of this fundamental American value.

David Handlin has analyzed the emergence of this peculiar view of houses and property in his book *The American Home: Architecture and Society 1815–1915*. He suggests that in the new democracy it was necessary for citizens to establish both their social identity and an appropriate morality through the houses they built and lived in. Especially in the initial period of urbanization, during the middle of the nineteenth century, Americans looked for stable forms and symbols of their roles in the new society, a rather chaotic, constantly moving population. The house, whether built on a farm or in an urban row setting, became that symbol of self.[1] Writers, architects, landscape gardeners, and pattern book companies supplied a wide range of model homes for Americans to choose from.

By the beginning of the twentieth century many of the types and styles of American dwelling were codified by region, class, ethnicity, and context. The ubiquitous Colonial, Cape Cod, Tudor, Spanish, and Mediterranean styles that are now common in real estate listings were well established in the periodicals, each vying for the title of "home sweet home" for the middle-class family. What the historian Alan Gowans has called "the Comfortable House" had arrived.[2] The codification of house styles, each of which has associations thought to be consonant with American values, represents one form of identity marker embodied in the dwelling.

A second, more powerful marker is present in the facade of a house that is part of a collective. Especially in Great Britain, where terrace or rowhouses make up the domestic fabric of nearly every city and town, people assess class status, ethnicity, and community solidarity both in individual houses and in the street frontage of groups of houses. London's famous terraces were generally built on land owned by the aristocracy. Only gradually were large urban parcels filled with houses. When the Duke of Bedford wanted to develop his city properties, he constructed uniform "terraces" and rented the houses to the emerging bourgeoisie. Many of London's eighteenth-century squares are named for their benefactors. Though none of the owners of these houses identify with a duke or an earl, they do associate places with names. Neighborhoods become associated with the original landowners long after their titles have passed to others.[3]

In America's first prosperous cities—Philadelphia, Boston, Charleston, and New Orleans—terrace houses were built by individuals and speculators as the most efficient form of dwelling to fill a city block. As most of the builders and occupants were from England, the rowhouse form was a shared standard that could be constructed with ease. All houses were attached to each other by a common "fire wall" that usually consisted of two adjacent brick walls roughly cemented together with mortar. Attached houses were more common in early America than detached ones and with this physical attachment came a social connection: residents of discrete rows or blocks could identify with others in the same location. The street front of each house was similar, though not necessary identical, to those adjacent to it, providing a form of collective identity as well as personal expression. As scholars such as Dell Upton and Frederick Starr have demonstrated, cities like New Orleans grew through the development of discrete rowhouse neighborhoods, or "faubourgs," according to the settlement patterns of new immigrant groups from France, Spain, England, and the Caribbean.[4]

As we noted in Chapter 2, the relationship between the facade or public face of a townhouse and its neighbors is demonstrative of social hierarchies in a city or community. Thus facades are apt to change in subtle ways as individual owners and the society in the neighborhoods interact with one another. The metamorphosis of some city houses is quite extreme, but generally these dwellings exhibit a kind of decorum based on shared cultural norms that shift gradually over decades, even centuries.

Millions of Americans live in attached or semi-attached houses, mainly in the older cities on the Eastern seaboard. Baltimore has a wide variety of rowhouse types, as do New Orleans, Savannah, and Mobile. As the architect Christine Hunter notes, attached rowhouses have a number of advantages over detached houses. They are economical, simple to construct, and very flexible. When a small family buys a larger rowhouse, there is often the opportunity to supplement

Rowhouses were the predominant form of housing in America's cities prior to the twentieth century. This row is in Savannah, Georgia. (Courtesy of Mark Alan Hewitt.)

yards formed by bay windows, stoops, or vestibules create subtle eddies of space along the slot created by walls of similar height. The rear yards are often treated as small gardens, with decks, balconies, and other private spaces decorated according to individual tastes. We'll talk about a fine example of this shortly.

Because of these characteristic spaces, rowhouses present particular problems for families wishing to expand them or alter their "faces" to the street. In this chapter we'll present several case studies of contemporary expansions, but before we do it is essential to understand the nature of the neighborhoods that give form to row buildings. Because Boston and Philadelphia are America's oldest English cities, we'll begin there.

income by renting floors to tenants. Structurally, rowhouses have the advantage of requiring only the two party walls for support. Plumbing and electrical systems can be located in risers, often near chimneys. And heating systems are very efficient because of the compact stacking of the floors, up to four or five stories.

Hunter also analyzes the powerful social and spatial characteristics of the rowhouse. The public domain of the street is very different from the private domain of the rear yard—formal and dignified versus informal and individual. Further, she notes that rowhouses "shape the open space around them," creating "outdoor rooms with varying degrees of enclosure."[5] In the front, the room is the street, and small

PHILADELPHIA AND BOSTON

Prior to the twentieth century, when the high-rise apartment house was developed, Boston and Philadelphia consisted entirely of residential neighborhoods filled with rowhouses. Upper-income neighborhoods—Society Hill and Rittenhouse in Philadelphia, Boston's Beacon Hill and Back Bay—still have many outstanding examples of this type of house. And hundreds of thousands still live in the working-class districts where attached houses are the norm. In contrast to the suburban ranches and split-levels we think of as the bedrock of American society, city houses encourage community and neighborhood security. That is one of the reasons why their public, street facades carry so much meaning. Moreover, as rowhouse districts developed in these cities, their characteristic styles and modes of construction gave flavor to neighborhoods, establishing a distinct sense of place.

Philadelphians are proud of their city and its fabric of row buildings. They should be, for the city of brotherly love contains the largest and most diverse collection of these houses in the nation. In 2003 the city's planning commission teamed with the National Trust for Historic Preservation in developing a short manual for homeowners of this building type. As the author notes, "Philadelphia rowhouses outnumber all other housing types as they have always been the most space-efficient and cost-effective way to provide homes for a rapidly growing industrial city."[6] The neighborhoods in which row buildings predominate have developed into historic places such as Old City, the Northern Liberties, Powelton Village, Spruce Hill, and Rittenhouse. In the booklet, nine distinct types of rowhouse are identified, three in each important period in the city's growth: Colonial and early nineteenth century, mid- and late nineteenth century, and twentieth century. Though names and sizes vary from the tiny "bandbox" or "Trinity" to the larger "Porchfront" and "Airlite," all are distinguished by their common-wall properties and high density. The diversity and adaptability of these house types has kept them viable over several centuries, and there is no reason to doubt that they will continue to provide quality space well into the future.

When Philadelphia rowhouse owners contemplate renovations or expansions, they seldom consider wholesale rede-

2300 Block of Delancey Street, Philadelphia. (Courtesy of Paul Hirshorn.)

sign or rebuilding as options. In other contexts an American family might see the need to express their individual tastes in a house, but in rowhouse neighborhoods the collective identity is of paramount concern. This has been the case ever since the first large-scale row developments were constructed during the eighteenth and nineteenth centuries by such architects as Robert Mills and John Haviland. In row buildings, the street facade carries all of the public significance and must convey a measure of decorum or good manners, while the rear facade is private, personal, and largely functional.

During the early 1980s, under the direction of professors Paul Hirshorn and John Blatteau, architecture students at the University of Pennsylvania fanned out through the city of Philadelphia to draw the best rowhouses as a means of studying precedents for new design. The result of their labors was the publication *A Comparative Study of Philadelphia Rowhouses*, now partially available online through Bryn Mawr College. One of the signal achievements of this study was to show the remarkable diversity that was possible within an otherwise highly constrictive building envelope. Another was the documentation of whole-block street facades, demonstrating the extraordinary persistence of collective identity throughout the various neighborhoods. Philadelphia's row buildings have maintained their coherence, scale, and meaning over decades, even centuries. Why are individual owners so faithful to the original dwellings made by their forebears amidst pressures to expand or demolish them?

Though no sociological studies have proved this, the likely reason for rowhouse continuity is that people work for

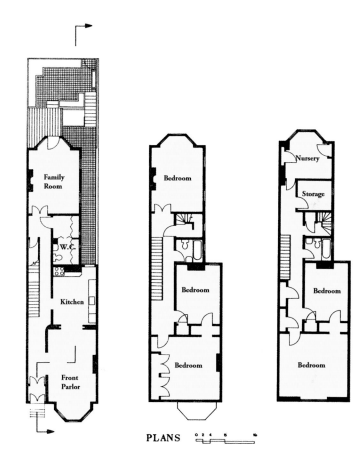

Right: Comparative study of Philadelphia rowhouses, plans of 2318 Delancey Street. (Courtesy of University of Pennsylvania School of Design.)

Below: Drawing of the 2300 Block of Delancey Street, Philadelphia, showing whole block elevation. (Courtesy of Paul Hirshorn.)

George A. Nickerson House (1897) on Commonwealth Avenue, Boston, by McKim, Mead & White. (From the Library of Congress Prints & Photographs Division, HABS, MASS,13-BOST, 112.)

the common good when it is in their best interest to do so. When their property values, public persona, and street security are bound up with the houses directly beside and around theirs, homeowners work collectively to preserve the whole neighborhood. True, many Philadelphia neighborhoods are in historic districts that levy some restrictions on changes to house facades, but this does not explain why virtually all economically viable districts in the city have well-kept rows of similar houses. Moreover, studies by preservationists in Pittsburgh during the 1970s proved that when one homeowner spruces up a facade and maintains her yard, others follow out of pride and a desire to maintain the community.[7]

The same kind of attitude prevails in Boston, America's oldest English city. Charles Bulfinch set the standard for terrace house design with his Tontine Crescent (1793–1794), a bow-shaped row of nearly identical houses centered on a monumental gateway. The beautiful brick Federal houses of Beacon Hill are a testament to Bostonians' collective munificence during the late eighteenth century, when the city led the nation in culture and politics. Significantly, when Charles McKim and Stanford White looked to townhouse precedents during the Colonial Revival, they used Beacon Hill mansions as their inspiration. All of the original models for these houses came from London.

In what was probably the largest municipal land expansion of the nineteenth century in the United States, Boston responded to a new wave of immigrants by leveling its hills and filling in the western edge of the Shawmut Peninsula in the 1850s. The resulting planned development was the Back

Boston's Back Bay was built entirely on landfill dredged from Boston Harbor. This early photo shows the development of the broad avenues in the district. (From the Library of Congress, Prints & Photographs Division, Detroit Photographic Company.)

Bay, an elegant district of Victorian townhouses that followed the city's early pattern of terrace and row buildings. Centered on Commonwealth Avenue, with its midline strip of gardens and street trees, the Back Bay has maintained a cachet as Boston's cultural hub for almost two centuries, benefiting from the construction of Copley Square on the west end and the Public Garden on the east.[8]

Bainbridge Bunting's classic study of Back Bay houses demonstrates the vitality, diversity, and influence of the buildings constructed in the district from the 1850s through the early 1900s. More important, his documentation of facade designs shows how typological standardization of plans could provide fodder for endless invention when architects and developers worked in succeeding styles. Academic French,

The distinctive bays in Back Bay houses create spatial rhythms and plays of light that give the district its sense of place. These 1868 houses are at 72–80 Marlborough Street. (From the Library of Congress Prints & Photographs Division, HABS, 13-BOST, 129.)

181

Gothic, Queen Anne, Colonial Revival, Richardsonian Romanesque—virtually every style popular in America during the nineteenth century is represented in the area. As in Philadelphia, however, uniform cornice lines, setbacks, common window types, and predominant brick and brownstone materials create a harmonious sense of place that is zealously protected by residents.[9] In this way Back Bay houses demonstrate the "unity with diversity" that Americans treasure in society and culture.

With its burnished gold past, it is not surprising that the Back Bay was one of the first urban districts in the United States to develop preservation organizations, local history groups, and technical resources to help homeowners maintain their houses. In 1989 the Boston Landmarks Commission (BLC) teamed with Historic New England to create a booklet on the care of historic brownstone facades, one of the earliest such resources available.[10] Guidelines for building owners in the large historic district were also published when the BLC began its work in 1975. The Gibson House (1859–1860) on Marlborough Street is a public house museum that provides period rooms complete with family artifacts and furnishings.

While restrictions on facade alterations are a deterrent against wholesale changes in the Back Bay historic district, homeowners understand that not only is the aesthetic coherence of each block dependent on their care for individual houses, but the social fabric of the neighborhood is also a responsibility shared by all. As in Philadelphia, few facades are altered except to restore damage or repaint trim and cor-

Hall-Wister houses, Philadelphia. Rowhouse neighborhoods change slowly, as the continuity of each block is essential to its identity.
(From the Library of Congress Prints & Photographs Division, HABS.)

nices every so often. The coherence of this unique area of historic Boston depends on such communal values and standards of care.

The same is true for rowhouses in all the older American towns and cities. New Orleans is particularly rich in variations on the rowhouse type, and also has the wonderful Garden District of detached houses. There, as elsewhere, a neighborhood loses some of its flavor when any owner alters or destroys a constituent building. There are nevertheless times when a rowhouse in an established district or on a particular square must have a new facade, or when expansions causes an owner to combine two or more lots in search of better accommodations. The English were the first to experiment with such changes in a row or terrace, so it is appropriate to begin with an example from London.

JOHN SOANE'S HOUSE

The most notable example of a rowhouse expansion and renovation in history is undoubtedly the London house of Sir John Soane (1753–1837), one of England's most eccentric and creative architects. Ostensibly built for his family in 1794, the house grew for more than thirty years as the architect assembled a remarkable collection of artifacts (including an Egyptian sarcophagus). At his death Soane provided for an endowment to establish a public museum in the house, recognizing that he had created more than just a domicile. It has enchanted visitors ever since.

The original Soane home at No. 12 Lincoln's Inn Fields proved too small by 1808, so the architect arranged to purchase the wider adjacent house, No. 13, from his neighbor. He took possession of only the rear portion of No. 13, demolishing the stable block and creating spaces to house his small museum, continuing to live in No. 12. In 1812 he arranged for the tenant occupying the front of No. 13 to move out and rent the house at No. 12. The architect demolished the front portion of No. 13 and built the ingenious house/office that exists there today. He also created a party wall between his old house and the new one, so that No. 12 could be rented. At this time Soane developed a scheme for joining not two but three facades in a joint composition. The center house would have a limestone front and a projecting loggia to make its dominance clear. The side dwellings would resemble most of the other brick lodgings taking shape around the square. Because his offices and teaching studio were to be located at No. 13, it was appropriate to give it a more public character than the average terrace house. He purchased No. 14 to make a trio of dwellings in 1823, demolishing that house and rebuilding it. He was then able to link the three back buildings to create a larger museum area.[11]

In addition to claiming more attention for the public front of No. 13, Soane also connected the rear yards of all three houses, making them the property of the center house. In this way he could maintain rental income from the neighboring dwellings while gaining more space for his collections. The entire breadth of the rear yards was filled with a kind of teaching menagerie of architectural artifacts and paintings:

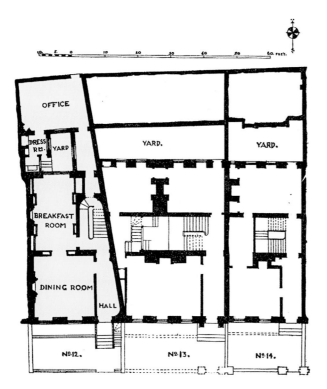

Soane House in 1796

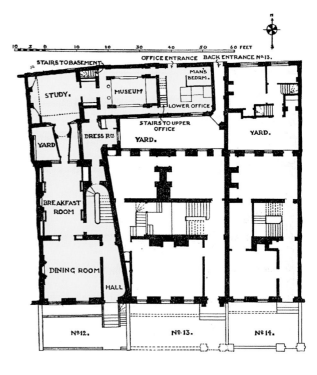

Soane House in 1810

Above and opposite: The plans of John Soane's houses at Lincoln's Inn Fields show a gradual accretion and spatial development that is exemplary in the growth of urban dwellings. (Courtesy of the Trustees of Sir John Soane's Museum.)

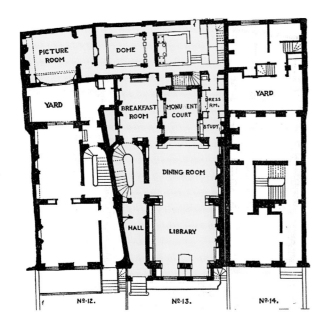

Soane House in 1822

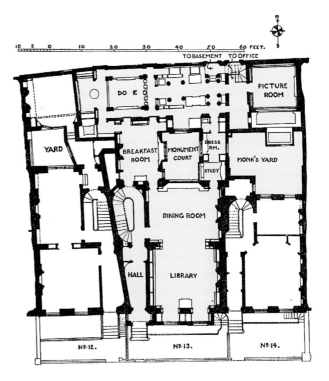

Soane House in 1837

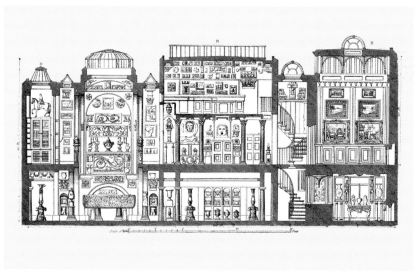

The section through the house shows Soane's menagerie of antiquities and works of art, framed by toplit spaces of his own invention. (Courtesy of the Trustees of Sir John Soane's Museum.)

Left: The facade of the combined houses is a masterful composition that belies the haphazard process by which the houses were assembled. (Photo by Martin Charles; courtesy of the Trustees of Sir John Soane's Museum.)

the New Students Room, the Dome Room, the Colonnade, and the Picture Gallery. In order to provide natural light to these spaces Soane created three tiny courtyards; the most intriguing was the "Monk's Yard" adjacent to the Picture Gallery. In this space the architect concocted a Gothic fantasy odd enough to be part of a Mary Shelley novel. The four rooms in the rear block are the most intense and monumental small spaces ever created in a house. As the American architect Charles Moore put it, "Soane's poignant exploitation of the almost trivial is peerless, beyond any hope of emulation." Lessons abound here for homeowners and architects wishing to frame a collection.

More significant for rowhouse designers is Soane's brilliant integration of the three house facades into a seamless, organic whole. English terraced houses are notably free of ostentation, probably a cultural trait as much as an architectural one. Lincoln's Inn Fields is no different than Grosvenor Square or the houses abutting Regent's Park: neighboring dwellings share scale, materials, and details so as to make a unified picture of discipline and propriety, just as the Horse Guards and Buckingham Palace sentinels do in their elaborate rituals. Visitors to the Soane Museum are often surprised at the gentle and abstract lines of the facade of No. 13. Though the Greek key string courses and subtle projections in the limestone cladding are consistent with Soane's mature style, they establish a simple order of similar lines and details

Photos looking up from the cellar to the skylight show the spatial interpenetration Soane wanted to achieve.
(Courtesy of Mark Alan Hewitt.)

among the three buildings. Moreover, the architect created the illusion of spatial continuity by carrying the brick materials of the flanking houses through the third and fourth levels of the center house. Originally the second-floor library loggia was to have been an exterior porch, similar to the balconies of the side houses. This too would have visually fused the three facades. What architects like to call hierarchy—a clear distinction between the center and the periphery, or the public and private—is much in evidence here. Seldom has an architect made so compelling and beautiful a statement about the public/private nature of the rowhouse.

EXPANDING THE AMERICAN TOWNHOUSE

Among New York's storied neighborhoods, Greenwich Village and the Upper East Side are probably the best known to nonresidents. Both districts are chock a block with fine rowhouses that have survived decades of boom-and-bust cycles in the real estate market.

Both experienced significant gentrification during the late twentieth century, resulting in socioeconomic changes that caused wide disparities between wealthy and working class residents. New York's rent control laws lessened the impact in some cases, but often created new conflicts between neighbors when a new owner sought to restore a house from multifamily to single occupancy.

Such was the case at 74 Perry Street, an 1866 brownstone designed by Robert Mook in the heart of the West Village historic district. The original house, built for a gold dealer, had an identical twin next door. Both stood in the middle of the block between Bleecker and West 4th Streets. In 1985, when Mark Alan Hewitt Architects were retained by a Wall Street attorney to restore No. 74, the neighborhood was still largely multifamily, the result of postwar conversions of the single houses into apartments. Many of the facades had been badly defaced by insensitive renovations. There was little coherence to the community, as most residents were transient renters. What was once a thriving artistic center had become rundown and dirty. No. 74 had lost a magnificent Italianate doorway and stoop in its last renovation. Its brownstone facade was painted a dull off-white, concealing the details that gave it character and life. Our first task was to restore the face of the building to its former glorious state.

The owner also had an ambitious plan to make the house into a comfortable single-family residence for himself and to provide a ground-floor apartment for a caretaker to mind the place when he was away on business. Every floor had been converted into a one-bedroom apartment, so there was work to do in order to restore the room arrangements and decor of the original building. Moreover, a top floor tenant refused to vacate his rent-controlled apartment despite generous offers to buy him out. The plan for restoration of both the building and its original use were further complicated by the city's traffic department, which did not want to grant permission to replace the historic stoop that had been removed in the 1940s. Only intervention by New York's Landmarks

74 Perry Street in New York's Greenwich Village was restored in 1987. The block had deteriorated after most houses were converted into floor-through apartments during the Second World War. A sympathetic owner replaced the missing stoop and front door, and converted the building back into a single-family residence. (Photo by Elliot Kaufman; courtesy of Mark Alan Hewitt Architects.)

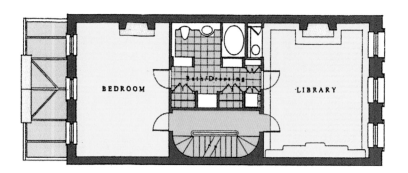

SECOND FLOOR PLAN

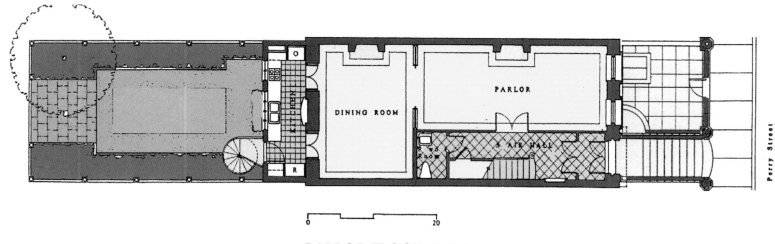

0   20

PARLOR FLOOR PLAN

Plans of 74 Perry Street. Except for the small kitchen addition facing the garden, the first floor was restored to its nineteenth-century arrangement. (Courtesy of Mark Alan Hewitt Architects.)

Preservation Commission, which endorsed the plans heartily, caused the department to back down.

Probably the most daunting challenge in the project was occasioned by zoning regulations. In order to prevent unwanted development of bulky apartment buildings in the West Village, the current zoning prohibited substantial additions to the rear of larger townhouses such as those on Perry Street. Since the original kitchen, manned by servants, was on the lower floor now occupied by a caretaker, the owner needed to create a kitchen adjacent to the rear parlor on the first floor, which would serve as a dining room. When we removed the entry pavilion from the street facade to reconstruct the stoop, we found that the sixty-six square feet it contained could be added to the rear to accommodate a small kitchen.

Adding a dark, slender lean-to on the back of the house was hardly a palatable solution, so we went to work to design something different. Since the rear facade was common brick, contrasting with the brownstone front, we chose to design a kitchen that would occupy the space between the existing wall and a new one, only 3.5 feet to the south. We used the ubiquitous carriage house often seen in the rear yards of rowhouses as our metaphoric precedent. The new brick wall was designed with generous openings, and we designed a continuous skylight as the roof. Although the kitchen measured 3.75 by 20 feet, it seemed surprisingly large and airy by virtue of the high skylight and its natural illumination.

The remaining interiors had significant remaining features, such as cornices, pier glasses, and doors. Working with Taconic Builders, a superb contractor, we were able to

The pier glass and mantel in the back parlor was intact and restored. (Photo by Elliot Kaufman; courtesy of Mark Alan Hewitt Architects.)

rebuild damaged plasterwork, repair walls, and refinish hardwood floors in the two main parlors. Upstairs, the new master bedroom, library, and bathroom suite were less beholden to

The small addition at the rear was designed to allow easy access to the garden via a metal stair. It contains only a kitchen. (Courtesy of Mark Alan Hewitt Architects.)

historic decor, as most had been gutted when the apartment was installed. The owner was amenable to a palette of period colors and wallpaper in the main rooms. In the master bath he wanted a more modern mode in the decor and fixtures, a common request when renovating an older house that has had plumbing issues in the past.

The face of the house was another matter of concern. When we prepared a plan to restore the brownstone facade in 1985, our intent was to use the least intrusive methods possible, as recommended by our Columbia University conservator, Frank Matero. Paint covering the entire facade obscured the degree of damage to the original brownstone. When we removed the 1940s-era coatings we found a wall heavily eroded and damaged by poor treatment over its 125-year lifespan. New York brownstone is a porous form of soft sandstone, generally quarried from beds in New Jersey and Connecticut. It was often improperly quarried, with slabs cut along the bedding plane rather than perpendicular to it. This led to extensive spalling and eventually to the total destruction of the face of the stone. At the time of our restoration, no American quarries were in operation, limiting our choices to getting replacement stone from Germany or resorting to the common stucco treatments that have sufficed in New York for decades.

We considered all possible restoration options, presenting the owner with advantages and disadvantages, especially relative to cost. One of the attractions to using newly quarried stone was novelty—there hadn't been a brownstone replacement in Manhattan in decades. Unfortunately, the price of cutting and shipping stone from Europe was prohibitive. We

Inside the addition, the kitchen gets extra light from a continuous skylight in the roof. (Courtesy of Mark Alan Hewitt Architects.)

In the stair hall a small powder room was inserted in a former broom closet. (Courtesy of Mark Alan Hewitt Architects.)

went to Plan B, a stucco resurfacing and reconstruction of missing features. We were lucky to get a superb stucco contractor, Mark Adami of Brooklyn, who not only helped us create an exact match in color and texture but also found the best mechanics to execute the details.

Using the house next door as a model, Spanish stucco craftsmen went to work on the facade. They carefully cut back the old brownstone to create a "key" for the new stucco before applying their scratch and brown coats. The final coat of stucco was a mix of cement binders and fine particles of actual brownstone taken from New York buildings. The stoop and front door surround, both destroyed in the previous renovation, were carefully sculpted from pieces of old brick and new stucco. The resulting restoration was remarkably true to the texture and color of the old brownstone at No. 76. The house won awards from the National Trust for Historic Preservation and from local groups.

The most inspiring result of our restoration on Perry Street was the rebirth that occurred following our project. Gradually houses on the block began to evince greater care and pride, with flower boxes, restored ironwork and stoops, and window repairs. Then, surprisingly, other houses changed hands. New owners found restoration craftsmen to work on their abused facades. Some houses were converted from multifamily to single family. The street became a showplace for Victorian brownstones in the West Village.

An even more remarkable neighborhood transformation occurred on the Upper East Side nearly two decades later.

Horace Trumbauer's classical Amory S. Carhart Mansion at 3 East 95th Street, built between 1913 and 1916, was sold in 2001 to owners who wished to convert it into condominiums. For decades the landmark townhouse had been in institutional use as a classroom building for the Lycée Français and had little of the original interior intact. Though large by East Side standards, the house would need an addition in order to support multiple residential units. This was possible because the Lycée also sold the developers a 1950s building to the east, directly adjacent to the Carhart house. The ensuing development process for the two parcels, monitored by the powerful New York City Landmarks Preservation Commission (LPC), took several years and involved three architectural firms.

Initial studies for the two lots by Brian Connolly proved that a unified facade could be developed from Trumbauer's three-bay townhouse by repeating the same window and door patterns in the proposed addition. The property changed hands following his design work and the new owner chose to hire Beyer Blinder Belle, a well-known preservation firm, to design the project. Rejecting the approach taken by the first architect, BBB produced a frankly contrasting modernist scheme for the addition that pleased many on the LPC but made real estate agents blanche with terror. The approved modern scheme was put on the shelf for a year while marketing studies tested the waters.

Like many rowhouse blocks in this wealthy area, East 95th Street maintains its exclusive identity by resisting wholesale changes in the streetscape. Moreover, this block was noted for its classical townhouses and four-story cornice lines amidst taller apartment towers on the nearby avenues. Sales agents worried that a "new" style facade on the block would spoil its air of calm and dignity, and with good reason: they had trouble preselling the units with the advertised

modern addition to the kind of wealthy owners who wanted a residence in the upscale neighborhood.

In 2002 the owners threw off the BBB scheme and retained Connolly's new firm, Zivkovic Associates Architects, to produce sympathetic partner for the Carhart house. John

The Carhart Mansion on East 95th Street was for many years part of a private school. In 2005 new owners converted it back into condominium housing, adding a sympathetic addition. The architects were Zivkovic Connolly of New York, assisted by John Simpson of London. (Photo by McKay Imaging; courtesy of Zivkovic Connolly Architects.)

The school constructed a building next to the mansion to serve as overflow space. The new owners removed it to construct a more compatible addition. (Courtesy of Zivkovic Connolly Architects.)

The addition that replaced the other building was designed to complement the original mansion without replicating its details exactly. This pediment is robust and more English than French in character, as befits the work of John Simpson, its designer. (Photo by McKay Imaging; courtesy Zivkovic Connolly Architects.)

Right: To inflect toward the landmark Fabbri mansion next door, the architects designed a beautiful roof terrace, complete with a temple motif—as a doorway on the terrace and a roof termination on the side facade. (Photo by Jonathan Wallen; courtesy of Zivkovic Connolly Architects.)

Simpson, one of England's finest classical architects, served as a consulting designer on the project. Well acquainted with Soane's work, he produced a design that would have done the master proud.

Directly adjacent to the new parcel on its east side stood the Fabbri mansion (1914–1916), a city landmark by Ernesto Fabbri and Grosvenor Atterbury. This fine brick house was set back from the street to create a small courtyard adjacent to its entry pavilion. Simpson and Connolly recognized that this unusual space could be used to advantage to provide a second face for their new building. They were also sensitive to the massing and detail of the original house, noting how Trumbauer used subtle changes in plane to create drama in his composition.[12]

The resulting addition is one of the finest works of residential architecture New York had seen in two decades. Winner of the prestigious Palladio Award, the combined townhouses demonstrate the potential for creativity within the tightly constrained compass of the terrace house type. Like the three Soane houses, the adjacent buildings are different enough to elicit surprise, but otherwise maintain horizontal and vertical lines and key rhythms along the street. The surprising element is a small "temple" at the attic level of the addition that is visible most prominently at an oblique angle from the east. As the addition turns the corner into the adjacent courtyard, the architects mark the transition with two antefixae (ornaments attached to the eaves) and a stepping parapet. The addition appears more unified and massive than the main house because it has no implied pilasters—the

The interior of the original mansion was restored to its 1916 appearance, as seen in the grand staircase. (Photo by Catherin Tighe; courtesy of Zivkovic Connolly Architects.)

windows are grouped in threes at each level. Such subtle differentiation establishes the secondary role of the addition but does not reduce it to a pale mimic of the main residence. This important example shows how architects with an understanding of classical principles, the vernacular of the town-house type, can expand and augment a residential property according to principles outlined in Chapter 2: massing, modules, and facade composition.

The Charleston Single House is one of the most distinctive dwelling types in America, studied by scholars and prized by residents. It is rare that a truly fine example comes on the market, and rarer still to find one capable of restoration. Such was the case with the William C. Gatewood House, an 1843 Greek Revival gem that was purchased by a film-industry veteran and a management consultant in 2003. The couple, one of whom is a tenth-generation Charlestonian, were ready for a full-scale restoration and upgrade, but perhaps not one that would take four years.

Charleston is home to one of the few institutions in the U.S. to grant a college degree in building restoration trades: the American College of the Building Arts, located in a former jail downtown and on a low-country plantation up river. It is also home to the College of Charleston, which offers preservation courses as well as training in classical architecture.

Taking advantage of local talent, the new owners of the Gatewood House retained Richard "Moby" Marks as the contractor on their project. Known locally for his knowledge of low-country houses, Marks has taught preservation for years in addition to running his specialty restoration firm. Gil Schafer, a New York architect renowned for his classical houses, joined the team as the design professional in charge.

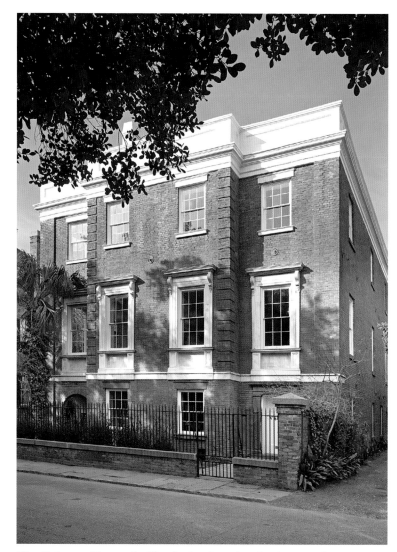

The Gatewood house in Charleston is a classic nineteenth-century town house that had fallen into disrepair. Architect Gil Schafer joined with Moby Marks, a contractor, in helping the new owners restore it in 2003. The project took four years to complete. (Courtesy of G.P. Schafer Architects PLLC.)

Schafer was impressed by the expertise and passion Marks brought to the job, and entrusted him with more than the execution of the construction documents.

Marks does what many restoration contractors do before starting construction: he removes sections of walls, floors, and ceilings in order to discover the hidden features that tell the story of the building's construction. Only when all the "ghosts" and structural secrets are known does he begin to work. Schafer appreciated having a detective on the premises to give him cues on how to design and renovate.

The house had serious structural problems that were uncovered during this discovery phase, issues that had escaped the inspector before the home was purchased. Much of the building had to be disassembled and put back together, augmented by discreet structural reinforcement. Marks located an original floor plan of the house in a local archive and used an early inventory to gauge the degree of finish and furnishings in its early days. Once this information was culled, the restoration team went to work on an authentic restoration.

Schafer intended to modernize the bathrooms and provide large closets for his clients, but they would have nothing that wasn't provided in the original house—no walls would be moved to create additional space. That meant that Schafer would have to hide new amenities in nooks and crannies, such as disused servant rooms and the like. In the end he and the contractor managed to update the house with six new bathrooms, two kitchens, three extra staircases, central heating and air conditioning, new wiring, high-speed data

The characteristic piazza has a window to the street to conceal its presence as a circulation space. (Courtesy of G.P. Schafer Architects PLLC.)

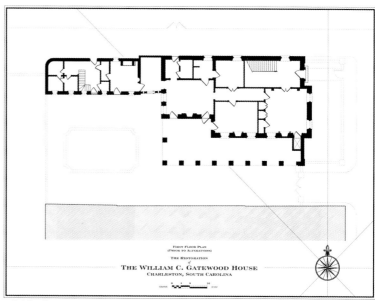

(a) before

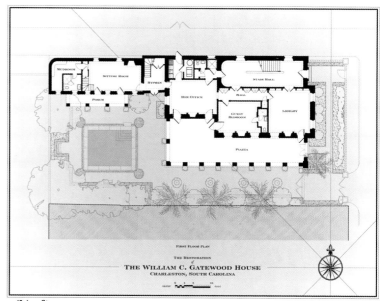

Plans of the Gatewood house renovation show subtle changes in the spaces. Though no major walls were moved the architect managed to add bathrooms, stairs, and other amenities for a modern family.

(Courtesy of G.P. Schafer Architects PLLC.)

(b) after

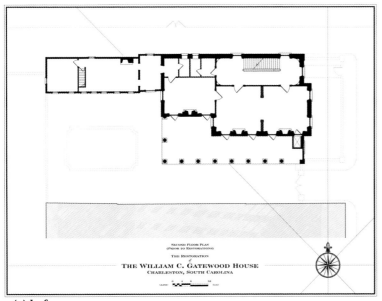

SECOND FLOOR PLAN
(PRIOR TO RESTORATIONS)

THE RESTORATION
of
THE WILLIAM C. GATEWOOD HOUSE
CHARLESTON, SOUTH CAROLINA

(c) before

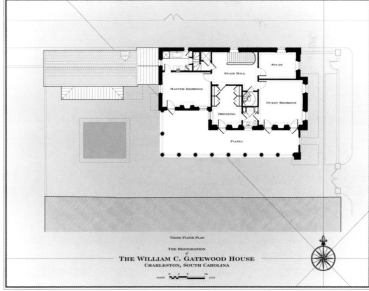

THIRD FLOOR PLAN
(PRIOR TO RESTORATIONS)

THE RESTORATION
of
THE WILLIAM C. GATEWOOD HOUSE
CHARLESTON, SOUTH CAROLINA

(e) before

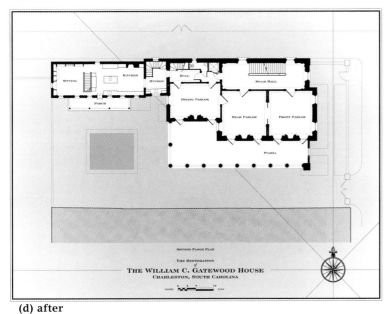

SECOND FLOOR PLAN

THE RESTORATION
of
THE WILLIAM C. GATEWOOD HOUSE
CHARLESTON, SOUTH CAROLINA

(d) after

THIRD FLOOR PLAN

THE RESTORATION
of
THE WILLIAM C. GATEWOOD HOUSE
CHARLESTON, SOUTH CAROLINA

(f) after

201

On the opposite side of the house is the beautiful stair hall, with its Greek Revival door surrounds and sinuous stair. (Courtesy of G.P. Schafer Architects PLLC.)

Fitting a bathroom into one of the guest bedrooms was a difficult trick—the architect managed to use a built-in wardrobe to conceal the small room. (Courtesy of G.P. Schafer Architects PLLC.)

The new kitchen occupies the space taken by the old kitchen wing, which was extensively rebuilt after structural problems were discovered. (Courtesy of G.P. Schafer Architects PLLC.)

lines, and a passenger elevator. So what seems to be a literal restoration turns out to be a modern renovation after all.

Like most Charleston single houses, the Gatewood House has a robust piazza with Doric columns that is concealed behind a street wall. That street wall, or facade, represents the proper public persona of the house and its occupants. Behind are the private things that support the family: the porch, the garden, service buildings, and so forth. The original property had a substantial carriage house and rear yard, but these were subdivided and sold as a separate residence some years ago.

Remarkably, the Gatewood House retained its detached kitchen house, built to protect the main house from fires. This was converted into guest rooms. Monumental triple-hung windows on the *piano nobile* were restored with their elaborate enframements on the interior. But the large new kitchen got an upgrade and a more rustic interior to fit with the informal lifestyle of the clients. Despite the conservative posture of maintaining only "original" features, this vintage house got a facelift, a fresh coat of paint, and a lot of comfortable amenities not known to 1840s residents of this beautiful city.

When the owners of the Gatewood House used their old kitchen building as space for additional amenities, they followed a practice that is increasingly useful to vintage house buffs: adding or renovating outbuildings. In the next chapter we'll look at the ways in which this strategy can make an expansion less daunting, especially when the original house needs to be left alone.

The staircase ends on the first floor with a distinctive scroll newell.
(Courtesy of G.P. Schafer Architects PLLC.)

8

OUTSTANDING OUTBUILDINGS

IN THIS CHAPTER WE ADDRESS THE SUBJECT OF EXPAN-sions to a house that involve buildings other than the main dwelling. Occasionally, if the main house is perfect and untouchable, owners must locate needed spaces in outbuildings out of necessity. More often, outbuildings are constructed in order to accommodate recreation, outdoor living, swimming, services, and other ancillary functions. We won't cover buildings built purely as garden follies, though these have their role to play on larger estates. The design of compatible outbuildings is as challenging as any other part of a renovation project. The examples in this chapter are fascinating for their style, ingenuity, and craft.

HAPPY MOTORING

Architects spend inordinate amounts of time designing the connections between the parked automobile and the busy family, even in new houses. So it is no surprise that many renovation projects begin with the vital link between the driveway, the garage, and the mudroom—a relatively recent amenity that virtually defines the life of today's soccer mom or dad. These rooms, and the circulation to and from them, have taken on a major role in house planning. Notwithstanding the hope for new forms of green transportation, it appears that some form of car space—especially given the current trend toward three-car garages—will be a part of American life for the foreseeable future.

The garage, not yet invented during the nineteenth century, became an intimate part of houses by the Roaring Twenties. Yet when vintage house owners contemplate changes to eighteenth- or nineteenth-century gems that predate the auto, a garage can sometimes seem like an invader from outer space. Fortunately, homeowners and designers wrestled with the same issue over a century ago, and their experiments can help define the issues, and lead to ideas,

Early garages were often repurposed building
types, such as barns or carriage houses (left);
or mail-order portable buildings (right).
(Courtesy of National Archives Associates.)

for how to house the four-wheeled member of the modern family.

When the first horseless carriages appeared around 1900, they were stabled very much like their predecessors—often in a repurposed outbuilding some distance from the main residence. Indeed, many a carriage barn was converted into a car barn, with little consideration for the functional requirements of the machine. Whatever their former use, these outbuildings were related in function and architecture (if any) with the grounds and support of the house—not the car—almost always looking like a stable or workshop. By the Tin Lizzie era of the 1910s, the growing numbers of cars on the road surpassed the supply of outbuildings, so to speak, and spawned a brief boom in supplying structures specifically designed for cars. Many of these were kit or prefabricated buildings from companies such as Hodgson and later Sears that were already in the business of supplying easy-to-erect summer cottages, hunting camps, and play houses. These early garages were typically sited in a backwater part of the property, and while designed specifi-

cally for sheltering cars, with convenient doors and windows for light, architecturally they were at best nondescript and functional, relating neither to the main house nor to any of the familiar types of outbuildings. In a few cases designers and manufactures tried to concoct garages that didn't look like buildings at all, as was the case with the Pergola Garage—a structure that hid the garage under vine-covered trellis and columns. Early underground garages (common in hilly communities) accomplished the same thing. By the 1920s the garage had become a standard part of new house design in the cold-weather parts of the country. The landscape historian J. B. Jackson likened its appearance to the addition of a family member to the household—the car no longer stayed in the guest room but had a room of its own.[1] Whether for the average homeowner with a single-car garage at the back of his lot, or for the captains of industry and banking who displayed their automobiles like prize thoroughbreds in buildings fit for a king, the garage was increasingly related architecturally to the main house. Gatehouses are a good example seen era of the house; a unique building designed for the auto, but not related to any other building—or even a building; or a residential type of building architecturally tied—even connected—to the main house.

Thomas Norman Rajkovich is a Chicago architect noted for his work in the elite enclaves of that city's North Shore—places like Lake Forest, Evanston, Lake Bluff, and Highland Park. A student of the work of David Adler, Howard Van Doren Shaw, and Harrie T. Lindeberg, Rajkovich is a deft designer in many classical and eclectic styles. He has restored or added

This early design featured hinged barn doors, an impractical solution (though a traditional garage look) that was replaced when the rolling door was invented. (Courtesy of National Archive Associates.)

A detached garage by Thomas Norman Rajkovich near Chicago brings similar forms and materials to the historic house by Arthur Heun. (Photo by Tony Soluri; courtesy of Thomas Norman Rajkovich Architect, Ltd.)

in early twentieth-century estates, and since a chauffeur was available day and night, the garage could be a mile from the main house. By the 1930s architects were even incorporating the formerly off-limits garage as part of the house—the attached garage. Chauffeurs are harder to come by these days, and most owners want their cars within shouting distance. So the attached or semi-attached garage has come to be an accepted part of estate planning.

Ancient history aside, what this tells us is that basically there are three approaches to designing a new garage for a vintage house: an agricultural/homestead outbuilding of the to the houses of many noted architects, in addition to designing distinctive traditional houses.

In his garage/studio for a Norman Provincial house, Rajkovich shows how a small outbuilding can add richness and distinction to a residential compound. A sympathetic roof form and fine materials were the keys to success in this design. The main house had roofs that were picturesque and distinctive—a corner turret, elaborate eaves, and traditional hipped configurations that are associated with this early twentieth-century style. Rather than mimic these forms precisely, Rajkovich used a "jerkinhead" roof, knowing that it was also common to the French/Norman idiom. The garage thus maintains its separate identity while also resonating with the style of the house.

The scale and roof forms of the addition fit perfectly with the tower and jerkinhead roof of the older house. (Photo by Tony Soluri; courtesy of Thomas Norman Rajkovich Architect, Ltd.)

Left: The doorway to the garage features heavy timber details similar to those of the original house. (Photo by Tony Soluri; courtesy of Thomas Norman Rajkovich Architect, Ltd.)

Employing similar materials and details in this design was tricky, since the cream-colored "ironspot" brick in the original house was not available from current brickworks. Many early twentieth-century houses employed materials that are difficult to locate today, except in salvage yards. The architect found a compatible and beautiful brick that marries well with the original and benefits from a slight contrast since it is not directly attached to the house.

Other design touches that enliven this small building are subtle but critical. The slate roof is detailed with dramatic sweeping eaves and elegant copper gutters according to formulas available only in old books on construction. Not every architect has such sources in his library, or the savvy to know when to consult them. The architect also handled the entrance to the garage with uncommon skill. Oak lintels complement the color and texture of the brick and are finished to emphasize the rustic quality of an old French farmhouse. The oak carries through to the area above the small porch, suggesting heavy timber construction. The garage doors and dormers continue the rustic theme with their slate-blue colors. Perhaps the most subtle touch is the treatment of the gable ends of the garage—the architect found a wood shingle that matches the house nearly perfectly, suggesting that they were designed together, not seventy-five years apart.

Another of our encounters with the work of Harrie T. Lindeberg occurred when a client called about a garage for his stable of antique cars. Like the house in Lake Forest, this fine 1920s example had steep, sweeping roofs and a prominent stair turret that made emulation difficult. But Lindeberg had made clear references to half-timbering and heavy timber construction in the otherwise brick masonry building. The porches were constructed of English-style cruckwork, and there were places where brick and half-timbering were combined, a typical Lindeberg touch. This gave us our cue to build a modern garage with traditional English medieval methods. In this way we could acknowledge both the source (Tudor houses) and the quotation.

Unbeknownst to most Americans, there is a thriving industry in heavy timber construction using traditional wood-to-wood joints. The Timber Framers Guild keeps this craft knowledge alive by training interested carpenters in

A garage for a historic Tudor house in New Jersey features real heavy-timber construction, even though the original house is built primarily of brick masonry. (Courtesy of Mark Alan Hewitt Architects.)

The timber frame was engineered and manufactured for assembly on the job site. The brick walls and slate roof are just a "skin." (Photo by Jerry A. Bruno, Jr.; courtesy of Mark Alan Hewitt Architects.)

The garage doors were framed with timbers in order to reflect the aesthetic of the Harrie T. Lindeberg house. (Courtesy of Mark Alan Hewitt Architects.)

the methods that our ancestors used to frame barns and houses before the invention of nails. Their workshops and publications are essential for restoration artisans who work on wooden buildings from the Colonial period to the Greek Revival.[2] In this case, the Guild led us to several companies that engineer and fabricate entire frames for delivery to the job site. We designed a four-bay garage using five "bents" or frames, connected laterally by timber plates and purlins. We knew that even if the frame were covered with brick veneer, it would give the garage interior an authentic ambience. And construction would be quick—the frame could be put up in one day, with sheathing and masonry to follow in short order.

The owners loved their house, and seeing a garage that echoed its style gave them a thrill, especially during construction. The new building was gingerly attached to one side of the Lindeberg house to allow access in inclement weather, but otherwise stood very much on its own. The materials and details were closely studied—a graduated slate roof was a must, given the prominence of the material elsewhere on the building. Our only license was to make a stucco design in the exposed gable to accentuate the timbering. Otherwise the brick and door framing were nearly exact matches with the older materials. And most important, the pitch of the new roof was precisely that of the main house.

A garage for a Colonial Revival house in Madison, New Jersey was set back from the street, but still reflects the vocabulary of the 1916 architecture. (Courtesy of Mark Alan Hewitt Architects.)

A number of our renovation projects have called for fully detached garages. One of the most challenging was on a sloped site with difficult edge conditions in Madison, New Jersey. The original house, built at the time of World War I, had a rather meager garage in its lower level. Access to the space was difficult as the driveway sloped steeply toward the back of the property, without adequate space to turn the car back toward the garage doors. So the owners resorted to parking their cars on the sloped driveway and scurrying for the front door with groceries during inclement weather.

Our design for the large addition to this house envisioned a path from the garage to one of two new back entrances: one to a raised porch off the main stair hall, the other to a recre-

ation/mudroom on the ground level. The latter was designed with a comfortable stair direction into the new kitchen and family room. Thus, when constructed, the new garage could be linked as directly as possible with the rear of the house, where most people now enter.

In style, the garage in Madison was deliberately intended to be a miniature version of the main house. The cove cornice and eave details were roughly equivalent in both buildings, and trim moldings were also similar. Though not immediately visible to drivers passing by, the garage makes a welcoming statement for pedestrians. The family makes certain

The building is not connected to the house, but a path leads from it to a basement mudroom and the kitchen. (Courtesy of Mark Alan Hewitt Architects.)

to be noticed: there is always a large flag hanging below the front porch.

SWIMMING WITH THE TIDE

The swimming pool is largely a twentieth-century invention that has proliferated throughout the United States, even in less temperate climates such as the Northeast and upper Midwest. Houses from earlier centuries seldom had outdoor pools unless they were part of a garden or resort environment. In recent renovations to larger historic houses, it has been common to include pools and pool buildings.

Oakley Farm, a National Register property in the northern Virginia horse country, has an unusual provenance. Originally constructed for Richard Henry Dulany (1820–1906) in 1852, it has been associated with equestrian activity for more than a century. Dulany was the founder of the Upperville Colt and Horse Show, the oldest event of its kind in the United States and still a draw for horse lovers from around the world. Originally the horse farm was known as Welbourne, a reference to Dulany's Scottish heritage. The estate passed through marriage to the family of A. C. Randolph, a member of one of Virginia's colonial planter clans.

The main house is an unusual variation on the mid-nineteenth-century Italianate Villa popular in the mid-Atlantic states. Its design comes from Samuel Sloan's popular pattern book, *The Model Architect* (1852). Sloan (1815–1884) was a prominent Philadelphia architect who had a prolific career both in the North and the South. His most famous house is Longwood in Natchez, Mississppi, built for Haller Nutt from 1858 to 1864 but left unfinished. Sloan was a technically innovative architect who worked in many styles, often including eccentric details and features in his buildings.[3] These qualities are omnipresent at Oakley Farms and were appreciated immediately by Peter Pennoyer, the New York architect who designed a significant expansion to the house and grounds from 1997 to 2002.

Snout Houses

A building trend that puts the cart before the horse, architecturally speaking, is the so-called snout house—a house appended to a garage, rather than the other way around. While attached garages are neither novel nor inherently offensive, what makes the snout house so noxious in some cases is its in-your-face orientation. Invariably, the garage not only faces the street (the better to make the shortest possible driveway distance), but also dominates the house by jutting out from the main facade to make the eponymous "snout." Appearing in both new construction and remodeling, snout houses have become ubiquitous to the point of being infamous—especially when they harbor today's multi-car garages. The Internet is rich in debate over their value, and communities like Portland, Oregon, have even gone so far as to make their construction illegal.

(Photo by Barbara Krankenhaus.)

The distinctive two-story porch was rebuilt to allow access to the upper floors. (Photo by Scott Frances; courtesy of Peter Pennoyer Architects.)

Opposite: Oakley in the Virginia horse country was designed in the 1860s by Samuel Sloan, the noted Philadelphia architect. His projected cupola was not constructed until 2002, during an extensive renovation program by Peter Pennoyer Architects. (Photo by Scott Frances; courtesy of Peter Pennoyer Architects.)

The main house at Oakley had seen better days when Pennoyer and his team came on the scene. "It was well loved but decayed," the architect recalled recently. "The back porch swayed in the wind; there was a washing machine in the attic and a cistern on top." His clients, a couple who were based on the West Coast, had more than a sentimental attachment to the place. The husband is a descendent of Theodora Ayer Randolph, whom the *New York Times* called "the first lady

The grand stair hall is now lit by the lantern above. Interior designer Katie Ridder added the distinctive red wall covering.

(Photo by Scott Frances; courtesy of Peter Pennoyer Architects.)

of the fox hunt" in Virginia. They wanted a retreat for their family where they could entertain a large crowd, but the farm had to maintain its familiar features for the benefit of the local population. The architects were charged with not only with maintaining the character of the house and grounds, but with inserting period details and elements that were left out of the buildings by Dulany for lack of money. "Our plan was to make it greater than its original glory," says Pennoyer.

That meant removing an unsightly second-floor porch added during the mid-twentieth century, restoring a terne metal roof, installing period-appropriate moldings in many rooms, and building a cupola for the villa that had been planned but never completed. Working with project architect Greg Gilmartin and designer Katie Ridder, Pennoyer created a house that positively glows with nineteenth-century ambience. One problem that they could not solve was the

The small kitchen gained storage space with high china cabinets. (Photo by Scott Frances; courtesy of Peter Pennoyer Architects.)

The pool house was designed to increase the potential for entertaining. (Photo by Scott Frances; courtesy of Peter Pennoyer Architects.)

comparatively small kitchen and bedrooms in the villa. When entertaining for a large crowd, additional space would be needed elsewhere on the site.

Fortunately, there were outbuildings on the 455-acre estate that could be reused or extended to serve recreational functions. An existing tenant house was retrofitted for guest rooms. Landscape architect Madison Cox designed a small parterre garden to front the guesthouse and connected it with a path

With the addition of the cupola, and the porches restored, the house regained its nineteenth-century elegance. (Photo by Scott Frances; courtesy of Peter Pennoyer Architects.)

The small classical porch designed by the architects adds character and inflects toward the double-story porch of the house nearby. (Photo by Scott Frances; courtesy of Peter Pennoyer Architects.)

to the side of the villa. Pennoyer created a bookend for the small building with a similarly scaled, board-and-batten pool house, accessible from the garden. Visitors walking along the new paths would be unaware that a large pool was nearby—a nod to the local preservationists who wanted nothing changed on the site. Similar nineteenth-century materials and details in the new and old building created a sense of permanence and continuity. Even the color scheme, a buff rose for walls and a red terne metal roof, evokes antebellum memories.

Inside the pool house, the architects provided enough amenities that the family, with or without guests, could hang out all day during warm weather without having to trek back to the villa. A kitchen, bathrooms, changing rooms, and a large living/dining area give the building a domestic feeling. At the same time, the design team recognized that the outside of the building could not appear to be a second dwelling or the coherence of the place would suffer. Hence the long facades were treated informally, with a verandah on one side and small dormers on the other. The only wink at the present century occurs on the gable end facing the house, where the architects placed a temple like portico around the side door.

The restoration brought back details in this bay window as well as the stucco surfaces of the old house. (Photo by Scott Frances; courtesy of Peter Pennoyer Architects.)

Such playful but sophisticated design marks this project as exemplary of what an old house connoisseur can achieve with the right resources, goals, and consultants. Though not an addition to the main house per se, the outbuildings at Oakley Farm are integral to the character of the place as a historic landscape and a remnant of a grand era in our nation's history. In this way they support and extend the qualities that define this and other horse farms in northern Virginia. Residents of this precious environment fought to keep a Disney theme park from encroaching on their piece of paradise, and would have been intolerant of any but the most authentic interventions at Oakley. Indeed, Mrs. Paul (Bunny) Mellon, a neighbor and grand dame of the Middleburg gentry, praised the project, noting the landscape design as distinguished even for its locale. With her approval, the hounds will run on familiar ground when the next hunt comes to Oakley Farm, with nary a whisper about changes to a beloved old place.

No less impressive for its elegance and resonance with a historic landscape is the pool pavilion designed by John Murray in Connecticut. As we saw in Chapter 5, this New York architect has a deft touch with historic details and a feeling for authentic materials that keeps him in the front rank of the city's traditional designers. His remarkable pavilion won the prestigious Palladio Award from the editors of *Period Homes* in 2005.

The premise behind the pavilion was different from that at Oakley. Since this estate was part of a designed landscape,

John Murray's project in Connecticut also included a pool pavilion, placed downhill from the house. The architecture of the pavilion complements that of the addition and the original buildings. (Photo by Durston Saylor; courtesy of John B. Murray Architect, LLC.)

and all the houses had their own distinctive materials and idioms, it was imperative that the pool building relate directly to the house, as a smaller but similarly styled structure. The axial relationship between a large tree near the house and the pavilion provides a strong visual connection. In the 1920s pool pavilions were rather small, lacking the facilities demanded by today's affluent families. So Murray and his staff were compelled to invent some Tudoresque features that would not have appeared on any historic prototypes.

The most obvious is the outdoor fireplace that occupies the center of the poolside facade. This unusual feature grounds the entire pool-and-house composition, providing a

A shallow vault in the porticoes reflects the light in the evening. (Photo by Durston Saylor; courtesy of John B. Murray Architect, LLC.)

The pool facade combines Tudor details with classical porticoes, a synthesis that is appropriate given the nature of the building. (Photo by Durston Saylor; courtesy of John B. Murray Architect, LLC.)

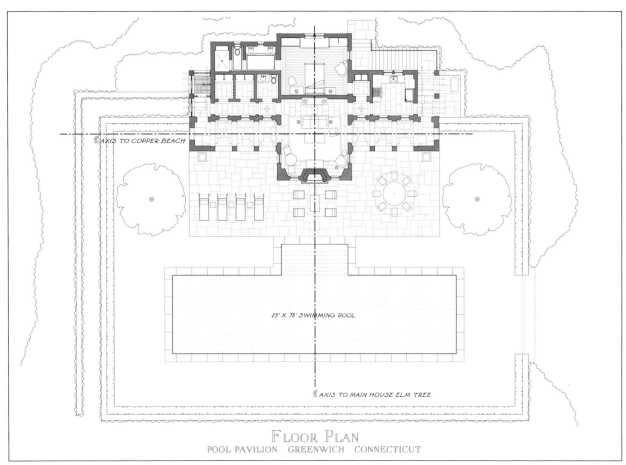

AXIS TO COPPER BEACH

25' X 75' SWIMMING POOL

AXIS TO MAIN HOUSE ELM TREE

FLOOR PLAN
POOL PAVILION GREENWICH CONNECTICUT

Murray's disciplined plan integrates the pool, the pavilion, and the stone terraces beautifully.
(Courtesy of John B. Murray Architect, LLC.)

warm glow in the evening when bathers are relaxing after a day in the sun. The room behind is an impressive living space, more like that of a modest house than a pool pavilion. And indeed, there is also a bedroom in the building, so that guests may stay on the grounds. Other amenities include a full-size kitchen, changing areas, showers, and a steam room.

In an area known for its Wall Street extravagance, this pool house is surely a candidate for "best in show."

The exterior of the building retains the same understated elegance as the addition to the main house. Limestone and stucco details, such as the shell cartouche in the main gable and the rusticated Tuscan columns in the two

222

loggias, mark this design as the work of a classical architect with years of experience. And although the building has a flat roof, its massing and robust stonework suggest a building from another era. Continuity with traditions older than the 1920s imparts a timeless quality to the site that the Olmsted brothers would have appreciated. In their English-influenced landscapes, they reached back to the days of the Picturesque movement in the eighteenth century for inspiration. Murray and his team were well aware of this when they created the pool terrace.

With Americans' passion for fitness, sometimes an outdoor pool is not sufficient to satisfy a swimmer's needs. This was the case when a Princeton resident asked Philip Kennedy-Grant, FAIA, to design a natatorium adjacent to his fine 1920s Georgian house a few years ago. For those not familiar with the term, a natatorium is an indoor pool, often sized for lap swimming.

The architect also had other requirements to consider when studying the site and program: a request that the new building be designed in the Georgian style of the original house, that it be unassuming and deferential to the landscape, and that it be sited to allow maximum use of an existing side yard. Moreover, the new building was to accommodate an exercise room, a shower room, a laundry, a lounge with kitchen facilities, and a separate guest bedroom.

Despite these constraints, the architect created a building that not only fits perfectly into the landscape setting but also is a distinguished classical design in its own right. Both

an existing lawn space and a stately copper beach tree were undisturbed by the renovation. Measuring only 40 x 60 feet, the natatorium is set back from the line of the house to provide a wall-like backdrop for a new garden terrace. Engaged Doric columns punctuate the terrace elevation, and there are two graceful pergolas to frame the limestone patio, one of which is also an outdoor spa.

Recalling ancient Roman baths, the building is vaulted on the interior to emphasize the shape of the pool and pro-

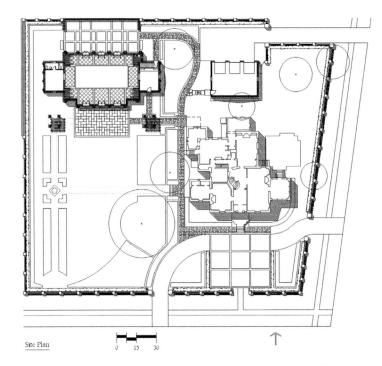

Site Plan

0   15   30

The site plan of a pool house addition in Princeton shows how the integration of gardens and outbuildings play a key role in any successful vintage house project. (Courtesy of Kennedy-Grant.)

The suppression of the pool house at the back of the site gives the main house primacy. The sympathetic materials and vocabulary of the new building are fully integrated with those of the house. (Photo by Durston Saylor; courtesy of Kennedy-Grant.)

Philip Kennedy-Grant's mastery of classical architecture was essential to the success of this project. (Photo by Durston Saylor; courtesy of Kennedy-Grant.)

vide a dramatic space for a collection of fine art. Temple-like spaces for the lounge and bedroom flank the pool space, and each is treated as a peristyle on the exterior. Inside, the ends of the natatorium walls are simple vaults, under which are openings framed by Tuscan columns in antis. By using these familiar elements in a surprising way, Kennedy-Grant

The architect used the Tuscan order to reflect the sybaritic nature of a natatorium in a classical garden. (Photo by Durston Saylor; courtesy of Kennedy-Grant.)

Tuscan columns, placed *in antis*, frame the two ends of the pool and give access to changing rooms and a small sitting room. (Photo by Durston Saylor; courtesy of Kennedy-Grant.)

The classical vocabulary extends to the interior, where a shallow vault covers the pool space. (Photo by Durston Saylor; courtesy of Kennedy-Grant.)

establishes a consistent theme resonant with classical garden buildings dating back to antiquity.

In his subtle contribution to this historic house and garden, Kennedy-Grant complements Georgian idiom of the 1920s house while also enriching the classical character of the neighborhood and the colonial heritage of Princeton itself.

FARM AND FIELD

We conclude our brief examination of outbuildings with a case study that is unusual in its breadth but universal in its

lessons about the continuity of good houses, gardens, and ancillary buildings in a rural environment. Like Oakley Farm, Mount Fair is located in the picturesque Virginia countryside that has attracted Americans from Thomas Jefferson to Paul Mellon. Part of the charm of Virginia's rural landscapes stems from their origins as plantations founded by the "Virginia cavaliers" under patents from the kings of England. Since immense landholdings remained in families for generations, parts of the countryside around Richmond, Norfolk, and Charlottesville and along the Rappahannock River retain their eighteenth-century vegetation, fauna, farm plots, roads, and burial grounds. Virginians have gone to great lengths in recent decades to preserve these historic landscapes.

Mount Fair is located in a valley called Brown's Cove, some twenty miles northwest of the city of Charlottesville, in Albemarle County. As its name suggests, the valley was settled by Benjamin Brown between 1747 and 1760, and once comprised over six thousand acres. Mount Fair became the family seat upon passing from Benjamin to his son Bezaleel in 1762. In 1845 the house built by Benjamin burned. Its then owner, William T. Brown, constructed a two-story Greek Revival house on the foundations of the early dwelling. In 1851 Brown insured his new house for $2,000, a little less than it had cost him to build it.

The farm remained in the Brown family until 1930. It was then purchased by the first dean of the architecture department at the University of Virginia, Edmund S. Campbell, who resided in the house for twenty years. It has had only three owners since that time. In 1990 it was listed on the National

Mount Fair is a horse farm near Charlottesville that has a distinguished Antebellum history. When the owners from Connecticut bought it, they hired Mark P. Finlay Architects to design a master plan for the site before proceeding with renovations. (Photo by Durston Saylor; courtesy of Mark P. Finlay Architects.)

The historic house built in 1851 by William T. Brown was carefully restored, and a minor addition was built that is discretely hidden from the main viewpoint. (Photo by Durston Saylor; courtesy of Mark P. Finlay Architects.)

A pergola directs the eye toward one of the small outbuildings on the property. (Photo by Durston Saylor; courtesy of Mark P. Finlay Architects.)

From the opposite direction, the house is visible on the left. (Photo by Durston Saylor; courtesy of Mark P. Finlay Architects.)

Register of Historic Places. The nomination cited the property as "one of the largest and best preserved antebellum farms in Albemarle County."[4]

While the buildings on the Mount Fair property were important for their history and distinction, it was likely the landscape and the two historic burial grounds that caught the attention of historians. While many plantations concealed or destroyed evidence of slave burials, Mount Fair's owners maintained both a family and a slave cemetery for decades following the Civil War. The open fields and farm plots surrounding these sacred places remained agricultural until the

1930s, when the Campbells converted it to a country estate of seventy-five acres. That might have changed in 2003, when a family from Connecticut decided to purchase the estate as a horse farm and country retreat.

The new owners, who had raised three sons in New England, hired Mark P. Finley Architects, a noted Connecticut firm, to create a master plan for the property. They quickly realized the challenge of working on a Virginia and U.S. landmark—though as private owners they were not legally restricted from changing the contributing buildings, they had a moral obligation to avoid conspicuous alterations to the original architecture. Before beginning design, the architectural team carefully researched the historic site to ensure that the master plan would respect the existing archi-

The kitchen was completely renovated in keeping with the rustic style of the house and its surroundings. (Photo by Durston Saylor; courtesy of Mark P. Finlay Architects.)

The new stable resembles a Victorian farm building, adding greatly to both the farm's functions and its historic landscape. (Photo by Durston Saylor; courtesy of Mark P. Finlay Architects.)

The interior of the stable is equipped with state-of-the-art accommodations for every horse. (Photo by Durston Saylor; courtesy of Mark P. Finlay Architects.)

tecture and keep all historical elements intact. The owner's ambitious program included a complete renovation and restoration of the nineteenth-century main residence as well as a new kitchen, mudroom, breezeway, garage, hunting room, exercise room, and indoor pool. Not limiting their designs to the main house, the architects also renovated a historic ice house and spring house to serve as guest quarters, and they designed a new horse barn, a hay storage shed, and a new caretaker's cottage on the site. With such a complex array of new and old components, the one thing that could most suffer was the property's most significant feature: the landscape.

The Finlay team devised a subtle and entirely sympathetic design for the necessary additions to the main house. Virtually invisible from the front, the service wing and ancillary buildings in the rear are arranged to take advantage of a rise in the hilltop site, concealing their configuration somewhat. In a brilliant planning strategy, the architects connected existing outbuildings using a new glass breezeway aligned with a door to a rear terrace to make an enfilade. The roof volumes of the existing service wing marry beautifully with the new roofs and merge with the agricultural character of the farm buildings in the service yard. Inside, the designers created evocative rooms that maintain the genteel feeling of the original decor while updating appliances, lighting, and furnishings.

The pastures around the house have been groomed and fenced to make a proper horse farm, and views of the surrounding hills are spectacular. What is even more remarkable is the extent to which Finlay's design for the new stable and ancillary buildings enriches the landscape by evoking Victorian agricultural types. Clad in modern stucco and standing-seam metal roofs, these new buildings maintain the massing, rhythm, and detail of earlier farm buildings. In this way they become modern frames for a mature landscape. When one surveys the entire ensemble there is no discordant note to spoil the splendor of the valley farmstead that Brown purchased 250 years ago. Even the new plantings and trees are placed to resemble old patterns of agricultural land use.

The stable is particularly handsome and well outfitted for its purposes. Its warm wood interior and heavy timber framing resonate with stories of the landed gentry in the Old Dominion. Immediately beside the stable yard is a fenced area that might be mistaken for another pasture, but for the old stone markers arranged haphazardly inside. This, of course, is the historic burial ground in which family members are interred. Beside it is the slave burial ground. Here the land and its history sing out like a spiritual, and the new stable building does not spoil the music.

This final case study brings our inquiry into the vintage house to an appropriate close. Nearly every practice we've advocated is persuasively demonstrated at Mount Fair. There is even a plan for a large solar field that will help power the buildings in the near future. The site planning done in 2003 built on a strong existing armature, changing nothing that did not require an upgrade. Understanding the rural landscape and building types was a key to the plan's success—modular repetition of room shapes, roof grammar, consistent application of structural logic—it all fit together. Moreover, the design team and the owners valued the identifying characteristics of the house and grounds above all other things; they did not touch the burial grounds, and they did not impinge on the views of the front of the house. The modesty and sensitivity that guided their approach is seldom seen in today's residential marketplace.

One last component remains to our study of additions and renovations to vintage houses: the all-important question of how to find authentic materials, details, and craftspeople to execute your project. In the pages to come we'll discuss some tricks of the trade and rules to follow when building adjacent to "good old work."

9

THE REAL DEAL

MANY HOMEOWNERS WRING THEIR HANDS WHEN considering the problem of finding materials to match the patina, quality, and texture of the roofs, walls, windows, and masonry on their vintage houses. Most people recognize that the quality and detail found in traditional craftsmanship and materials will distinguish a run-of-the mill renovation from the kind of projects we've illustrated in this book. Thirty years ago there was a definite paucity of choices for those wishing to create an "authentic" look with replacement materials. Today, however, getting the real deal in building restoration is simply a matter of knowing where to find resources and trade experts. In this chapter we'll discuss a few ways of assessing the types of materials and elements in your house, and then finding sources for them.

Form, volume, and the organization of spaces are what determine the success of most additions from the inside, but it is the choice and use of exterior materials that often makes

an addition look "right" from the outside—especially for a vintage house. These exterior materials—principally roofing, windows, and wall claddings (from wood siding and shingles to bricks)—are the vital components of the building's "weather envelope," a thin skin that protects the framing and interior finishes from the onslaught of rain, wind, and sun.

In vintage houses, however, traditional exterior materials also function as a critically important architectural cloak. It is their textures, colors, and associations that contribute the details of a building's historic style, as well as embody the essence of its historic character, such as age or how it was created. Though traditional exterior materials are too often taken for granted when already present—and blatantly ignored when it comes to repairs and major alterations—when they're respected and used knowledgeably in new work, they can go a long way in continuing to tell the unique story that is a latent part of every vintage house.

ROOFING

Covering as much as 40 percent of the exterior of any house, and invariably uniform in color and installation, roofing makes a monumental architectural statement. What's more, as a consistent, all-embracing material, roofing has the power to visually tie together the other, often disparate, parts of a building into a coherent, unified whole. When it comes to additions, this can be of great value because, generally, if you get the roof right, there's a lot more latitude in what you can do with the rest of the materials. To help make that happen, here are the most common materials and issues you need to know about when expanding or replacing a vintage house roof.

When the slates are smooth-faced with consistent dimensions— whether the roof is plain or patterned, say, with tails cut in geometric shapes or with a mix of colors— it's a standard roof, by far the most common type. (Photo by Barbara Krankenhaus.)

SLATE

Always high-end, with a complexity and heft that requires skilled installation, slate is nonetheless among the most cost-effective of roofing materials because of its legendary longevity—seventy-five to a hundred years or more. Though slate has covered roofs for centuries in Europe, it was rare on American houses until after 1850, when railroads made it practical to ship the weighty material beyond markets close to quarries. Decorative slate was popular for Victorian houses with European roots, like those in the Second Empire style, but the real heyday of the slate roofing industry was the period from about 1897 to 1914, when there were as many as two hundred quarries in operation. Interest in slate roofing remained strong during the building boom of the 1920s, as is evidenced by the creative ways the material was used, and slate has enjoyed something of a renaissance since the 1990s, for both new houses and historic restoration projects.

Slate, of course, is stone—any one of several sedimentary rocks laid down as silt in ancient oceans and mined in mountainous regions called slate belts. But slate colors— commonly ranging from black, gray, and blue-gray to shades of green, brick red, and deep purple—are only part of the design of the roof. Historically, slate roofs were divided into three different types. In standard slate roofs, the slates are smooth-faced and have consistent dimensions that produce a uniform roof. Whether the roof is plain or patterned—say with tails cut in geometric shapes or a mix of colors—it's still a standard roof, by far the most common type. The next type is textural: the slates vary in thickness, have uneven tails, and usually combine colors in a seemingly random pattern. Though in fact carefully planned, textural roofs evoke the haphazard accretions of medieval buildings and became very popular for houses in the Tudor and English Revival styles of the early twentieth century. The third type is the graduated slate roof: the roof is laid with the largest and thickest slates and the most exposure at the eaves, and the slates diminish in exposure and dimensions as they go up the roof. This produces a foreshortening effect that enhances the drama of a large roof. Some quarries expand this list to include Dutch lap, where the slates lap side-to-side as well as top and bottom.

As dimensions increase so does weight, and for a dense material like slate, thickness is an important consideration. Depending on thickness, slate roofs weigh in at 800 to 1,000 pounds per square (100 square feet) versus 550 pounds or less for asphalt shingles. What this means is that in order to safely install slate, the roof framing has to be strong enough to carry the weight. As a rule of thumb, you cannot expect to install slate on a roof that was not previously slated, unless

The seemingly random pattern of textural roofs, where slates vary in thickness, tail length, and color, is, in fact, carefully planned. Designed to evoke medieval handwork, textural roofs are seen widely on English Revival houses of the early twentieth century. (Photo by Barbara Krankenhaus.)

In a graduated slate roof, the largest and thickest slates are at the eaves, and diminish in exposure and dimension as they go up towards the roofline. This style enhances the drama of a large roof, such as this roof reconstructed with medieval Welsh slate. (Photo by Barbara Krankenhaus.)

Depending upon the source, roofing slates last sixty to 175 years, which makes them among the most "green" and historically appropriate option for major repairs and additions. (Photo by Barbara Krankenhaus.)

a structural engineer or experienced contractor has determined that the framing is sufficient.

When it comes to roofing period houses, the challenge is often to match material that's already on the building—whether for a major repair or an addition. Here the endurance of slate makes recycled material an attractive option. A recycled slate roof can last from fifty to a hundred years, depending on the slate type, and may cost 30 percent less than new material. It's often possible to cull a hefty percentage of good slates from an existing roof and reuse them elsewhere. A good slate roofer will be able asses the condition of each slate by tapping it with a hammer. Sound slates have

a characteristic "ring," while a slate on the way out produces only a dull thud.

CLAY TILE

With ancient origins, early clay tile roofs were used consistently for their resistance to fire, low maintenance, and long durability, but sparingly because the tiles were time-consuming to make by hand and always heavy. What really gave clay tiles a boost was first the Centennial Exhibition of 1876, which featured several tile-roofed buildings, and then the perfection of tile-making machinery in the 1880s. Clay tile in terra-cotta orange became the crowning touch for Richardsonian Romanesque buildings at the end of the nineteenth century, but it really came on strong for the new breeds of Arts and Crafts and Mediterranean Revival houses of the early twentieth century, especially with the advent multicolored glazes.

In contrast to flat, stiff slate, clay roof tile is a boundlessly plastic medium that is molded into scores of creative shapes and patterns—a wealth of options that basically divide into two categories: flat tiles and pantiles, which are generally any tiles with a half-round or barrel-shaped form. Today the most traditional types, such as Spanish tile or two-piece Mission-style tile, are called profile tiles in much of the industry. While such tiles are part of the architectural image of the Southwest and Florida, generally profile tiles represent less than 50 percent of today's market.

More common and far more diverse are the flat and

Clay tiles in half-round forms—broadly referred to as pantiles or profile tiles—are most closely associated with historic styles in the Spanish and Mission vein, especially in unglazed terra-cotta. (Courtesy of Ludowici.)

Colored glazes, developed in the early twentieth century, added another design dimension to clay tile roofs, and helped popularize them for Arts & Crafts houses. (Photo by Barbara Krankenhaus.)

interlocking tiles. Patterns range from straightforward, massive slab tiles to traditional English and French styles with sculpted surfaces and interlocking sides and tops. Color too is one of the signal beauties of clay tile. Beyond the ubiquitous earthen red-brown of the ceramic base, glazes in red, brown, black, purple, and green came on the scene by the late 1890s.

Like slate, the density of clay is what makes the material so durable as a roof but formidable as a load. Depending on type, clay tile can run from 800 to 1,000 pounds a square and more. While tiles in the 800-pound range are not necessarily over-heavy for houses built to recent building codes with

beefier framing, some clay tile manufacturers have introduced new lightweight products that, at around 600 pounds a square, are the equivalent in weight of an architectural asphalt roof.

Matching clay tile of the past with new tile is generally done on a case-by-case basis, often with the help of design services at major manufacturers who can research former products. It gets tricky, though, because decades ago there were more manufacturers, each offering lots of styles. Technology can be a hurdle too. Glazes from before the 1920s, for example, were often lead-based, and cannot be reproduced in the same way today.

Coming as close as possible to historic products is where recycled clay tile can be a boon. Industry suppliers say a recycled tile roof will last fifty to seventy-five years, subject, of course, to the tile type and the elements it endures. As with slate, this durability also applies to additions and alterations to an existing roof, making it very practical to remove and reinstall original tiles after completing repairs or changing the roof shape. Indeed, when there are problems with a clay tile roof, it is usually the flashing or fasteners that have given out—not the tiles themselves.

WOOD SHINGLES

In North America, where wood has always been the universal construction material, wood shingles have long been the oldest and most ubiquitous roofing. At first made by hand, shingles grew to be the garden-variety roofing for houses once railroads and machine production opened up the virgin softwood forests of the Pacific Northwest in the 1890s. If you don't know what kind of roof was originally on a house—even one built as late as the 1930s—and it is not a grand building, chances are it was originally wood shingles.

In the 1970s the use of woods shingles—and shakes, their neo-rustic cousins—enjoyed a renaissance of sorts for new as well as historic buildings. As luck would have it, this increased interest intersected with a dwindling supply of the best materials—basically old-growth cedar—and fading experience about how to install and maintain them. The upshot is that a roofing material that had a reputation for lasting as

Shingles split from local woods, then carefully dressed and shaped, are the original roofing material of North America. Though common in museum buildings, such as George Washington's Mount Vernon, they can be tricky to use on the average house. (Photo by Barbara Krankenhaus.)

Shingles versus Shakes

When it comes to historically appropriate wood roofs for old houses, the difference between shingles and shakes is more than semantic. Whether handmade (by splitting them out from sections of straight-grained logs) or machine-produced (by band- and circular-sawing), wood shingles have always been smooth-surfaced. The thick, lumpy-surfaced version called a shake is a product developed in the 1950s for a rustic effect, but one with no real historic precedent.

Shingles (left) are machine-sawn and flat; shakes (right) are uneven, split, and date to the 1950s. (Photo by Barbara Krankenhaus.)

much as a generation was regularly giving out in about ten years—sometimes less. This and the fact that wood shingle roofs offer a minimum of fire resistance (they're banned in many communities) has led to a dramatic drop in their popularity. Nonetheless, if you insist on installing a wood shingle roof, or want to repair or maintain the one you already have, consider the following points.

Western red cedar is basically the preferred roof shingle wood because it has a high content of tannins and rot-resisting extractives. This is not to be confused with eastern white cedar, which is a traditional cladding material in New England. Eastern white cedar is renowned as siding for the way it turns silver gray in a salty marine environment, but is not as durable as western red cedar when used on a roof.

The ideal shingle has a thick butt and is knot-free with vertical grain—that is, the annual growth rings run perpendicular to the face of the shingle. This gives the shingle greater durability (because there is less exposed softwood) and resistance to warping. Less desirable is a flat-grain shingle, where the annual rings run more or less parallel to the face, producing the characteristic flame pattern on top. More softwood is exposed and the shingle is more likely to warp. In fact, a good carpenter will saw such shingles in half to give them more of the characteristics of a vertical-grain shingle.

The most important factor, though, is ventilation. Historically, wood shingle roofs were installed on an open deck or nailers—strips of wood that spanned the rafters with considerable spaces in between. This practice allowed the shin-

American Thatch: Shingles Sublime

By the 1920s, wood shingle roofs started to take a hit—first from building codes that raised the issue of fire safety, and then from a totally new, upstart roofing material: asphalt shingles. Asphalt roofing manufacturers claimed that their material had better fire resistance, and it could be had in attractive colors. To meet the challenge, a couple of companies out of upstate New York started marketing color-impregnated wood shingles by the late 1920s.

But the final creative flurry of the wood shingle was in the late 1920s and early 1930s, with the vogue for thatched-effect roofs. This fashion—almost a fad—was probably inspired by the appeal of all things English in the years between the two world wars and represented a different look than say, the sharply gabled roofs of a Tudorbethan manor or a Cotswold cottage. For this technique, the roof framing was embellished with half-round eaves, rakes, and ridges. Wood shingles, carefully steam-bent to calculated radiuses, were installed over the framing to produce a Hansel and Gretel look. Another technique was to create undulating course lines by varying the lengths or angles of the shingles sometimes called a wave effect. Both techniques were often used at the same time.

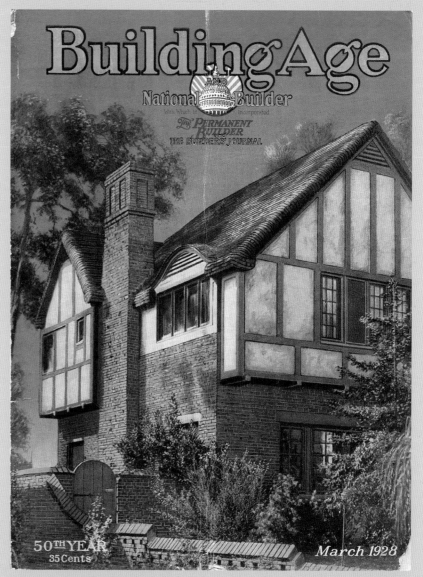

Thatch-effect roofs created by steam bending shingles over roll-formed eaves became the roof "du jour" for cottage-style houses of the 1920s.
(Courtesy of the National Archives Associates.)

gles to breath from both the top and the bottom, and it can still be practical for many buildings, especially where there is no finished living space in the attic. But what has proven to not be a good practice is to lay shingles right on a closed roof deck—that is, plywood or other sheathing running continuously over the rafters, the typical condition over a finished attic. In this situation, moisture collects under the shingles, contributing to warping and rotting of the wood.

One solution is to simulate the condition of an open deck by installing nailers or battens on top of a closed deck and laying the shingles on them in the conventional manner. (This detail has been in carpentry literature since the 1920s, but seemed to have been forgotten by the 1970s.) Generally, the closed deck is covered with 15 lb. felt; then furring strips are attached as nailers to provide air movement under the shingles. Rakes at the edges are left open for ventilation (though usually covered in screening to exclude animals), and gaps are added between nailers to allow for moisture movement. Some carpenters even pitch the nailers slightly down-roof to promote moisture collection runoff.

METAL

Sheet lead and copper have been used for expensive American roofs and low-pitch conditions since colonial times. In fact, besides silversmithing, one of Paul Revere's enterprises was a rolling mill for making sheet copper. Both copper and lead can be soldered into a flat-seam roof that is essentially a watertight membrane, but the more common use of copper is in a standing-seam roof made of multiple pans that are joined in seams about 1" high. Done right this is a very durable, long-lived, and almost maintenance-free roof that does not require painting because the copper will weather to a protective patina.

Copper makes a great roof, but also an expensive one, leading to a search for a less dear metal, commonly called a tin roof. The earliest such roofs were not tin but actually sheet iron (later steel) coated with a tin alloy. Since the late nineteenth century, the perfected version of this roofing has been known as terne or terneplate, and the version sold today (a proprietary product of the Follansbee company) is marketed as TCS III. Like copper, a terne metal roof is remarkably long lived—a hundred years years is common—if it is kept painted with a high-oil-content paint.

By the 1860s someone had the bright idea to combine the affordability of sheet metal with the beauty of slate and wood shingles, and came up with metal shingles. Advertising of the time was not shy about promoting the idea that these products eliminated the need for a skilled carpenter to install them. Metal-shingled roofs were very popular in some areas from the 1880s to the 1910s and many of them are still hard at work today.

The typical metal shingle of the late nineteenth and early twentieth centuries is about the size of a roofing slate, but instead of being flat it is embossed with some sort of raised pattern. While often decorative, the embossing had the practical purpose of helping the thin sheet metal hold its shape and adding the appearance of thickness to the shingle. Seams along the edges interlock with the adjacent shingles and maintained the integrity of the roof. Of course, today there's a whole industry based on metal shingles for contemporary styles and buildings, but a handful of manufacturers also still make a historic pattern or two specifically for the restoration market.

ASPHALT

The most widely used roofing material on any house, new or old, is the asphalt shingle: a fibrous base (traditionally made of organic felt, but now usually fiberglass mat) imbued with modified bitumen and covered with ceramic granules to add color and weigh. Perfected after 1915 as a fire-resistant alternative to the wood shingle, asphalt shingles in their earliest forms are now considered historic materials in the own right. Asphalt shingles once came in a wide variety of sizes, shapes, patterns, and colors, and although this variety has shrunk dramatically since the 1970s, knowing something about the traditional types of asphalt roofs still on the market can be useful background for picking a sympathetic new roof today.

Three-tab—Manufactured as early as the late 1920s and still the ubiquitous, garden-variety shingle type, three-tab shingles are 12" x 36" strips of single-thickness material die-cut with two slits along one side so that the strips can be quickly installed but appear to be three individual shingles in the final job.

Hexagonal—Once three-tab shingles caught on in the 1920s, tab pattern variations (as well as colors) became important selling points. One of the most enduring types was the hexagonal tab, which remained common through the 1940s. Hexagonal-tab strip shingles faded from the market through the 1960s but have been making a comeback of sorts since 2000 in asphalt products that emulate slate roofing.

French Method—As the asphalt shingle industry came into its own in the 1930s, one of the most common products for over-roofing an old wood-shingled roof was the French method shingle—a diamond like shape 12" or 16" on a side, so named because it resembled the chateaux roofs of the Loire valley. French method shingles added new life and a distinctive flair to many older houses, and because the shingles were made with storm-resisting tabs they were still available in some Midwest markets until the late 1990s.

Interlocking—The last of a once common breed of giant individual shingles is the interlocking shingle—typically a large T shape cut with ears and tabs that fit into with those of its neighbors, similar to a cereal box lid. The point of interlocking shingles is practical—to keep edges from lifting in wind- or storm-prone regions—but their effect is also architectural, producing a basket-weave appearance. These shingles are still sold in regional markets.

Laminated—Among the most popular asphalt shingle types sold today is the laminated or architectural strip shingle, which first became common in the 1980s. Laminated shingles are composed of two or more layers of asphalt roofing manufactured in such a way that they give the appearance of thickness and natural materials associated with wood shingles. One way manufacturers achieve this effect is by die-cutting tabs in a dragon's-tooth shape (similar to an inverted keystone) so that the tabs extend through the first strip (from which they are cut) to rest on a second sheet or backer strip. (Dragon's-tooth tab shingles might in fact be considered a historic shingle type on their own right, because they date to at least the 1940s.)

While they would never be mistaken for historic roofing materials like wood shingles or slate, laminated asphalt shin-

Asphalt shingles that interlock in basket-weave patterns are still sold in some storm-prone regions to resist wind-lift. (Photo by Barbara Krankenhaus.)

Large, diamond-patterned French Method shingles in asphalt or asbestos cement were once common for over-roofing, but are now available only in metal or some new plastic products. (Courtesy of the National Archives Associates.)

gles are often an appealing and appropriate choice for old houses because of their dimensionality and range of colors. As an added bonus, the thickness of these products generally means they have a good service life and are very forgiving on older roofs—that is, not readily showing dips and uneven-ness. Where the goal is to emulate the look of wood-shingle roof, avoid the lighter tans and browns that suggest freshly cut and installed shingles. Look instead to darker tones that

243

might mimic a few years of aging, and therefore appear a bit more realistic.

SLATE AND WOOD STAND-INS

Throughout the twentieth century, the building materials industry has looked to replicate natural materials with man-made versions that were lighter, cheaper, more uniform, or more profitable, and roofing has always been an area of keen interest. One of the earliest and most successful, the asbestos-cement shingle, is still in service on thousands of buildings, but has been out of production for at least two decades because of the asbestos component. Manufacturers have since tried a variety of other formulations and materials that continue to come and go as the technologies evolve. While there are no industry standards to date, some of the more common material types fall into six general categories.

Fiber-cement—Similar to asbestos-cement shingles but without the asbestos content, fiber-cement shingles are marketed by manufacturers for use beyond the snow belt where the potential of delamination due to freeze-thaw cycles are not an issue.

Rubber—Recycled rubber (typically from industrial waste) has been the basis of simulated slate products manufactured in Canada and the United States, sometimes for the "green building" market.

ABS plastic—Manufacturers have also turned ABS (acrylonitrile butadiene styrene), an easily molded plastic used to make auto bumpers, as a light, tough material for casting slate and shingle look-alikes.

Clay and concrete tile—Several producers of clay and concrete tile roofing have from time to time offered products shaped and colored to emulate slate or wood. While on the heavy side (especially compared to wood shingles), some products are made in lightweight versions that are comparable to laminated shingles.

Composition—Various composition products—such as slate particles in a man-made binder molded into realistic-looking slates—have been tried by manufacturers in recent years.

Asphalt—Taking a cue from the success of laminated/architectural asphalt shingles that evoke the ambiance of wood, since the late 1990s almost every manufacturer has come out with a strip shingle line that produces a slatelike appearance though the clever use of tab cut-outs, backer strips, and graduated coloring of granules.

Many of these materials and technologies are relatively new, with a limited track record of performance under the demanding weather and sun exposure of roofs. (Curling and color shifting, rather than actual leaks, seem to be the most common concerns to date.) On top of this, in the view of strict historic preservation standards, such as the Secretary of the Interior's guidelines, these are technically substitute materials. Nonetheless, used sensitively on the right project—say on nonprimary roofs—these substitute materials can often get a cautious nod from historic review boards and other design authorities if they make a convincing effort to maintain the

The Skinny on Membrane Roofs

A class of man-made roofing materials that definitely do not have a long history but are nonetheless increasingly useful for special roofs on historic buildings are generally called membrane roofs because they are single-ply and installed to form a continuous, seamless watertight surface. Basically flat with no architectural character of their own besides a limited range of colors (typically black and white), the materials are a welcome alternative to traditional materials, such as standing-seam sheet-metal or hot-mopped asphalt built-up roofs, for use on low-slope roofs, such as porch roofs, rowhouses, or the upper, nearly level portions of double-pitch mansard roofs. Membrane roofs are generally of two kinds:

EPDM

An acronym for ethylene propylene diene terpolymer, EPDM is a synthetic rubber developed during World War II for lining man-made ponds. By the 1960s it had found a new application as the liner for large, flat-roofed commercial structures, such as department stores and factories. An EPDM roof is created by running multiple six-foot-wide strips over a specialized underlayment board and then fusing the strips with a torch to make a watertight seam.

Modified Bitumen

Similar to traditional roll roofing but more sophisticated, modified bitumen roofing is a fiber base saturated with asphalt and, depending upon the manufacturer, sometimes rubberized compounds; it is often covered with mineral granules similar to asphalt shingles, to add color. Modified bitumen typically comes in 48" wide rolls that are laid over an appropriate underlayment and joined with cement.

Ice and Water Underlayments

Not roofing per se, but an increasingly popular accessory material, ice and water underlayments are thin, sticky membranes made in a variety of formulations—most major roofing manufacturers have their own proprietary products and trade names. Originally intended to be run as an undercourse at the eaves to prevent ice-dam water from finding its way under the roof, these materials have also become popular in lieu of black paper under valleys and between courses of roofing where wind-driven water is a concern.

Changing Roofs in Midstream

Keeping roof materials consistent can help integrate an addition into an existing building. Nothing screams "incompatible" like an unexpected switch in roofing materials—say, clay tile to asphalt shingles. However, two exceptions to this rule apply. First, roofs with exceptionally low pitch (such as porch roofs or shed roofs) or no pitch (such as dead flat roof areas) by nature require a switch to roofing material that won't allow water to penetrate between courses—for example, a standing-seam metal roof (commonly used in the past) or one of the modern membranes (such as modified bitumen or EPDM). Second, as with wall cladding, historically, clearly subordinate additions were frequently roofed with materials that were less expensive or complex than those used on the main structure—say, wood shingles on the summer kitchen of a slate-roofed house.

original architectural intent of the roof in place of expensive or impractical original materials.

WINDOWS

Windows rank behind roofs in importance as part of the weather-shedding envelope, but when it comes to alterations and additions they can be among the most critical—and contentious—elements in the house. Just proposing to change the windows in a vintage building to different shape or design can put an architectural review board on high alert—and even derail a tax incentive application or National Register nomination. The reason is that relative to their surface area, windows make an outsized contribution to the architectural character of a vintage house. And it's not only the patterns of the panes of glass (or lights) that are a concern, but also the size and number of windows and their placement—or, to put it in fancier terms, the fenestration.

Fortunately today's windows market—especially the growth in specialty suppliers and lines of historical windows—has made it more feasible than ever to find windows for an addition that are the same or very close in size and details to those that are on the existing building (see list of suppliers at the back of this book). Where this is not possible, however, a good guideline is to consider the same type of window (double-hung, casement) with the same general proportions (height to width), and then to choose a glazing pattern that, if not exactly the same, is at least consistent with the era (for example, 6 over 6 instead of 9 over 9). The following rundown of historic window designs can be a good point of reference.

WINDOWS BY TYPE

First we'll look at the four major kinds of windows you're likely to encounter, depending on the age and style of your house.

Double-hung sash windows—With two frames or sashes that slide up and down like guillotines within the window opening, these are the ubiquitous, workhorse windows of North America. Though colonists coming from Europe knew well the casement window (which opens like a door), the sash window proved better adapted to the colder winters in the New World.

Casement windows—Casements appeared in some of the first New England houses during the early settlement period of the seventeenth century, but they saw only limited use thereafter for evoking an Old World appearance, as in the Gothic Revival style of the 1840s. By the turn of the twentieth century, however, Frank Lloyd Wright and other architects of the 1910s who were searching for new, indigenous forms of American houses eagerly adopted the casement because it could be readily ganged in multiple units to produce large, wide expanses of window. By the 1920s, the immense popularity of English Revival house styles, such as Americanized Tudor and Norman, spread the casement window to every suburb across the continent, especially in the form of metal

The Secret Life of Wavy Glass

Ever peer out an old window to find that your view is subtly distorted, like a reflection in a fun-house mirror? Wavy window glass is something residents of recent houses seldom see or think about because they are accustomed to *float glass*—an optically perfect product first manufactured in the late 1950s. Vintage house owners, however, may have wavy glass of one degree or another in almost every window. Since this antique material is increasingly recognized and valued as an important part of a building's historic character, it is worth knowing a bit about so it can be appreciated, saved, and even restored, when desired, by using salvage or new reproduction glass.

Window glass in older houses is wavy not because of advanced age—or, as myth would have it, the effects of not-quite-solid glass sagging at a glacial pace over decades—but simply due to a fascinating manufacturing process. For centuries, window glass was an offshoot of the bottle-making craft, and by the 1850s glass-blowers had perfected their method into what is called *cylinder glass*.

To start, the glass-blower gathers a blob of molten glass at the end of a hollow rod and begins to blow it into a bubble, as if for a bottle. Next, he continues to grow the bubble, but into a long, sausage-shaped bulb by alternately blowing into the rod and then swinging it like a pendulum. Through this process the glass-blower produces an elongated cylinder, 36" or more in length, that, when cooled, is cut open at the ends and slit lengthwise with a hot iron to form a *shawl*. When the shawl is placed in an oven of the correct temperature, slit up, the sides begin to wilt, and what was once a cylinder unfolds to become a large sheet of flat glass.

The cylinder glass method was capable of producing much larger window glass (and more of it) than the earlier method of *crown glass* (in which thin glass is spun out of pizza-like discs), but it was not a perfect method. Even when the cylinder process was mechanized after 1900, the glass might still be left with minor imperfections, such as waves or ripples (the side effects of coaxing the inner and outer circumferences of the cylinder into a flat sheet) and air bubbles and protruding bits of glass (the flotsam and jetsam of the blowing). To be sure, homeowners and architects of the past always sought the best view possible for important windows by selecting as much top-grade glass as the budget allowed. However, when it came to secondary windows on the upper floors or in service rooms, less expensive, second-grade glass with occasional ripples or *seeds*—those little football-shaped bubbles that lie suspended in the thickness of a pane—was usually just fine.

So, while vintage wavy glass may not be as smooth and lucid as modern float glass that is flame-polished to precision clarity, may people cherish it for its hand-manufactured charm and the way it gives each window a unique personality, which is what owning a vintage house is all about anyway.

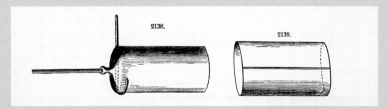

Old window glass has ripples and minor imperfections thanks to a technique that continued well into the twentieth century. The glass began as a large, bottlelike cylinder that, when slit lengthwise, could be wilted into a flat sheet. (Photo courtesy of The National Archives Associates.)

Casement windows, which open like doors, became a favorite of Arts & Crafts and Prairie School designers in the early twentieth century because they could be ganged in two's and three's to make large windows. (Photo by Barbara Krankenhaus.)

Most of the windows in this unassuming house are double-hung, two-over-two sash—the ubiquitous late-nineteenth century window type—but the gable end at the top is lavished with a three-part Palladian window. (Photo by Barbara Krankenhaus.)

sashes and frames either imported from England or made domestically.

Picture windows—Large, unobstructed sheets of glass that are fixed in place have their origins in the landscape windows marketed by sash manufacturers starting around 1900 (see below). But the idea really took off with the post–World War II housing boom, when big expanses of glass became more affordable, thereby adding a modicum of architectural distinction, and a sense of space and light, to Cape Cods and other basic tract houses of the time.

Palladian and ornamental windows—These distinctive windows have been used singly, but constantly, through almost every era and style of houses. Palladian windows and other types of three-part windows are the classical focal points in Georgian and Colonial Revival houses—typically centered in the second story over the front entrance—but they may also appear in gable ends. In contrast, ornamental windows, such as oval "cameo" windows and oriels, appear as jewel points in secondary or unexpected places, often also lighting a stairway or hall.

WINDOWS BY ERA

Because the technological advances in windows have been—and still are—defined by predominantly by glass, windows can be pegged to generally defined eras by the size, shape, and number of lights as well as other characteristic indicators, such as the profiles of the muntins (also called glazing bars).

1620 to 1720—First period houses—that is, those built by the first generations of North American settlers and closely modeled on medieval houses from their home countries—are believed to have had casement windows composed of many small diamond-shaped pieces of glass, or quarrels, held in lead bars called cames.

1700 to 1780—The Georgian style imported from England brought with it the double-hung sash window with each sash composed of twelve small panes of glass—commonly called a 12 over 12 window—set in a grid of wide muntins shaped with a quarter-round ovolo moulding. Common variations on the glazing patterns included 8 over 12, 9 over 9, and 6 over 9.

Georgian-style windows of the pre-revolutionary era had sash with thick muntins and many small lights, such as 12 over 12 or 8 over 12. (Photo by Barbara Krankenhaus.)

The Window Change Game

The way remodeling salesmen and TV advertisements pitch replacement windows with the promise of everything from lower energy consumption to easier cleaning, you might assume that the idea is a creation of our time, but that is far from the case. In fact, swapping out windows has been a favorite American practice for at least 150 years and probably a lot longer. New, more up-to-date windows were pushed as early as the 1850s as the ideal way to give a house an instant stylistic makeover—say, for making a thirty-year-old Greek Revival farmhouse look more in tune with the Victorian 1870s. By the 1930s window manufacturers added the incentive of lower maintenance and increased comfort to help drive business in a limp economy. The back-to-back oil crises of the 1970s injected energy efficiency into the argument—a talking point that was reborn as "green building" for the twenty-first century.

The point is that while the windows in your vintage house could well be decades old, the chances that they are original—that is, the same windows that came with the newly built house—get slimmer the more birthdays the house has had. If you hope to discover the oldest windows in the building, don't expect to find them on the first floor or the front of the building. These are the most prominent windows in the house and therefore the most likely place homeowners of the past would spend their window-changing budget. Instead, check out upper levels and out-of-the way places or service spaces. Like many valuable mementos, the oldest windows in your house may actually be waiting for you on the third floor or in the attic.

The clue that the windows in this late-medieval house in Litchfield, Connecticut have been changed is the muntin pattern—a 6 over 6 grid that dates from the Greek Revival era of the 1840s. (Photo by Barbara Krankenhaus.)

By the late-nineteenth century, affordable glass combined with romantic tastes to make popular the picturesque or cottage sash with complex muntins in the top sash, and a single pane of glass in the bottom. (Photo by Barbara Krankenhaus.)

1780 to 1820—The Federal style that followed the American Revolution brought more refined and subdued windows with narrower muntins than the Georgian style, and slightly larger glass, typically in 9 over 9 patterns but also in other combinations.

1820 to 1850—The Greek Revival style, America's first homegrown house idiom, popularized the 6 over 6 window with muntins based on the echinus, a convex Grecian molding shape derived from geometry.

1850 to 1870 (and later)—The mass production and widespread shipping of window glass, as well as window sash, found its ideal form in the 12" by 24" pane, producing the iconic 2 over 2 windows of the early and mid-Victorian era.

1870 to 1910—By the 1870s the Industrial Revolution had made large window glass economical enough to be used as the sole pane in a sash. Ironically, just as muntins became all but obsolete technically, they bounced back in highly complicated patterns for ornamental purposes. The most famous of these is the Queen Anne sash, a single, central piece of glass bordered by multiple small panes, often of colored glass. An elaborate Queen Anne sash was often used in the top half of a window over a single-paned sash—a combination sometimes called a picturesque or divided-top window.

1880 to 1910—Following the Queen Anne model, houses with early Colonial Revival detailing or in the Shingle style might use an upper sash with a grid of diagonal muntins that evoked the medieval quarrels of colonial houses. Avant-garde houses might also combine a small sash with a complex muntin pattern (or stained/leaded glass) over a much larger single light sash—a combination called a cottage front window.

1900 to 1920—Prairie School houses of the Midwest and Arts and Crafts houses such as bungalows did their best to incorporate innovative, ahistorical windows and muntin patterns. Highly popular for both casement and sash windows was the nine-light grid—basically a Queen Anne sash with selected muntins eliminated.

1920 to 1940—The widespread popularity of English Revival style houses, as well as the influence of European modernism, fueled an increased use of casements windows in both traditional and innovative ways. While many medieval-looking casements used patterns of small lights in either rectangular or diamond-shaped grids, they also appeared with totally twentieth-century large fixed lights or arranged in groups as bay windows. Large metal casement windows adapted from industrial architecture became the hallmark of modernist houses built in the International style.

1920 to Present—After World War I, the Colonial Revival movement reinvigorated the interest in houses with Georgian and classical details. When recast for the automobile suburbs of the twentieth century, the result was that the 6 over 6 window was adopted almost universally.

WOOD CLADDINGS

The third most important group of exterior materials, in terms of their appearance on vintage houses and what they contribute to alterations, are wood claddings. As ever, wood is the principal building material of North America, and early on carpenters devised cunning ways to fashion it into a variety of "skins" for protecting walls—principally horizontal and vertical siding and shingles. Each of these has their own symbolic visual identity that, when manipulated by changing the dimensions of open space and shadow lines (or combining with other claddings), produces wall treatments that are characteristic of particular styles and eras—valuable to know for creating changes that look "right."

Clapboards—The iconic siding of colonial New England houses, and one emulated in many other forms and eras across North America, is the clapboard. Plain, beveled boards that take the form of a thin triangle when viewed on the end, clapboards are installed horizontally so that they lap 1" to 1.5" at the upper edge to form a weather-shedding surface. The earliest clapboards from the seventeenth century were split out of logs by hand, of limited length and width, and typically installed with a relatively narrow weather exposure of about 3". Machine manufacturing in the 1800s made possible wider clapboards of up to 4.5". In the early twentieth century, when the broad woods of the West Coast became available, clapboardlike siding with an exposure as wide as 9" became both feasible and fashionable.

Matched flush siding—Many high-style houses of the eighteenth and nineteenth centuries—particularly in the Greek Revival style—were clad with horizontal boards that carpenters carefully edge-jointed and surface-planed to produce a flat, smooth wall. This matched flush siding was

Clapboards are the original horizontal wood siding and have been used since the eighteenth century for a durable, refined cladding. (Photo by Barbara Krankenhaus.)

typically employed to form a highly refined wall that, when painted shades of gray or brown and decorated at the corners with wood quoins, would simulate a facade of carefully dressed stone.

Vertical Boards and Battens—In the 1840s and '50s, tastemaker Andrew Jackson Downing and his collaborator, architect Andrew Jackson Davis, popularized a new form of wood siding: vertical boards capped at the joints by narrow strips or battens. Designed to be an economical way to add picturesque charm to the cottages and Gothic Revival houses they advocated, board-and-batten siding continued on as the all-purpose cladding for farm buildings.

Drop and novelty siding—Beginning around 1865, the increased sophistication of steam-powered millwork machinery made possible an industrialized cousin of the clapboard. Called variously drop siding or novelty siding, depending on the time and place, these materials are installed horizontally like clapboards to produce pleasing shadow lines, but differ in that they are nailed up flat against wall studs and integrated in a shiplap joint to make a weather-shedding surface. These sidings were milled in decorative patterns, such as the ubiquitous cove (sometimes called German siding)—as many as two dozen standard profiles by the 1920s.

Wood shingles—Though shaped wood shingles are known to have been used on roofs in the 1700s, it took Andrew Jackson Downing to help promote the idea of wood shingles for walls. In his book *Country Houses*, Downing featured a design for a Swiss cottage adapted to the American environment, clad with "an external coating of shingles cut in

The Exterior Enigma: Same or Different?

When it comes to adding onto a house in a historic district or attempting to qualify for the National Register of Historic Places, an owner or restorer may face a vexing question: should the new exterior match the existing structure—or be clearly different?

At first blush, the second option may sound illogical, but if the building is subject to a local historical/architectural review board, or if the owner is hoping to qualify for historic tax incentives, the decision can indeed be serious. Review boards are guided by the Secretary of the Interior's Standards for Rehabilitation (see www. nps.gov/hps/TPS/tax/rhb/stand.htm), and when it comes to additions, one of the tenets of these guidelines is to make a "visual distinction between new and old." The intent is to not only preserve the historic character and historical significance of the older building—that is, to make it clear to the casual observer what is the historic part of the house—but to also leave a clear record of what is new. This way, many years from now when the addition has aged, future observers and researchers will not confuse the more recent work with the earlier or original house.

In the eyes of preservationists, one of the principal ways to make this distinction between new and old is through a clear differentiation of materials. In some high-profile and public buildings, this concept has stirred controversy because of the jarring juxtapositions it can foster—for example, a concrete-block elevator shaft hanging off a brick Victorian courthouse. In the case of houses, though, the practice need not be at odds with history (see "The Exterior Enigma: Take Two"), nor as radical. The differentiation can be made through the choice of the materials themselves—shifting from, say, clapboards to shingles—or through the design or installation of the new materials—for example, altering the exposure dimensions of the siding, the detailing, or even just the color.

The Exterior Enigma: Take Two

Whatever you make of today's philosophical arguments about changing exterior materials between new and old work, the idea of not having identical materials on all walls of a house has many

In early New England, well-to-do homeowners had no problem flaunting expensive clapboards on prominent facades, then using economical brick elsewhere. (Photo by Barbara Krankenhaus.)

longstanding precedents. For example, in preindustrial New England clapboards were the siding of choice and a sign of prosperity as well as taste. Nonetheless, it was a frequent and socially acceptable practice to lavish these expensive materials primarily on the front of the house—the featured facade—or just the front and sides, and to clad the back in a lesser material, such as matched boards or even brick.

Additions too were regularly (though not universally) clad in different materials than the main house, also primarily for economic reasons. A kitchen ell built off the back might not only be dimensionally smaller than the main building, it often was constructed of more economical materials—wood siding, for example, for a stone house, or rough boards or shingles for a finely clapboarded house.

This tradition of using commoner exterior materials for later ells and wings can be a useful guideline today. Generally, additions run the risk of looking precocious or out-of-scale when their exterior materials are more substantial or expensive those of than the main house. But if they appear less sophisticated or more garden-variety, they can help a new addition read as subordinate, common practice, and something that has always been there.

Victorian house styles, such as the Queen Anne, were quick to capitalize on novelty as well as the fruits of the Industrial Revolution, and often changed cladding materials one or more times up the wall. (Photo by Barbara Krankenhaus.)

an ornamental pattern." Downing called this design a cottage ornée, meaning that it was fancifully picturesque and ornamental. Today we see the skeleton-like framework of boards filled with ornamental shingles as the prototype wall treatment for the Stick Style houses that proliferated across the American landscape in the 1860s.

In the 1870s decorative wood shingles reinforced the popularity of another style that became synonymous with the Victorian house: the Queen Anne. When American architect Henry Hobson Richardson reinterpreted the houses of English architect Richard Norman Shaw on these shores, he swapped out the ceramic tiles Shaw used on the upper

255

walls in favor of more American (and more affordable) wood shingles, and both the style and the use of shingles caught on. When the Queen Anne morphed into what's now called the Shingle Style at the end of the nineteenth century, plain wood shingles (colored with new creosote stains) swathed the entire volume of the building, but beyond occasionally wavy course lines, decorative shapes and effects were minimal.

By the early 1900s wood shingle siding bounced back as a natural, honest cladding for bungalows and other new house types of the Arts and Crafts era. While architects and builders eschewed ornamental shingles as artificial and busy, they had no problem creating eye-catching walls with unexpected course lines and installation patterns using plain shingles. One of the most common techniques is ribbon coursing: shingles of the same size laid up in a double layer, but with the top layer raised to expose 1" of the bottom layer to produce a single ribbon at the course line. Or shingles of consistent width could be laid up with every other shingle raised 1" to produce and up-and-down pattern called staggered coursing.

BRICKS AND MORTAR

Masonry may form the solid walls of a house, or it may just be a veneer over another material, such as wood framing or structural tile, but either way, it too can be a common exterior material, and the most widely seen masonry exteriors are made of brick.

Bricks have been used for millennia in cultures as diverse as ancient Rome, Mesopotamia, and southwestern North America. The kinds of brickwork that a vintage house owner is likely to encounter are relatively few in relation to that spectrum, but nevertheless present special problems that bewilder even the experts.

A brick is like a loaf of bread—it consists of a hard, baked crust and a porous interior. Considering how it is made, the analogy with baking is perfect. Clay and sand are mixed with water, packed into a mold, and baked for several days in a kiln. When cool, the finished units are durable enough to stand weathering for hundreds of years—that is, if properly installed and maintained.

Among the many types of historic brick used in houses, three are particularly important because of their widespread use during particular eras: oversize English handmade bricks from the Colonial era, "pressed" bricks from the Federal and Greek Revival eras, and late nineteenth-century sand-lime bricks, generally lighter in color than earlier types. The sand-lime process was patented in Germany in 1881 and quickly came to the United States. So-called pressed bricks became popular during the early nineteenth century, particularly in townhouses, because of their smooth texture and uniform color. Hydraulic pressed brick, a proprietary process for molding very refined bricks with plain or embossed-pattern faces, became popular in the late nineteenth century. Laid with a minimum amount of fine mortar, walls of pressed brick are extremely difficult to put up. Few masons are capable of grinding mortar and executing these "butter" joints less than 1/8" thick. There are no manufacturers of these bricks in operation today, so salvage material must be found to do restoration work, or terra-cotta manufacturing firms must create custom molds for specific forms and colors.

Light-colored brick, often with "iron spot" (iron oxide) textures in the outer face, became fashionable around the turn of the twentieth century, most often in commercial buildings. In cities with German populations, such as Philadelphia, St. Louis, Chicago, and Milwaukee, these bricks were often used in combination with colorful terra-cotta ornaments. Made without clay, they were fired at higher temperatures to produce dense and somewhat brittle characteristics. Though limited in color and texture, iron spot and lighter sand-lime brick are widely available today.

In order to achieve the patina, color, texture, and durability of historic brickwork, masons must sample the existing brick and look carefully at its composition. Occasionally there will be a maker's mark stamped into the units, but in the earliest buildings local kilns were the likely suppliers of common brick. At Colonial Williamsburg in the 1930s, restoration architects had to recreate the historic burning process in special kilns using local clays and sands to get suitable results. Larger English brick are produced today in the traditional manner using small, stacked "clamps," fired to between 800 and 1200 degrees C. Most handmade bricks were laid with sand-lime mortars, with joints approximately ¼" thick.

When restoring or replicating historic brick masonry, getting the proper color and texture in the bricks is only half the battle. It is perhaps more critical to match the mortar and joint types. Strangely, old-house owners often tolerate brick

This rowhouse in Washington, DC is a showcase of late-nineteenth-century brickwork: smooth, precise, wire-cut brick set in thin, red "butter joints" for a monolithic appearance, with pressed brick decorating window and door headers. (Photo by Barbara Krankenhaus.)

repairs using mortar that is not even close to the color and texture of the original wall. Why? Often they are told that better results can't be achieved because the materials and skills are not available. This is seldom the case; the key is finding a highly skilled mason.

Two predominant types of mortar are found in brick walls today. If the building was constructed before about 1875, it will usually have lime-and-sand mortar, often hidden behind subsequent pointing, but sometimes intact on the surface. These "soft" mortars contain no additives or colorants—all the color is provided by the sand. The only binding material holding the aggregates together is lime, the product of processing limestone or seashells. Such mortars appear "natural" because they come from the earth near the house, not from thousands of miles away.

For buildings built after about 1900, and any new buildings, the most common form of mortar is composed mainly of sand and Portland cement, a product manufactured from a combination of ingredients. Portland cement mortars are harder and more durable than lime-sand mortars, which is why Portland is mixed with large aggregates to make the concrete that fills our modern world. Introducing Portland cement mortar into soft brick and stone walls, however, can have deleterious effects. The most common problems we encounter in either stone or brick masonry are caused by the improper use of hard Portland cement mortars for repointing aged mortar joints (the "mortar mismatch" we mentioned in Chapter 3). Mortars with a high percentage of Portland cement are much harder and less resilient than most of the brick made before about 1880. As a result, during the freeze-thaw cycles common in many American regions, bricks will expand, but the Portland cement mortar won't give like softer lime-and-sand mortar, so as the bricks continue to expand pieces break off or spall.

When all the ingredients are in place, a properly restored or infill brick wall will astound you—and that is no exaggeration. Americans are not used to seeing superlative masonry materials and craftsmanship in brick buildings. Though the mason's union provides some training in historic techniques, few go on to master them to the high standards of the past. Go and find a truly experienced master mason, and your efforts will be rewarded. And do not assume that a competent stonemason can lay brick in difficult patterns, or a brickmason can lay stone. Look at a sample of the work before you make your choice.

STONEWORK

Stone masonry is not only an ancient and highly durable exterior building material—serving for generations with a minimum of maintenance—it is among the most evocative and beautiful, the product of craft and design traditions that have been worked out over centuries.

Stone masonry that is exposed derives the bulk of its appeal, as well as strength, from the stone itself. Even after the invention of railroads, the weight of stone made it daunting to ship, so it has traditionally been used not far from

Historic Masonry Is All in the Match

Modern bricks are harder and more brittle than bricks used during the eighteenth and nineteenth centuries. They are most often shaped by wire-cutting rather than molding, and thus have a more regular appearance. They are easier to lay than handmade brick; hence there are fewer masons with the skills to do old-fashioned work. The first rule to follow if you have a historic brick house is to hire the best possible mason, and one with vintage house credentials.

When we first became involved with old house restoration thirty years ago it was difficult to find specialty brick to match or approximate the myriad types used in eighteenth- and nineteenth-century buildings in the United States. Today the market is full of excellent manufacturers who cater to the preservation trade. Of course, getting new brick to perfectly match a wall that has weathered for two centuries is impossible, so often salvage brick is the best alternative for large areas of infill masonry. The salvage brick market is generally local, so it pays to have a local mason who can find sources for your particular needs.

In restoration, we generally perform a detailed mortar analysis to find out exactly what materials and compounds make up the original mortar. If your mason or architect can do this for you, by all means take advantage of the service. If not, ask your mason to crush some of the mortar and assess the composition visually. Then ask him to erect a "test panel" of new brick to match with an old wall nearby. When you and your architect are satisfied with the mortar match, proceed, but not before.

Creating a matching mortar for historic masonry is not just about obtaining a mix that is the right hardness—that is, softer than the brick or stone it binds—but also obtaining the correct color by using sand that matches the original. (Photo by Barbara Krankenhaus.)

where it was quarried—which might even be the building site—making it an architectural expression of the local natural geology. Suffice it to say that for repairing or extending existing stonework on a vintage house, finding the closest possible match to the stone itself is critical, and local quarries (or salvage from nearby structures) are the place to start the search.

Of the many kinds of rocks present in the earth's crust, only a few are suitable or practical for building construc- tion—that is, are sufficiently strong (to withstand compression for building), hard (to resist wear for carving and detailing), attractive (with pleasing appearance and durable color), and present in sufficient quantity to be obtained at a reasonable cost. Basalt, sandstone, limestone, granite, marble, gneiss, and slate are among those used in masonry. Stone masonry also derives its beauty from how the mason selects and places the stones in the wall, as well as the way the stones—especially the faces—are detailed. The amount of detailing generally places stone masonry into one of two broad types, rubble and ashlar.

Rubble masonry employs stones that are irregularly shaped—that is, not squared or otherwise worked except for removing awkward points or protrusions. Rubblestones are used just as they come from the quarry (sometimes because the stone's nature makes it difficult to cut) or, in the case of rounded river stones or cobblestones, as they are found in a riverbed or field. Rubblestone walls are generally either *uncoursed rubble*, stones laid without any conspicuous courses (intentional horizontal layers), or *coursed rubble*, laid in rudimentary courses at intervals up the wall; the course heights are not uniform and the stones are random sizes.

Traditionally, rubble masonry was the functional stuff of rough walls for foundations or the hidden backing behind more expensive masonry or a coating of parge (see the section on stucco). But masons often played up the irregular beauty of uncoursed rubble by dressing the mortar into raised joints that highlight the random patterns of the stones, sometimes coloring the mortar as well. By the 1890s uncoursed rubble

What Is Cast Stone?

Cast stone is a product similar to concrete, but should never be confused with the stuff you see on sidewalks and in parking garages. Whereas concrete is formulated with Portland cement and indiscriminate aggregates of sand or pebbles, cast stone is made of real crushed stone. When you see very regular areas of what looks like limestone, you may actually be looking at a form of cast limestone made in a factory under highly controlled conditions. Indeed, cast stone has been used since the nineteenth century where large areas of masonry were required and the price of real stone was outside the budget. The proportion of crushed stone to Portland cement (a binder substituting for natural heat and pressure underground) in cast stone is very high, as would be the case in the natural product. As with any material, one should consult references and technical specifications before considering cast stone in any application.

Rubble masonry seems unsophisticated because it employs undressed stone, but it takes great skill to lay and has been highly prized for rustic-style buildings and Arts & Crafts houses, such as this bungalow. (Photo by Barbara Krankenhaus.)

with dressed corner stones or quoins was fashionable for an informal yet cultured treatment in country churches and suburban buildings. At the same time, rounded boulders and fieldstones were being widely used for consciously rustic-style buildings (sometimes as the facing over a lesser stone backing)—a vogue that took on increased popularity with the Arts and Crafts buildings of the early twentieth century. Throughout its long history stone has been used for building solid, load-bearing foundations and walls, but since the 1920s its use in houses has usually been as a veneer material over other masonry, such as brick or structural tile or even wood framing.

Ashlar masonry is readily distinguished from rubble masonry because, in whatever style it appears, the outside, facing stones are always cut. The refined appearance of ashlar masonry is a result not only of cutting and finishing the stones, but also the straight, plumb, vertical joints this produces. The stones may be laid to create *coursed ashlar*, where all the stones are uniform in size and the horizontal joints are continuous, or *broken ashlar*, where the stones vary in size and horizontal joints run continuously for no more than four feet or so before they are interrupted by a large stone. When the stones in broken ashlar are laid up so that the vertical joints do not align over each other with any regularity, the masonry is sometimes called *random-coursed ashlar*.

Coursed ashlar masonry using stones with uniform, tooled faces, but detailed with specialized corner stones and belt courses, is most often seen on public and office buildings rather than houses, unless they are very large or built within

Fig. 18

Ashlar masonry, with its straight edges and tooled faces, is most often seen in its refined versions in public buildings like banks and courthouses, but the random, coursed ashlar shown here is popular for houses. (Courtesy of the National Archives Associates.)

a specific historical design tradition, such as the Italian or Beaux-Arts styles. More common, perhaps, since the late nineteenth century is using smooth-faced ashlar masonry for a sheer, monolithic surface, especially where stones such as limestone or brownstone were both fashionable and plentiful. Broken ashlar masonry customarily uses rock-faced stones, and though this would seem economical, laying up the irregular shapes actually makes this masonry more expensive than coursed ashlar. Therefore it was often reserved for particular architectural expressions or styles, such as the Richardsonian Romanesque style.

Ashlar masonry is invariably applied to a cruder, less

expensive stone or brick backing. Thickness typically varies between 4" and 8" for stones 12" and under in height, and it was often varied to ensure a better mechanical connection with the backer wall. Some popular ashlar stones like marble or sandstone are only 2" to 4" thick, so metal anchors are added to help tie the stones to the backing.

STUCCO

As an exterior material, stucco inhabits a unique position because, although it functions as a protective cladding with a strong architectural identity—it can be highly ornamental to the point of masquerading as stone or brick—until it is mixed and skillfully applied, it has a minimum of material qualities of its own. Also called exterior plaster, roughcast, and parge, stucco is basically masonry mortar applied like cake frosting over another material to protect it and often improve appearance. In preindustrial North America, stucco was used to cover structures ranging from the log buildings of pioneer settlements to farm houses to the European-styled mansions of the wealthy. In the early twentieth century it found a vast new popularity as the convincing finishing touch to revival-style suburban houses, from myriad mini-villas in the Spanish and Mediterranean mode to the ersatz half-timbering found in Tudor-style manors. Besides being highly versatile and cost-effective, stucco was also fireproof and worked well as a remodeling material.

Stucco is as old as building construction itself, and for

Stucco, or exterior plaster, is an ancient cladding method with many variations that found new popularity in the early twentieth century as a perfect expression of the Arts & Crafts and Prairie styles. It is also an economical make-over material. (Photo by Barbara Krankenhaus.)

263

centuries it was based on the ancient inventory of masonry ingredients, starting with clay, sand and stone dust, and lime. By the 1920s the advent of new industrial cements and building materials had expanded the menu of constituents so that the building industry recognized three common stucco types, lime, Portland cement, and magnesite stucco.

Lime stucco is a traditional mix of lime, sand, and aggregates (pebbles, stone dust, or the like), often including a small amount of Portland cement by the 1920s. Portland cement stucco is a mixture of sand, aggregates and (in addition to a small amount of lime) modern, quicker-setting Portland cement in either gray or white, depending on desired color. Magnesite stucco is one of several proprietary products (now obsolete), formed by mixing magnesium carbonate (magnesite) with a liquid chemical. Some magnesite products are also known to have included novel ingredients, such as mica chips (for a reflective glint) and asbestos (as a fireproof binder). Though originally promoted as being highly weatherproof, in some cases magnesite stucco has proved to be far less durable than traditional stucco mixtures after several decades of exposure.

Like traditional interior plaster, stucco is applied in two or three coats. It can be applied directly to a masonry wall, and for many vintage houses it is the original, intended final finish over rubble stonework or common brick. More commonly for recent houses, however, stucco is troweled onto wood or metal lath nailed to a wood frame, especially where it is used to simulate medieval wattle-and-daub in half-timbering, or to cover over another cladding as a remodeling upgrade

The wide range of decorative effects possible with stucco are legendary and often based on the building traditions of regions and ethnic groups around the world. Reinterpreted in North America, they have been adapted and manipulated by builders and tradesmen over the last 150 years to meet the ebb and flow in architectural fashions, not to mention the shifts in methods and economics of the construction industry. The upshot is that when it comes time to replicate an existing stucco finish on a vintage house for either an addition or an infill repair, the methods that produced it can often

Beware of Men Carrying Trowels!

The stucco industry in the United States has historically been dominated by immigrants from the Mediterranean, Mexico, and South America, where the craft is practiced widely. Many of the best stucco craftsmen still come from these areas of the world. In more recent decades, companies offering spray-on, synthetic, and acrylic forms of "stucco" have entered the market in large numbers. Beware of salesmen offering the advantages of stucco for half the cost, or varieties of stucco that do not contain mainly sand and cement or lime. Though some products offer legitimate, durable exterior finishes, none will replicate the character of real stucco. Don't be fooled. There is no substitute for a three-coat stucco finish applied by a master craftsman.

be maddeningly elusive to decipher. Though the tools and techniques are typically not elaborate—sometimes as prosaic as old towels or buckets of gravel—they are often a part of a trade tradition that is oral, not written down. Moreover, the craftsmen behind finishes from as recently as the 1950s are now long out of the picture, taking their skills and experience, as well as this lore, with them.

Nonetheless, by carefully examining the original stucco and finding a contractor willing to experiment, it is often possible to come very close—sometimes amazingly and easily dead-on—to a historic stucco effect. But first you'll want to familiarize yourself with the most popular treatments and finishes.

COLOR

The color in the best stucco work is not paint but is inherent in the material. Lime stucco is white by nature, but historically it was also enhanced with materials such as white marble dust for added brightness. Traditional colorants, such as brick dust or modern lime-fast pigments, were also used to produce other shades or colors, as in the colored stuccos popular for Prairie-style houses in the early twentieth century.

AGGREGATES

The nature of the sand used is a big influence on both the color and texture of stucco. For example, common aggregates of the early twentieth century—perhaps the golden age of modern stucco—included colored pebbles, crushed granite, marble in various colors, sandstone, quartz, and gravel.

TEXTURE

The craftsperson can produce an assortment of classic (as well some unique) stucco textures simply by the way he or she manipulates the wet mortar with trowels and simple mason's tools like a broom or float (often just a board). Examples include stippled finish (a smooth-troweled finish patted with a broom or brush end while wet), sand-floated finish (smooth stucco rubbed with sand while partially set), and sand-sprayed finish (smooth stucco sprayed or dashed with a creamy slurry of cement, water, and sand by throwing it from a broom or brush).

DASHING

Creating a stucco effect by embedding conspicuous aggregates in the surface of wet mortar is a centuries-old practice. Though collectively called applied-aggregate finishes in trade manuals, these methods are better known by time-honored descriptive names, such as spatter-dash (sand or finely crushed stone forcibly thrown against smooth, wet stucco) and pebble-dash (clean, round pebbles ¼" and larger, thrown against the wall and then pressed into the wet stucco with a clean wooden trowel). In some regions and traditions, dashing is finished with a smattering of brightly colored stones or pieces of glass—even a few child's marbles—for jewel-like highlights.

Seth Thomas House, Morristown, New Jersey. (Courtesy of Mark Alan Hewitt.)

10

THE LONG VIEW

IF THIS BOOK HAS A MANTRA IT IS THIS: TAKE CARE OF the past and the past will take care of you. This does not mean that we advocate nostalgia over optimism for a better future. In fact, we advocate a point of view that is broader and more cognizant of future realities than the narcissistic, consumer-oriented, antienvironmental posture taken by many in our society. By encompassing the "good old work" done by our spirited predecessors in our view of the future, we take a longer and more salient view than many of our more technocentric colleagues. The French call this "la longue durée."

What do they mean? Decades ago a group of young historians forged a quiet revolution in their field by studying broader and more temporally ambiguous subjects than their teachers thought advisable. Most of the group taught in France, where the terrain of historical material had been pretty well covered. The key events, powerful leaders, cul-tural forces, and economic currents in each epoch had been established using unimpeachable research. Yet something was missing in these slices of historical narrative—a sense of the slower and more durable world of common people, their families, and their struggles to survive shifts in economic and social structures while much of their immediate environment stayed the same.[1]

The theories behind this shift in historiography were somewhat complex, but the result was that the dominant modernist/Hegelian view of history—as a series of discrete and readily definable epochs that waxed and waned in a dia-lectic—was dealt a fatal blow. It was no longer possible to ignore the longer preindustrial past in favor of Western his-tory. Nor was it possible to privilege certain epochs or cultures as hegemonic in the development of the human species over thousands of years. It was as if contemporary intellectuals realized that they stood amidst the primitive, mythic structures of their ancient ancestors, on an equal footing rather than on a pedestal. Widening the lens of history liberated it from parochial points of view in many arenas.

One of the many liberating concepts that came from this shift was one we have woven through this book: that our homes are not just documents of a moment in history that can be frozen like a snapshot, but rather the shells of members of a human species that change slowly over decades and centuries. The denizens of individual dwellings are tied to a particular place that informs their lives and gives meaning to their families over generations, not just fleeting years or short-lived fashions. When we alter our places of habitation we also alter our culture, for better or for worse. Yet organic growth in our home places continues, with changes that make it possible for us to maintain our families in "historic" environments without limiting ourselves to our own temporal frame, whatever zeitgeist happens to be sanctioned now.

Unfortunately, not all preservationists, or all architects, accept this view of history as a long, slow continuum in which "progress" is not necessarily an end in itself. The predominant view that each age has its own discrete zeitgeist is still attached to some important preservation standards, like the famous Venice Charter of 1964 and the Secretary of the Interior's Standards in the United States. That is unfortunate for buildings in residential historic districts, because it overly restricts the kinds of changes that individuals can make to their own houses. Steven Semes has written a critique of contemporary architecture that rails against Hegelian "historicism" as a framework for judging the built environment.[2] He argues persuasively for a different framework from which to view change in the built environment, but his is a minority position. The Institute for Classical Architecture and Classical America, which sponsored his book, has been a consistent supporter of this point of view. Until very recently the American Institute of Architects stuck to the opposite view, that all good architecture is Modernist architecture.

Everyone living in a historic neighborhood has a horror story about a neighbor or friend who tried to erect a fence, paint a front door, or expand a kitchen, only to be told that her changes would have to be deemed "appropriate" by a local preservation commission. On the one hand, applicants are told that their changes must be entirely in character with the "original" house, while on the other they are discouraged from designing or decorating in the *style* of the original house. Instead, their architects must tread the fine line of making something "of its own time" (contemporary, modern) while also making something entirely "appropriate" to the historic dwelling. More than a few projects have been approved that satisfy neither one of these oxymoronic rules, but instead result in an addition that is ugly, out of scale, and apt to be torn down as soon as the next owner with some taste comes along. In the face of critiques such as Semes's, and of much popular scorn for the Modernist bias in preservation laws, the U.S. government is likely to revise the standards in the near future.

In the foregoing pages we have explored several successful strategies for renovating and expanding vintage houses. Our framework for looking at growth in houses reflects the "longue durée" that many now accept as a better way of looking at time and change in buildings. And we believe that the examples in this book prove that houses can grow and change while respecting the style and intentions of their first builders. The five parameters outlined in Chapter 2 provide a framework within which designers can respond to changing family needs without forsaking the traditions that guided the original makers of your house.

These tips and resources are just a beginning, for any such project demands painstaking care and hard work. But beyond the sweat and economic privation that you've endured, what makes your house important to the society at large when you leave it to the next owner, even if that owner is your relative? Why, ultimately, does the continued life of your vintage house matter to others?

In this concluding chapter, we share some ideas about those key questions, and we hope to tie some of the concepts presented earlier into a wider theme: the endurance of historic places on a changing planet. Three current trends related to our quality of life are particularly meaningful to vintage house owners: new ways of looking at the value of houses and properties, new attitudes toward environmental conservation, and a new awareness of the importance civic engagement.

THE SHIFTING SENSE OF VALUE

One of the startling new realities of a planet that is imperiled by climate change, extinctions, and energy shortages is the

A familiar "disjunctive" addition to a Beaux Arts building in Milwaukee that might be deemed acceptable by some historic district commissions in the United States. (Courtesy of Mark Alan Hewitt.)

necessity for living with less. Economists and planners are changing their models for predicting future trends because twentieth-century macroeconomic systems are unsustainable for a population of seven billion, let alone double that amount fifty years hence. Recently a group of Quaker scholars proposed the consideration of a "whole earth economy" that values every market transaction in terms of its ultimate effect on the earth's flora, fauna, and ecosystems.[3]

Although many argue that humans have not yet reached the crisis point at which draconian changes must occur in consumption and lifestyle, there are things that intelligent people can do to reduce their footprint now to forestall a disaster. One of them, we have argued, is to preserve and maintain their own houses and gardens.

In the face of the environmental crisis, societies throughout the world are reevaluating their attitudes toward the historical built environment. In the coming years buildings will no longer be valued merely as artifacts, or additions to real estate, or investments, or inherited property. The age value and material culture embodied in houses will come to mean more to humans as more and more people compete for scarce resources. The embodied energy in craftsmanship and fine materials will increase exponentially in value as we develop new means of assessing our built environment in terms of its contribution to a sustainable planet. Old houses, the best of their style or type, will become treasured cultural icons as well as savvy investments, and the public will monitor their stewardship more and more closely. Why? The answer is obvious to those who have guarded and coddled great houses,

but less so to most government officials, business leaders, and policy analysts. Vintage houses bear the stamp of quality, craftsmanship, aesthetic value, and embodied energy, and our appreciation for them will only increase as we live with less in our daily lives.

We have only begun to experience the sense of loss that scarcities will bring during the next century. If only for that reason, the "green building" movement will embrace preservation more sincerely and with greater urgency. Your investment in a historic house, and the care you put into the house during your period of ownership, will advance the cause of sustainability more effectively than the construction of ten high-tech "energy zero" houses. Whatever these new "green machines" offer in terms of life-cycle energy savings will be outweighed by the enormous energy resources used to construct them in the first place. Building new houses with recycled materials, though better, is also expensive because these materials must be processed and transported to far-off sites for reuse. A vintage house stays where it was built because it belongs there, and it will only get better with age. That is, if we take care of the land it sits on.

As we pointed out in Chapter 1, the multiple values we place on property, historic buildings, and the historic human-made environment are largely determined by culture and society. Age value, historic value, embodied energy, real estate value, and replacement value in current dollars all affect our willingness to invest in older buildings. The relationship between these often conflicting measures determines how we allocate resources to maintain our cultural patrimony, the term used to denote all artifacts deemed worthy of protection by the society at large.

If the trends noted in this book continue, we believe that outstanding historic houses in private hands will enter the realm of things that our society wishes to protect or watch over—the meaning of the Latin roots of "conserve"—for the public good. Legal scholars continue to debate how much control our government should have over private property, but notwithstanding their positions, the scarcity of these resources will only increase as the population increases. We believe that it is unlikely that governments in developed nations will abandon decades of conservation policy favoring individual houses or those in historic districts. Indeed, the future augers well for those who care for their vintage houses, for their value can only increase. And the better the quality of maintenance and upgrades in a home, the more that value will grow.

THE CONTINGENT ENVIRONMENT

Being baby boomers, the authors of this book participated in the first Earth Day celebrations in 1970. High schools throughout the country announced the event with great fanfare, and there were "teach-ins" about a new ethic for treating our fragile planet with respect. In those days there was much hope for a utopian future in which humans would value and care for the planet to help ensure a balance in its ecosys-

tems. We know today that, despite the projections, we have not cared for the earth very well since 1970. The current crisis is the legacy of twentieth-century excess. Our future will be contingent on the degree to which we can solve climate, food, population, and energy problems during the next fifty years.

The strained negotiations over the Copenhagen greenhouse-gas reduction treaty may portend ill for environmental regulations everywhere, but there is little question of the necessity for complex agreements over the use and abuse of the earth's resources. That is why all of us should look at our immediate environment as contingent on the actions of our fellow humans as well as the actions of Mother Nature. Every intervention made by humans in an ecosystem will cause a reaction in the balance of that system. Areas of predictable stasis will help climate scientists make models of future patterns, just as planners build roads and infrastructure based on predictions of population growth and economic activity in cities. And everything conserved or maintained, as long as it has achieved balance in the system, will contribute a measure of stability.[4]

All planning in the future will be comprehensive, environmental planning. We will cease to look at city and country, park areas versus core areas, or transit corridors, because these are merely the components that make up "spaceship earth," or the biosphere. When these components are connected to climate, atmosphere, geological resources, water, and all the other things that affect regions of the globe and the planet as a whole, the entire practice of planning will enter a new phase, complete with new schemata and new terminology. Historic houses and neighborhoods will be understood within this larger framework. The closest analogy we have now to the future of these places are the so-called historic centers of great European towns like Oxford, Florence, Venice, or Bruges.

As we begin to look at regions and urban areas comprehensively, as both buildings and landscapes shaped by humans, it will become clearer that patterns of historic land use can be preserved over larger and larger areas. For example, when farms are destroyed for McMansion developments, the fabric of the agricultural landscape is damaged, but not necessarily irreparably. As local foods become more desirable, the agricultural landscape may return in areas that are historically and culturally rich. Good policy, sound practice, and conservation planning could bring historic land use patterns back, thereby strengthening both the environment and society at large in a whole region. Some European countries, such as the United Kingdom, have tied heritage conservation to regions, seeking to protect whole cultural areas rather than just cities and countryside. Theorists in the United States are starting to consider such measures.

While it may seem odd to evaluate an individual house on a small plot in relationship to whole regions or ecosystems, that is precisely how prescient planners are beginning to map the earth and its resources. What is more, historians of the built and natural environment are creating complex, layered databases and maps containing information about the past conditions of these regions. In some cases, national

Local organic farms like this one are changing the way Americans eat while promoting environmental conservation. (Courtesy of Mark Alan Hewitt.)

parks have been created using this information—witness the heritage landscape areas in France and Spain, for instance. Such parks have been a boon for tourism, while maintaining traditional crafts, art, and food stalls in the protected areas.

What if your own house were considered vital to such an urban or regional heritage corridor? Public funds might become available for facade maintenance and repairs, helping you to care for the place during your period of ownership. In a few U.S. neighborhoods and urban zones, such as Old City, Philadelphia, such programs are already in place. Indeed, coherent historic districts are spurring economic and civic rebirth throughout the country. Most of these districts contain primarily single-family houses. One by one, the maintenance, upgrades, and preservation of these historic dwellings will contribute to the greening of our nation and planet. They also contribute to the collective sense of place we all treasure in great neighborhoods.

THE NEW CIVIC RESPONSIBILITY

In 1965 Charles W. Moore, soon to be dean of the Yale School of Architecture, was asked by Yale graduate students to write an essay about monuments and urbanism in California. What monuments? What urbanism? The incredulous architect produced an essay that was not only entertaining but also profoundly prescient: "You Have to Pay for the Public Life." While many architects took issue with his thesis that Dis-

neyland was the only place where compelling public spaces could be found in Southern California, his critique of American attitudes toward the public realm was devastatingly on target. Moore was one of the first well-known architects to warn that sprawl and superhighways could destroy America's cities. "The most evident thing about Los Angeles," he wrote, "is that, in the terms of any of the traditions we have inherited, hardly anybody gives anything to the public realm."[5]

Today the United States is blighted with "public" places such as shopping malls, playing fields, county and city parks, and sports arenas where people congregate but do not experience a collective sense, a feeling of community. Increasingly, Americans cannot find "public life" in public places. They behave largely as individuals or family units, with little connection to their neighbors or the surrounding landscape. Moore's prediction that theme parks would supplant Main Street or the bandstand in the town square as places where Americans go to enjoy a communal experience has come true. You have to pay money to feel a part of something larger than yourself.

In order to turn the tide, two of Moore's students, Andres Duany and Elizabeth Plater-Zyberk (best known as the designers of the planned community of Seaside, Florida) have worked assiduously to bring civic values back to the American city. In 1994 they helped write the Charter for the New Urbanism, a profound document that has encouraged an old-fashioned sense of responsibility for urban and small-town neighborhoods—what used to be called "civics."[6] Paradoxically, what they called "new" in the charter was in fact a

273

well-established pattern of human settlement that only came under attack after the automobile and the Modern Movement in architecture. The Congress for the New Urbanism has made it a priority to promote planning that uses the lessons of great traditional cities, in an effort to combat the rapacious tendencies toward uncontrolled growth that have plagued the United States for half a century. The models often cited in their "Traditional Neighborhood Developments" are precisely the kinds of neighborhoods and districts that vintage house owners seek out: places like Back Bay in Boston, Chestnut Hill, Pennsylvania, Montclair, New Jersey, Old Santa Fe, New Mexico, and Shaker Heights, Ohio. These planned residential districts are filled with excellent vintage houses. More importantly, the houses are arranged in patterns that encourage security, community, and civic engagement. Unlike contemporary subdivisions, railroad and streetcar suburbs were designed to promote the kind of civic values that used to be part of America's democratic ethos. Traditional civics is virtually nonexistent in most U.S. suburbs, which have replaced it with rancorous planning board sessions in which competing interests threaten each other to achieve the upper hand.

Because most historic neighborhoods were built before the automobile became a necessity for U.S. families, they tend to attract buyers who believe in community and civic responsibility. Vintage homeowners are generally engaged with their towns and cities, volunteering time on boards and committees for civic improvement. They recognize that their investment goes beyond the upkeep of their own residences. Partly in order to encourage further investment in historic

Seaside, Florida is a town associated with the New Urbanism movement. (Courtesy of Mark Alan Hewitt.)

neighborhoods, many owners of older houses have created civic organizations that foster pride in the collective heritage of specific places.

There is an increasing awareness that cities thrive only when such civic engagement becomes the norm, especially as governments shrink neighborhood services. The rising number of nonprofit community organizations in U.S. cities is a sign of this trend. Even urban environmentalists have tied their improvement efforts to community organizations. Like everyone else, they recognize that people experience their sense of belonging to a place by virtue of the houses and streets that make it up. If love and attention are given to those streetscapes, commensurate with the care and art that people put into their construction over time, we all sense this. We too are at home, comfortable, and secure.

Indeed, the strongest citizen organizations in America's cities are often neighborhood coalitions whose missions are to conserve the social and architectural fabric of their home places. New York's community boards routinely fight overdevelopment when the city's planning commission has stepped away from controversies. In the Old City district of Philadelphia, the Civic Association organizes neighbors in clean-up drives, community policing, tree planting, zoning controls and many other vital services for the area. And we've mentioned in Chapter 7 the spirited groups that support Back Bay in Boston. Post-Katrina New Orleans is a poster child for the benefits of civic organizations, as the city has only been able to begin to rebuild in neighborhoods with strong community cohesion. Most of these are full of vintage houses.

WHAT'S AHEAD

While it may seem paradoxical to end this book with a glance at the future, the ultimate purpose of good conservation is to ensure the continued viability of the works of humanity in the natural environment. The "good old work" of housewrights, patrons, architects, and vernacular artisans must be protected if humans are to continue to live peacefully and resonantly with the work of their ancestors. To expand a vintage house successfully, homeowners should be looking ahead to understand the effect their actions will have on the next genera-

The historic neighborhoods of New Orleans are emerging from the Katrina disaster thanks in part to civic groups that care about their vintage houses. (Courtesy of Mark Alan Hewitt.)

tion and beyond. This is another meaning of "the long view."

We began this book by sketching the process by which vernacular builders "grew" their dwelling houses using centuries-old principles—understanding the site, the structure, the module, the roof massing, and the facade composition of their houses. We noted the technical challenges that builders and architects face when inserting new systems and materials into older buildings. We looked at the challenges of particular types of expansion—within the existing footprint, outside the footprint, in neighborhoods with continuous facades, and in outbuildings. We concluded with some advice on how to achieve authentic details using both traditional and new materials.

As the nations of the earth move cautiously into a new age of sustainable economies and ways of living, we believe that more people will insist on the protection of the built environment in concert with the so-called natural one. The key here is "in concert," not "in opposition" with. Environmental groups are increasingly teaming with building preservationists to formulate guidelines and laws that protect all the creations and interventions that humans have wrought upon the earth during hundreds of thousands of years. What's ahead for concerned citizens of the globe will depend on how successful these new partnerships and protections are in controlling the destruction of valuable resources while the population grows. Many planners are recognizing that it will not be possible to build our way out of the coming dilemmas posed by climate change, human sustenance, and the need for shelter as seven billion people procreate and multiply on an ever smaller planet.

Vintage houses are full of priceless craftsmanship, and all of it can be conserved. Here, master woodworker Paul Sellers cuts dovetail joints by hand in his Texas workshop. (Courtesy of Mark Alan Hewitt.)

A 2009 keynote before the American Institute of Architects by Peter Head, director at Arup Associates in London, made it clear that it will be neither possible nor desirable for societies to house their growing populations primarily in new buildings. He noted that perhaps 15 percent of the construction activity during the next century will involve entirely new structures. The rest will be targeted at what is already here, in cities and in the countryside: roads, bridges, power plants, railroads, infrastructure—and billions of units of housing that are sound and worth renovating. Making dwellings more energy efficient and reducing their carbon footprint is already a priority in most developed societies. But progress in this area has been slow. In the near future architects, planners, and environmental scientists will address this area with solutions that may or may not be kind to vintage houses.

One part of our aims for this book has been to create an awareness that our future depends on the careful and deliberate conservation of the best artifacts handed to us by past builders. Houses are by far the largest group of buildings on the earth. Though modern theorists have often argued that dwellings are the most likely structures to be torn down and rebuilt each generation, a new conservation ethic in the coming century will change that attitude. The result is that more and more houses, especially the ones we classify as "vintage" or historic, will need conservation and expansion. Looking ahead, there is an inevitability to the kinds of endeavors we advocate here. With foresight and careful preparation, countries like the United States can meet future conservation challenges. Without it, our society will suffer not only the loss of precious houses, but also an impoverishment in the culture at large.

In 1967 Ian McHarg published a far-reaching study of humanity's interaction with the environment, *Design with Nature*. His warnings about the coming crisis in the balance of natural and human-made forces in the biosphere were prophetic, if too conservative. He recognized sooner than most that creating human artifacts, including buildings, involves "the employment of energy and matter in raising levels of order." Energy, including the vast embodied energy already invested in buildings and infrastructure, would be inventoried and studied, parsed and doled out in ever-decreasing amounts according to increasing needs. What he called "the ecological view" of the earth and its resources would come to govern the work of architects and planners as well as politicians and economists.[7]

Ultimately, McHarg predicted, all human actions would be evaluated in terms of their net effect on the biosphere. Actions that upset the balances in ecosystems would be more costly and destructive than those that conserved existing resources. Conservation would increasingly govern the affairs of governments and societies. He wrote: "The world is abundant, we require only a deference born of understanding to fulfill man's promise. Man is that uniquely conscious creature who can perceive and express. He must become the steward of the biosphere. To do this he must design with nature."[8] We would add that he must design with the understanding that past creations, including vintage houses, are a constituent part of the biosphere, and thus have entered a larger compass, beyond the natural, to become a new "nature." As Robert Harrison has written, "We are both inside and outside of nature: this is our dismay, that we come up against its insurmountable limit. We gain our freedom not by overcoming but by recognizing that limit."[9]

By caring for our own houses, and increasing our respect and understanding of the importance of historic houses, we recognize the limits of our ability to manage the natural and human-made biosphere. We are designing with history in mind, and respecting the role that our ancestors had in creating our whole environment. In this way we are true to our own nature as well as that of the world around us.

FURTHER READING

Abramovich, Ingrid. *Restoring a House in the City.* New York: Artisan, 2009.

Birnbaum, Charles, and Robin Karson, eds. *Pioneers of American Landscape Design.* New York: McGraw Hill, 2000.

Brand, Stewart. *How Buildings Learn: What Happens after They're Built.* New York: Penguin, 1994.

Bunting, Bainbridge. *Houses of Boston's Back Bay: An Architectural History.* Cambridge: Harvard University Press, 1967.

Ching, Francis D. K., and Cassandra Adams. *Building Construction Illustrated.* 3rd ed. New York: Wiley, 2001.

Clark, Clifford Edward, Jr. *The American Family Home, 1800–1960.* Chapel Hill: University of North Carolina Press, 1986.

Cusato, Marianne and Ben Pentreath. *Get Your House Right: Architectural Elements to Use and Avoid.* New York: Sterling, 2007.

Dietz, Albert G. *Dwelling House Construction.* Cambridge: MIT Press, 1971.

Fisher, Charles E., and Hugh C. Miller, eds. *Caring for Your Historic House.* New York: Harry N. Abrams, 1998.

Garrett, Elizabeth Donaghy. *At Home: The American Family, 1750–1870.* New York: Harry N. Abrams, 1989.

Gowans, Alan. *The Comfortable House: North American Suburban Architecture, 1890–1930.* Cambridge: MIT Press, 1986.

Hale, Jonathan. *The Old Way of Seeing: How Architecture Lost Its Meaning (And How to Get It Back).* Boston: Houghton Mifflin, 1994.

Hewitt, Mark Alan. *The Architect and the American Country House, 1890–1940.* New Haven: Yale University Press, 1990.

Holohan, Dan. *The Lost Art of Steam Heating.* Bethpage, N.Y.: Dan Holohan Associates, 2002.

Howe, Barbara J., et al. *Houses and Homes: Exploring Their History.* Nashville: American Association for State and Local History, 1987.

Hull, Brent. *Historic Millwork.* New York: Wiley, 2003.

Hunter, Christine. *Ranches, Rowhouses, and Railroad Flats: American Homes: How They Shape Our Landscapes and Neighborhoods.* New York: W. W. Norton, 1999.

Jenrette, Richard Hampton. *Adventures with Old Houses.* Charleston, S.C.: Wyrick and Company, 2005.

Jester, Thomas C., ed. *Twentieth-Century Building Materials.* New York: McGraw-Hill, 1995.

London, Mark. *Masonry: How to Care for Old and Historic Brick and Stone.* Washington, DC: Preservation Press, 1988.

Massey, James C., and Shirley Maxwell. *House Styles in America.* New York: Dovetail Publishers 1999.

McAlester, Virginia and Lee. *A Field Guide to American Houses.* New York: Knopf, 1995.

Moore, Charles, Gerald Allen, and Donlyn Lyndon. *The Place of Houses.* New York: Holt, Rinehart & Winston, 1974.

Moss, Roger W. *Lighting for Historic Buildings.* Washington, DC: Preservation Press, 1988.

——, ed. *Paint in America: The Colors of Historic Buildings.* New York: Wiley, 1994.

Moss, Roger W., and Gail Caskey Winkler. *Victorian Exterior Decoration.* New York: Henry Holt, 1987.

——, *Victorian Interior Decoration.* New York: Henry Holt, 1986.

Murphy, Kevin D. *The American Townhouse.* New York: Harry N. Abrams, 2005.

Nash, George. *Renovating Old Houses.* Newtown, Conn.: Taunton Press, 2003.

Nylander, Jane C. *Fabrics for Historic Buildings.* Washington, DC: Preservation Press, 1983.

Nylander, Richard C. *Wallpapers for Historic Buildings.* Washington, DC: Preservation Press, 1983.

Rosenstiel, Helene von, and Gail Caskey Winkler. *Floor Coverings for Historic Buildings.* Washington, DC: Preservation Press, 1988.

Roth, Leland M. *A Concise History of American Architecture.* New York: Westview Press, 1979.

Semes, Steven. *The Future of the Past: A Conservation Ethic for Architecture, Urbanism, and Historic Preservation.* New York: W. W. Norton, 2010.

Shirley, Frank. *New Rooms for Old Houses.* Newtown, Conn.: Taunton Press, 2007.

Wright, Gwendolyn. *Building the Dream: A Social History of Housing in America.* Cambridge: MIT Press, 1983.

RESOURCES FOR VINTAGE HOUSE OWNERS

ARCHITECTS FEATURED IN THIS BOOK

Jacob Albert
Albert, Righter & Tittman Architects, Inc.
8 Winter Street
3rd Floor
Boston, MA 02108

David Bucek
Stern and Bucek Architects
1610 Commerce Street
Houston, TX 77002

Brian Connolly
Zivkovic Connolly Architects PC
511 West 25th Street
Suite 201
New York, NY 10001

Nick Cusano
Cusano Associates
5 Wilson Street
Mendham, NJ 07945

Anne Fairfax
Fairfax & Sammons
67 Gansevoort Street
New York, NY 10014

Mark Finlay
Mark P. Finlay Architects
96 Old Post Road
Suite 200
Southport, CT 06890

Allan Greenberg
Allan Greenberg Architect
1050 Thomas Jefferson Street NW
Washington, DC 20007

Milton Grenfell
Grenfell Architecture
910 Seventeenth Street NW
Suite 1090
Washington, DC 20006

Mark Alan Hewitt
Mark Alan Hewitt Architects
114 Claremont Road
Bernardsville, NJ 07924

Philip Kennedy-Grant
Kennedy-Grant Architecture
35 Mill Street
Bernardsville, NJ 07924

Ian Mactavish
Voith & Mactavish Architects LLP
1616 Walnut Street
24th Floor
Philadelphia, PA 19103

Howard Miller
The Johnson Partnership
1212 NE 65th Street
Seattle, WA 98116

John Milner
John Milner Architects
104 Lakeview Drive
Chadds Ford, PA 19137

John Murray
John B. Murray Architects LLC
48 West 37th Street
10th Floor
New York, NY 10018

Peter Pennoyer
Peter Pennoyer Architects
432 Park Avenue South
11th Floor
New York, NY 10016

Thomas Norman Rajkovich
Thomas Norman Rajkovich Architect
518–526 Davis Street
Suite 206
Evanston, IL 60201

Gil Schafer
G.P. Schafer Architect PC
270 Lafayette Street
Suite 1302
New York, NY 10012

Hiland Turner
Hiland Hall Turner Architects
47 Mine Brook Road
Bernardsville, NJ 07924

Mark Wright
Wright & Robinson Architects
63 Adams Place
Glen Ridge, NJ 07028

AIR CONDITIONING

Daikin AC (split AC systems)
972-245-1510
www.daikinac.com

Mitsubishi (split AC systems)
www.mehvac.com
866-323-4822

Spacepak (mini-duct AC systems)
www.spacepak.com
800-465-8558

Trane (conventional AC, geothermal)
www.trane.com

Unico Inc.(mini-duct AC systems)
www.unicosystem.com
800-527-0896

Water Furnace (geothermal)
www.waterfurnace.com
800-GEO-SAVE

ARCHITECTURAL HISTORY, TECHNICAL CONSULTING

Gordon Bock
National Archives Associates
3120 Lee Street
Silver Spring, MD 20910
www.gordonbock.com

BATH FIXTURES

DEA Bathroom Machineries (specialty toilets and sinks)
www.deabath.com
209-754-0601

Eljer (triangular tank toilets)
www.eljer.com
800-423-5537

Geberit Manufacturing (concealed tank toilets)
www.us.geberit.com
800-225-7215

The Renovator's Supply, Inc. (vast selection of antique fixtures)
www.rensup.com
800-659-2211

BRICKS AND MORTAR

The Belden Brick Co., Ohio
www.beldenbrick.com
330-456-0031

Gavin Historical Bricks (salvage brick)
www.historicalbrick.com
319-354-5251

Old Carolina Brick Co. (handmade bricks)
www.handmadebrick.com
704-636-8550

Old Virginia Brick Co. (wirecut and handmade bricks)
www.oldvirginiabrick.com
540-389-2357

Virginia Lime Works (traditional lime mortars)
www.virginialimeworks.com
434-929-8113

CERAMIC TILE

American Restoration Tile, Inc., Arizona
www.restorationtile.com
501-455-1000

Ruth Frances Greenberg, Portland (custom tile mosaics)
www.ruthfrancesgreenberg.com
503-235-2882

Tile Heritage Foundation (database on antique tile)
www.tileheritage.org
707-431-8453

Tile Source, South Carolina (encaustic Victorian tiles)
www.tile-source.com
843-681-4034

CLADDING AND SALVAGED TIMBER

Sylvan Brandt, Lititz, Pennsylvania (new milled stock)
www.sylvanbrandt.com
717-626-4520

Carlisle Restoration Lumber, Vermont (salvage timber)
www.wideplankflooring.com
800-595-9663

James Hardie Building Products (fiber cement siding)
www.jameshardie.com
888-542-7343

DECORATIVE PAINTING AND GILDING

John Canning Studios, Connecticut
www.canning-studios.com
203-272-9868

Evergreene Architectural Arts, New York
www.evergreene.com
212-244-2800

John Tiedmann, Inc., New Jersey
www.johntiedemann.com
877-600-2666

DOORS

Historic Doors (custom wood doors)
www.historicdoors.com
610-756-6187

Reilly Windows and Doors
www.reillywoodworks.com
631-208-0710

Vintage Woodworks (Victorian screen doors)
www.vintagewoodworks.com
903-356-2158

FLOORING

Bear Creek Lumber (hardwood flooring)
www.bearcreeklumber.com
800-597-7191

Echeguren Slate, Inc. (exotic slate and stone)
www.echeguren.com
415-206-9343

Forbo (linoleum)
www.forbo.com
41 58 787 25 25

Hull Forest Products, Inc. (FSC certified timber)
www.hullforest.com
860-974-0127

Mountain Lumber Co. (heart pine flooring)
www.mountainlumber.com
828-963-75224

Old Barn Wood (salvaged flooring)
www.old-barn-wood.com
608-356-8849

GLAZING AND STAINED GLASS

S. A. Bendheim, Ltd. (restoration glass)
www.restorationglass.com
800-606-7621

J. & R. Lamb Studios, New Jersey
www.lamstudios.com
201-891-8595

Rohlf's Stained & Leaded Glass Studio, New York
www.rohlfstudio.com
800-969-4106

Conrad Schmitt Studios, Inc., Milwaukee
www.conradschmitt.com
800-969-3033

HARDWARE

Ball & Ball, Pennsylvania (Early American hardware)
www.ballandball.com
800-257-3711

Blaine Window Hardware, Hagerstown, MD
www.blainewindow.com
800-678-1919

Craftsman Hardware (Arts and Crafts reproductions)
www.craftsmanhardware.com
660-376-2481

Crown City Hardware (Victorian and beyond)
www.crowncityhardware.com
626-794-0234

P. E. Guerin, Inc. (custom decorative hardware)
www.peguerin.com
212-243-5720

House of Antique Hardware (specialty hardware)
www.houseofantiquehardware.com
888-223-2545

Nanz Hardware (custom brass hardware)
www.nanz.com
212-367-7000

Walter Phelps Co. (window hardware) Brattleboro, VT
www.phelpscompany.com
802-257-4314

Wm. J. Rigby Co. (new old stock) Cooperstown, NY
www.wmjrigby.com
607-547-1900

HYDRONIC HEATING SYSTEMS

Beacon/Morris (kickspace heater)
www.beacon-morris.com
413-562-5423

Bell & Gossett (steam and hot water controls)
www.bellgossett.com
847-966-3700

Burnham (boilers, reproduction radiators)
www.usboiler.burnham.com
717-397-4701

Danfoss Automatic Controls (thermostatic radiator vents)
www.danfoss.com
905-285-2050

Mestek (kickspace heaters)
www.mestek.com

Tekmar Control Systems, Inc. (outdoor reset controllers)
www.tekmarcontrols.com
250-545-7749

Weill-McLain (boilers)
www.weil-mcclain.com
219-879-6561

LIGHTING FIXTURES

Ball & Ball Lighting, Pennsylvania (candle type fixtures)
www.ballandball.com
800-257-3711

The Federalist (eighteenth-century fixtures)
www.thefederalistonline.com
203-625-4727

Rambusch Lighting Jersey City, NJ (custom antique lighting)
www.rambuschlighting.com
201-333-2525

Rejuvenation, Seattle (Victorian and Early Modern fixtures)
www.rejuvenation.com
888-401-1900

St. Louis Antique Lighting Company (Victorian fixtures)
www.slalco.com
314-863-1414

METALWORK

Architectural Iron Company
www.architecturaliron.com
800-442-4766

Historical Arts and Castings, Utah (cast iron, bronze, brass)
www.historicalarts.com
800-225-1414

Les Metailliers Champenois (traditional French *forgerons*)
www.l-m-c.com
973-279-3573

Robinson Iron
www.robinsoniron.com
800-824-2157

MILLWORK

Agrel Architectural Carving, Ltd.
www.agrelcarving.com
415-457-4422

Hull Historical Architectural Millwork
www.hullhistorical.com
817-332-1495

Zepsa Architectural Millwork
www.zepsa.com
(704) 583.9220

PLASTER REPAIR AND MOLDINGS

The Decorator's Supply Company, Chicago
www.decoratorssupply.com
773-847-6300

Foster Reeve Architectural Plaster, Brooklyn
718-609-0090; www.fraplaster.com

San Marco Buildings Coating Systems, Atlanta
www.san-marcousa.com
698-907-5811

ROOFING

Cedar Shake & Shingle Bureau (wood roofing products)
www.cedarbureau.org
604-820-7700

CopperCraft (copper leaders, gutters, accessories)
www.coppercraft.com
800-486-2723

The Durable Restoration Company (slate, roof tile, specialty roofing)
www.durablerestoration.com
614-299-5522

Evergreen Slate (Vermont and Welsh slate)
www.evergreenslate.com
518-642-2530

Gladding McBean (terra cotta products)
www.gladdingmcbean.com
800-776-1133

Hendricks Tile (steel reinforced concrete tiles)
www.hendrickstile.com
800-276-8262

Ludowici Roof Tile (clay roof tiles)
www.ludowici.com
800-945-8453

W. F. Norman Corp. (metal roofing)
www.fwnorman.com
800-641-4038

Vande Hey Raleigh (clay and concrete roof tile)
www.vrmtile.com
920-766-0156

STONE AND CAST STONE

Bybee Stone Company, Inc. (Indiana limestone)
www.bybeestone.com
800-457-4530

Haddonstone (cast stone)
www.haddonstone.com
856-931-7011

Gerald Siciliano (sculptor)
www.geraldsiciliano.com
718-636-4561

Traditional Cut Stone Ltd. (Ontario, Canada)
www.traditionalcutstone.com
416-652-8434

WINDOWS

Allied Window (high quality aluminum storm windows)
www.alliedwindow.com
800.445.5411

Marvin (leading manufacturer of authentic wood windows)
www.marvin.com
800-537-7828

Seekircher Steel Windows (steel sash repair and replacement)
www.seekirchersteelwindow.com
914-734-8004

Zeluck Doors & Windows (custom wood and metal windows)
www.zeluck.com
800-233-0101

GLOSSARY

ACROTERION: A decorative element placed at the peak of a pediment in a classical building.

ARCHITRAVE: The main beam that rests on column capitals and forms the lowest part of an entablature.

ART DECO: An international style of architecture and decoration influenced by the 1925 Exposition Internationale des Arts Décoratifs in Paris. Also called Streamlined Moderne, Zigzag Moderne, Jazz Moderne.

ARTS AND CRAFTS: Late nineteenth- and early twentieth-century movement in design that was associated with the English writers John Ruskin and William Morris, emphasizing the connection between work and useful objects, especially handicrafts. Also called Mission, Craftsman, Stickley.

ATTIC BASE: The base of a column or pilaster that is associated with Greek architecture of the Attic period, consisting of alternating concave and convex moldings.

BALUSTRADE: A railing composed of a series of upright members, often in a vase shape, with a top rail and often a bottom rail.

BARGEBOARD: A decorative board running along the edge of a gable (often called vergeboard).

BATTLEMENT: A parapet wall at the edge of a roof with slots designed to afford defensive warfare during a siege.

BAUHAUS: Work associated with the artists and architects training or teaching at the German school founded by Walter Gropius and active from 1919 until 1933.

BAY: A unit of a building facade, defined by a regular spacing of windows, columns, or piers.

BAY WINDOW: An exterior wall projection filled with windows; if curved, called a bow window; in English houses, called an oriel window.

BEAUX-ARTS CLASSICISM: A term associated with the classical architecture and art theory taught at the École des Beaux-Arts in Paris (and its American offshoots), mainly from 1870 to 1930, when many Americans attended the school.

BOND: The pattern of overlapping brick joints that binds them together to form a wall (e.g., common bond, Flemish bond, English bond).

BRACKET: A decorative element supporting a wall projection, cornice, or other exterior element.

BUTTRESS: A mass of masonry or brickwork projecting from or built against a wall to strengthen it.

CANTILEVER: A projecting structural member, the end of which is supported on a fulcrum and held by a downward force behind the fulcrum.

CAPITAL: The crowning portion of a column or pilaster.

CARPENTER'S GOTHIC: A wooden version of Gothic Revival styles popular during the 1840s to 1870s in the United States, made possible by the use of lathes, jigsaws, and molding machines. Also called Gingerbread, Steamboat Gothic.

CARRARA GLASS: Pigmented structural glass (commonly black) with a reflective finish, used commonly in the 1930s and 1940s.

CASEMENT WINDOW: A window with hinges at one side.

CINQUEFOIL: Decorative element representing a five-leafed form.

CLAPBOARD SIDING: Tapered wood boards lapped one over another to form horizontal siding.

CLERESTORY: Windows located at the highest point of an exterior wall, usually for providing daylight to the interior.

COLONIAL REVIVAL: Style associated with the revival of interest in early American art and architecture following the 1876 Centennial Exposition in Philadelphia; generally appropriating elements and decoration from British colonial sources as interpreted by American artisans.

COLUMN ELEMENTS:
PLINTH: The lower square form at the base of a column.
FLUTING: Concave grooves running vertically up a column.
CAPITAL: The top, crowning feature of a column.

CORBEL: An incremented wall projection used to support additional weight, most commonly constructed of brick.

CORNICE: The decorative projecting element at the top of an exterior wall.

CRAFTSMAN: Furniture, architecture, and decorative arts associated with Gustav Stickley and his *Craftsman Magazine* (1901–1916); see also Arts and Crafts.

CRESTING: An ornamental ridging at the top of a wall or the peak of a roof.

CUPOLA: A small tower rising above a roof, usually with a band of small windows or openings, often crowned by a dome.

DENTILS: Rectangular toothlike elements forming a decorative horizontal band in a cornice.

DORMER WINDOW: A window and window structure that project from the slope of a roof.

DOUBLE-HUNG WINDOW: Window with two sashes, one above the other, each of which slides vertically.

EASTLAKE: A decorative arts term from the 1860s to 1880s sometimes associated with the British Gothicist Charles Eastlake.

EAVE: Lower edge of a roof extending beyond the exterior wall.

ECLECTICISM: A term applied to "the architecture of choice," meaning a plurality of elements and associations derived from high-style Western, Eastern, and vernacular sources, often in a single building.

ENGAGED COLUMN: A column integral with a wall surface, usually half round in form.

ENTABLATURE: The topmost horizontal portion of a classical building; it includes the architrave, the frieze, and the cornice. From the Latin word for table.

ENTASIS: The subtle bulge or taper in the profile of a classical column.

FACADE: Usually the front elevation or face of a building.

FANLIGHT: Fan-shaped window, usually located over an entrance door.

FASCIA BOARD: A flat, horizontal board between moldings, typically used with classical styles.

FEDERAL: An American neoclassical style popular in art and architecture from New England to Virginia during the early years of the American Republic, from 1790 until 1820. Also called Adamesque, Jeffersonian.

FINIAL: A vertical ornament placed at the peak of a roof, or on parapets.

FRIEZE: A decorative horizontal band located just below a cornice.

GABLE: The triangular section of exterior wall just under a double-sloped roof.

GAMBREL ROOF: A double-sloped barnlike roof, often associated with Dutch colonial architecture.

GEORGIAN: Strictly the period associated with the Hanoverian dynasty in Britain, from George I in 1714 until George IV in 1830. More generally, a classical style that uses brick surfaces enlivened by white stone or wood details.

GOTHIC REVIVAL: A generic term for a widespread architectural movement in Europe and the United States during the mid-nineteenth century, often associated with A. W. N. Pugin in England, which revived interest in medieval church forms and decoration. Also called High Victorian Gothic, Victorian Gothic, Ecclesiological.

GREEK REVIVAL: In North America, a widespread architectural movement that began in the early years of the nineteenth century, stemming from British neoclassical sources associated with Greek excavations in the mid-eighteenth century. Attains its greatest popularity during the 1830s, but seen until mid-century.

GROIN VAULT: A vault in which two arches meet on a perpendicular axis to form a crossing.

HIP ROOF: A roof with slopes in the direction of each elevation, commonly in four directions.

I-HOUSE: A two-story vernacular house type, usually one room deep, with a central hallway.

IN ANTIS: A Latin term for columns that are flanked by walls, usually marked with pilasters at their ends.

ITALIANATE: A generic term for eclectic neo-Renaissance or neo-Romanesque styles originating in England and Germany, and popular in America from the 1840s to the 1860s; generally featuring heavy molded window heads or pediments, and overhanging bracketed cornices. Also called Bracketed, Hudson River Bracketed, Round Arched, Villa Style.

KEYSTONE: Center stone in a masonry arch.

LABEL: A molding over a door or window.

LANTERN: A small turret with openings or windows all around, crowning a roof peak or dome.

LINTEL: The horizontal support over a door or window.

MANSARD ROOF: A steeply sloped roof covering the exterior wall of the top floor of a building, named after the French architect François Mansart and commonly associated with the Second Empire style.

MISSION REVIVAL: A term associated with the popular interest in colonial Spanish missions in California and the Southwest from the 1890s to the 1920s.

MODERNISM: Strictly speaking, the architecture of the European avant-garde from 1910 until World War II; generally partaking of an "engineer's aesthetic" of functionalist, abstract, and planar forms. Also called International Style, Modern, Modern Movement.

MODILLIONS: A series of simple brackets usually found in a cornice.

MULLION: The vertical member separating windows, doors, or other panels set in series.

MUNTIN: Wood pieces separating panes of glass in window sash.

NARTHEX: The entry vestibule of a church.

NEWEL POST: Wooden post located at the top or bottom of a stairway balustrade.

OCULUS: A round window.

ORIEL WINDOW: A projection from an upper floor of an exterior wall surface that contains one or more windows.

PALLADIAN: Associated with the Italian architect Andrea Palladio (1508–1580); also Palladianism, one of the most significant classical movements in Anglo-American architecture, from 1700 to 1760.

PALLADIAN WINDOW: Large window unit with an arched window in the center and smaller windows on each side, often called a Serliana in Italian.

PARAPET: An extension of an exterior wall projecting above the roof plane, commonly used to hide the plane of a low-sloped or flat roof.

PEDIMENT: The gable form at the top of the facade of a classical structure; also used over windows and doors.

PERIPTERAL TEMPLE: A temple form with columns encircling a central room or naos.

PICTURESQUE: Not a style but a philosophy of design popularized during the late eighteenth century in England and the Continent, usually associated with landscape design and painting, stressing variegated, irregular, and asymmetrical groupings of forms and natural settings.

PILASTER: A flat, rectangular partial column attached to a wall surface.

PITCH OF ROOF: The angle of a roof slope, expressed in a ratio of vertical to horizontal (e.g., 6:12).

PORTE COCHERE: A covered entrance for coaches or vehicles.

PORTICO: A covered porch attached to the main facade of a building, usually supported by columns.

PRAIRIE SCHOOL: The Midwestern school of architects associated with Louis Sullivan and Frank Lloyd Wright, practicing mainly between 1900 and the 1920s in and around Chicago.

QUATREFOIL: A decorative element representing a four-leafed form.

QUEEN ANNE: An ambiguous but widely used term for eclectic architecture from 1860 through 1900 in the United States, originally associated with the more specific British architects such as Richard Norman Shaw during the 1870s, often featuring broad areas of shingles, elaborate carved moldings, and decorative tiles.

QUOINS: Decorative stones at the corner of a building.

RAKE: The extension at the end of a pediment or gable roof.

RICHARDSONIAN ROMANESQUE: The neo-Romanesque work associated with Henry Hobson Richardson, primarily from the 1870s to the 1890s, usually featuring robust masonry arches, stout columns, and medieval details.

RUSTICATION: Large stone blocks or stone forms with deep reveal masonry joints.

SECOND EMPIRE: The period in France between 1852 and 1870, during the rule of Napoleon III; in the United States often associated with heavily ornamented government buildings and houses during the 1850s and 1860s.

SEGMENTAL ARCH: A partial arch form, usually a segment of a circle but sometimes formed of ellipsoidal components.

SHAKE: Hand-split wood shingle.

SHED ROOF: A single-pitched roof, often over a room attached to the main structure.

SHINGLE STYLE: An American style influenced by British Queen Anne architecture, always featuring broad expanses of wood shingles on both roof and wall surfaces; most popular from 1870 to 1890.

SIDELIGHT: Narrow vertical window located immediately adjacent to an entrance door.

SINGLE-HUNG WINDOW: Window with two sashes, one above the other; the lower slides upward, and the upper downward.

SOFFIT: The underside of an architectural element.

SPANISH COLONIAL REVIVAL: A popular architectural style in California during the 1920s, with motifs taken from Spanish missions and other old colonial buildings in the Southwest. Also called Mediterranean Revival, Spanish Revival, Mission Revival.

STICK STYLE: A narrow term applied to American domestic architecture in the Northeast from 1850 until 1870, associated with elaborate wood ornament, bay windows, gables, and dormers.

TERRA-COTTA: Baked clay blocks or tiles used for roof tiles or decorative surfaces.

TRABEATION: Architecture that is constructed of walls, posts, and beams rather than arches and vaults.

TRACERY: Traditional intersecting ornamental divisions found in Gothic windows.

TRANSOM: A horizontal window located immediately above a door.

TREFOIL: Decorative element representing a three-leafed form.

TUDOR REVIVAL: A popular style for American houses during the late nineteenth and early twentieth centuries, associated with the manor houses of the Tudor and Jacobean periods in England, generally featuring half-timbering, broad areas of brick or stucco, prominent steeply pitched gables, and strapwork ornament. Also called Tudorbethan, Jacobean Revival, Neo-Tudor, English Tudor, Elizabethan.

TURRET: A small tower located at the corner of a building, often containing a staircase.

VERGEBOARD: See bargeboard.

VERNACULAR: Not a style but a way of building: vernacular artisans hand-building methods and traditions down from generation to generation without explicit rules. Also called "architecture without architects."

WAINSCOT: A horizontal molding placed approximately at waist height, running around a room or space.

NOTES

1: Conserving Vintage Houses

1. For a discussion of the recent boom, see Daniel McGinn, *House Lust: America's Obsession with Our Homes* (New York: Doubleday, 2008), 89–119.
2. See Robert MacKay, Anthony Baker, and Carol A. Traynor, eds., *Long Island Country Houses and Their Architects, 1860–1940* (New York: W. W. Norton, 1997).
3. Richard Hampton Jenrette, *Adventures with Old Houses* (Charleston, SC: Wyrick and Company, 2005), 57.

2: How Do Houses Grow?

1. Stewart Brand, *How Buildings Learn: What Happens After They're Built* (New York: Penguin, 1994), 12–23.
2. Witold Rybczynski, *Home: A Short History of an Idea* (New York: Viking Penguin, 1986), 22–49.
3. For example, see Christopher Alexander, *A Pattern Language* (New York: Oxford University Press, 1980).
4. Fred B. Kniffen, "Folk Housing: Key to Diffusion," in *Common Places: Readings in American Vernacular Architecture*, ed. Dell Upton and John Michael Vlach (Athens: University of Georgia Press, 1986), 3–26.
5. Edward R. Ford, *The Details of Modern Architecture*, vol. 1 (Cambridge: MIT Press, 1990).

6. See John R. Stilgoe, *Common Landscape of America, 1540–1845* (New Haven: Yale University Press, 1980).
7. Dolores Hayden, *A Field Guide to Sprawl* (New York: W. W. Norton, 2004), 42.
8. Thomas Hubka, *Big House, Little House, Back House, Barn* (Hanover, NH: University Press of New England, 1984), 70–85.
9. See Henry Glassie, *Folk Housing in Middle Virginia* (Knoxville: University of Tennessee Press, 1975).
10. Virginia and Ward McAllister, *A Field Guide to American Houses* (New York: Knopf, 1995).
11. Clare Cooper Marcus, *House as a Mirror of Self* (Berkeley: Cornari Press, 1995), 17.
12. Philippe Boudon, *Lived-in Architecture: Le Corbusier's Pessac Revisited*, trans. Gerald Onn (Cambridge: MIT Press, 1972).
13. Marianne Cusato and Ben Pentreath, *Get Your House Right: Architectural Elements to Use and Avoid* (New York: Sterling, 2007).
14. Jonathan Hale, *The Old Way of Seeing* (Boston: Houghton Mifflin, 1994).

4: New Spaces in Old Places

1. See Mark Alan Hewitt, *The Architect and the American Country House, 1890–1940* (New Haven: Yale University Press, 1990).

2. See Mark Alan Hewitt, "Harrie T. Lindeberg," *Oxford American National Biography;* and *Domestic Architecture of H. T. Lindeberg* (1940), repr. with introduction by Mark Alan Hewitt (New York: Acanthus Press, 1996).

3. Kenneth T. Jackson, *Crabgrass Frontier: The Suburbanization of the United States* (New York: Oxford University Press, 1979), 234–238.

5: Additions That Stay in Tune

1. David Lowenthal, *The Past Is a Foreign Country* (Cambridge: Cambridge University Press, 1985).

2. James Howard Kunstler, *The Geography of Nowhere* (New York: Touchstone, 1993).

3. Frank Shirley, *New Rooms for Old Houses* (Newtown, CT: Taunton Press, 2007), 4.

4. See Mark Alan Hewitt, *The Architecture of Mott B. Schmidt* (New York: Rizzoli, 1991), 146–55, plate 20.

5. Christopher Hussey, *The Life of Sir Edwin Lutyens* (London: Country Life Ltd., 1959), 115 and 116.

6. Lawrence Weaver, *Houses and Gardens by E. L. Lutyens* (London: Country Life Ltd., 1913), 275–83; and Gavin Stamp, *Edwin Lutyens: Country Houses* (New York: Monacelli, 2001), 128–33.

6: Blowing Hot and Cold

1. Joan DeJean, *The Age of Comfort: When Paris Discovered Casual–and the Modern Home Began* (New York: Bloomsbury, 2009), 93–101.

7: Facing the Neighborhood

1. David P. Handlin, *The American Home: Architecture and Society, 1815–1915* (Boston: Little, Brown, 1979), 3–88.

2. Alan Gowans, *The Comfortable House: North American Suburban Architecture, 1890–1930* (Cambridge: MIT Press, 1986).

3. For classic studies of these developments, see Donald J. Olsen, *Town Planning in London: The Eighteenth and Nineteenth Centuries* (1964), repr. (New Haven: Yale University Press, 1982), 39–73; and John Summerson, *Georgian London* (Baltimore: Penguin, 1962).

4. On New Orleans houses, see S. Frederick Starr, *Southern Comfort: The Garden District of New Orleans, 1800–1900* (Cambridge: MIT Press, 1989); and Dell Upton, *Another City: Urban Life and Urban Spaces in the New American Republic* (New Haven: Yale University Press, 2008).

5. Christine Hunter, *Ranches, Rowhouses, and Railroad Flats: American Homes: How They Shape Our Landscapes and Neighborhoods* (New York: W. W. Norton, 1999), 184.

6. Rachel Simmons Schade, AIA, *Philadelphia Rowhouse Manual: A Practical Guide for Homeowners* (Philadelphia: City Planning Commission, 2003), 3.

7. Arthur P. Ziegler, Jr., *Historic Preservation in Inner City Areas: A Manual of Practice* (Pittsburgh: Ober Park Associates, 1974), 10–29.

8. Bainbridge Bunting, *Houses of Boston's Back Bay: An Architectural History* (Cambridge: Harvard University Press, 1967), 21–61.

9. Ibid., 63–286.

10. Sara Chase and Kim Lovejoy, *Brownstone: An Owner's Care and Repair Guide* (Boston: Society for the Preservation of New England Antiquities, 1989).

11. Dorothy Stroud, *Sir John Soane, Architect* (London: Faber & Faber, 1984), 89–96.

12. For an excellent treatment of the entire design process and ensuing controversy, see Steven Semes, "The Art of Conversation," *Period Homes Magazine*, September 2006, available at www.period-homes.com.

8: Outstanding Outbuildings

1. J. B. Jackson, "The Domestication of the Garage," in *The Necessity for Ruins and Other Essays* (Amherst: University of Massachusetts Press, 1980), 102–12.

2. The Guild offers a number of fine publications at its bookstore, www.tfguild.org; one of them is Tedd Benson, *Timberframe: The Art and Craft of the Post-and-Beam Home* (Newtown, CT: Taunton Press, 1999).

3. On Sloane's life and work see Harold N. Cooledge, Jr., *Samuel Sloan: Architect of Philadelphia, 1815–1884* (Philadelphia: University of Pennsylvania Press, 1986); and "Sloan, Samuel," in *Biographical Dictionary of Philadelphia Architects, 1700–1930*, ed. Sandra L. Tatman and Roger W. Moss (Boston: G. K. Hall, 1985), 730–35.

4. See Rhonda Lefever, National Register Nomination for Mount Fair, August 1, 1990, "Statement of Significance." Available at www.dhr.virginia.gov.

10: The Long View

1. The key document in the development of this product of the Annales school is Fernand Braudel, *La Méditerranée et le Monde Méditerranéen à l'époque de Philippe II* (1949), published in English as *The Mediterranean and the Mediterranean World in the Age of Phillip II*, trans. Siân Reynolds (Berkeley: University of California Press, 1996).

2. Steven Semes, *The Future of the Past: A Conservation Ethic for Architecture, Urbanism, and Historic Preservation* (New York: W. W. Norton, 2010).

3. Peter G. Brown and Geoffrey Garver, *Right Relationship: Building a Whole Earth Economy* (San Francisco: Berret Kohler, 2009). The book was undertaken by the Moral Economy Project of the Quaker Institute for the Future. For further details see www.moraleconomy.org.

4. For more on this argument, see Mark A. Hewitt, "Architecture for a Contingent Environment," *Journal of Architectural Education* 47, no. 4 (May 1994): 197–209.

5. *You Have to Pay for the Public Life: Selected Essays of Charles W. Moore*, ed. Kevin Keim (Cambridge: MIT Press, 2001), 111–41; quote on 112.

6. See Andres Duany, Elizabeth Plater-Zyberk, and Jeff Speck, *Suburban Nation: The Rise of Sprawl and the Decline of the American Dream* (New York: North Point Press, 2000).

7. Ian McHarg, *Design with Nature* (New York: Wiley, 1992), 196.

8. Ibid., 5.

9. Robert Harrison, "Toward a Philosophy of Nature," in *Uncommon Ground: Rethinking the Human Place in Nature*, ed. William Cronon (New York: W. W. Norton, 1996), 436.

Abbey House, England, 127
ABS plastic shingles, 244
Adam, Robert, 124
Adami, Mark, 194
additions. *See* expansion of houses
Adler, David, 207
age value, 22, 28
air conditioning, 161, 165–73
    calculating need for, 172
    conventional ducts, 166–67
    ductless (split) systems, 170
    geothermal alternative, 170–73
    humidity control, 172
    mini-duct systems, 167, *168*, 169–70
    retrofitting, 166, 169
air handler, 167, *169*
Aladdin, 16, *17*
Alexander, Christopher, 35
American College of the Building Arts, 198
American Institute of Architects, 73, 136, 268
American Tudor houses, 145
Amory S. Carhart Mansion, New York City,
    194–97, 194–95, 197, 204
anchor-bent framing, *41*, 41
applied-aggregate finishes, 265
aquastat, 157
Arthur Newbold house, Laverock, Pennsylvania,
    142

Arts and Crafts movement, 16–17, 59, 236, 248,
    252, 256, *261*, 262, 263
asbestos-cement shingles, 244
ashlar masonry, *42, 262*, 262–63
asphalt roofing, 240, 242–44
attached houses, 176–83, *177*
Atterbury, Grosvenor, 197
attics, 99, 101–2
Ayr Mount, North Carolina, *25*

Back Bay, Boston, Massachusetts, 180–82, *181*,
    274, 275
balloon-frame construction, 41, 45, 61–62, *62*
Baring, Cecil, 124
basements, 99
bathrooms, 96–97
Beacon Hill, Boston, Massachusetts, 180–83
beams, 71
Beaux-Arts style, 262, *269*
Benjamin, Asher, *American Builder's Companion*,
    13
Beyer Blinder Belle, 194–95
Blatteau, John, 178
boards and battens, 253
Boston Landmarks Commission (BLC), 182
Boston, Massachusetts, 177–78, *180*, 180–83,
    181

Boudon, Philippe, 50
braced-frame construction, 40–41, 60–61, *61*
Bradbury, Bruce, 21
Brand, Stewart, *How Buildings Learn*, 23, 31
Braun, John Frederick, 82
brick, 63–64, 256–59, *257*
Bridget Smith house, Ferromonte, New Jersey,
    43, *44*
British Thermal Units (BTUs), 172
broken ashlar, 262
Brown, Benjamin, 227
Brown, Bezaleel, 227
Brown, William T., 227
brownstone eczema, *69*, 69
brownstones, 12, 14, 188–94
building orientation, 37–39
building pathology, 55
building skeletons, 40–43, 59–64. *See also*
    building structure
building structure, 34, 40. *See also* building
    skeletons
building systems, 24. *See also* mechanical
    systems
built-ins, 32
Bulfinch, Charles, 180
bump-outs, 128
bungalows, 16–17, 90–91, *261*
Bunting, Bainbridge, 181

Burnham radiator company, 156
bustle back dormers, 90

Campbell, Edmund S., 227, 230
Cape May, New Jersey, 46–47
Carhart Mansion. *See* Amory S. Carhart
    Mansion, New York City
Carl Schurtz Park, New York City, 122
Carriage House, Somerset Hills, New Jersey,
    115, *116–18*, 117
casement windows, 246, *248*, 248
cast stone, 260
cedar, 238–39
ceilings, 72
Centennial Exhibition (1876), 236
central air conditioning, 161, 166
central heating, 161, 162
change, 28–30, 119–21
Charleston single houses, 38–39, 198
Charter for the New Urbanism, 273
Cherokee Construction, 84
Chestnut Hill, Pennsylvania, 274
chimneys, 70
chronologies, old house, 73–74
circulation, interior, 85–99, 161
circulator pump, 162, 163
city planning. *See* planning
civic responsibility, 273–75
clapboards, 252, *253*
Classic Radiator model, 156
Classical American Homes Preservation Trust, 25
classical style, 57
clay tile roofing, 236–38, *237*, 244
Cleveland Heights, Ohio, 39
climate, 37
coal, 160
Cochrane, H. H., 126
Coe, William R., 22
College of Charleston, 198
Colonial Revival houses, 59, 249, 252
Colonial Williamsburg, 257
comfort, 32, 155, 160–62
community organizations, 274
A Comparative Study of Philadelphia Rowhouses,
    179

composition roofing material, 244
compressor, 167, 169, 170
concealed-tank toilets, 96
concrete tile roofing, 244
condensers, 167, 172
conditions survey, 55
condominium building, Washington Street,
    Cape May, New Jersey, *47*, 47
Congress for the New Urbanism, 120, 274
connected farms, in Maine, *38*, *39*
connoisseurship, 25–26, 28, 30
Connolly, Brian, 194, 195, 197
conservation, 271, 275, 277
construction. *See also* building skeletons;
    building structure
        honesty in, 37
        limitations in, 41, 42
construction drawings, *73*
control relay, 157
convection heating, 162
cooling systems. *See* air conditioning
copper roofing, 241
corner-tank toilets, 96, *97*
Corto radiator model, 159
Cotswold-style house, Greenwich, Connecticut,
    145, *146–49*, 147, 149
cottage, ornée, 255
cottage sash windows, *251*
country estates, 19
Country Life in America (magazine), 142
coursed ashlar, 262
coursed rubble, 260
coursed stone construction, 42
courtyard houses, *57*, 57
cove siding, 253
Cox, Madison, 217
crack tell-tales, *66*, 66
cracks, 65–66, *70*, 70
The Craftsman (magazine), 17
craftsmanship
    connoisseurship regarding, 26
    conservation of, 276
    energy costs of, 23
    masonry, 258
    value of, 24
crown glass, 247

Cusano, Nick, Mendham, New Jersey house,
    101–4, 101–2, 104
Cusato, Marianne, *Get Your House Right*, 52
cylinder glass, 247

dashing, 265
Davis, Alexander Jackson, 253
decoration
    of facades, 49–53
    psychology of, 50
DeJean, Joan, 162
Dickerson, Mahlon, 43
discoloration of masonry, 68
Disneyland, 273
Donahue-Wood House, Norwich, Connecticut,
    13
door inspection, 71–72
dormers, 90
double house, 301–303 East Henry Street,
    Savannah, Georgia, *15*
double houses for miners, Ferromonte, New
    Jersey, 43–45, *44*
double-hung sash windows, 246, *248*, *249*
Downing, Andrew Jackson, 12, 14, 160, 253,
    255
    Country Houses, 253
drainage, 67
drop siding, 253
Du Pont family, 51
Duany, Andres, 273
ductless (split) air conditioning systems, 170
Dulany, Richard Henry, 213, 216
Dutch lap, 235

Eames, Charles and Rae, 110
Earth Day, 271
Edwards, Arthur Trystan, 51
Eichler homes, 99
electric circulator pump, 157
electricity, 164
Eljer, 96
embodied energy, 22–23, 270, 277
English country houses, 124
English Revival style houses, 246, 252

entrances, location of, 88, 138
environmental approach, 271–72
errors. *See* renovation errors
Estell Manor, Atlantic County, New Jersey, 51, *52*
ethylene propylene diene terpolymer (EPDM), 245
Evans, Edith, 82
evaporators, 167, 169, 170, 172
expansion of houses
    additions in keeping with the original, 120–54
    disjunctive approach to, 120, 123, 269
    issues concerning, 29–30
    materials used for, 255
    new spaces in old places, 75–118
    organic growth and, 31
    service wings, 76–85
    strategies for, 53–54
    traditional forms, 57–58
extrusion, 132

Fabbri, Ernesto, 197
Fabbri mansion, New York City, 196, 197
facades
    American townhouses, 188–204
    attached houses, 175–204
    Boston and Philadelphia, 177–83
    examples, *51*
    New York City, 188–97
    organic growth of, 49–53
    Soane House, 183–88
Fairfax, Anne, 128
farmsteads, 37–38, 149–50, 227–32, 272
faubourgs, 176
Federal Housing Administration, 18
Federal style houses, 251
fiber-cement shingles, 244
fifty-year upgrade cycle, 23, 32
Finn, Laurie, 79
fire stops, 62
fireplaces, 155, 160
float glass, 247
floors, 72
flow-control valves, 157

flow of space, 85–99, 161
Follansbee, 241
Folly Farm, Sullingstead, England, *126–28*, 126–27
forced-air heating, 161
Ford, Edward, 37
Forest Hills Gardens, New York City, 39
former parsonage, Madison, New Jersey, *49*
foundation, 67
foursquare houses, 56, *57*, 59
Frame/Harper House, Houston, Texas, *105–10*, 105, 108, 110–11
France, 273
Franklin, Benjamin, 160
Franklin stove, 160
freeze/thaw damage, 70
French method asphalt shingles, 242, *243*
French Norman house additions, Greensboro, North Carolina, *141–45*, 141–44
French Village, Chestnut Hill, Pennsylvania, 145
front-gabled one-story houses, 56, *57*
front-gabled two-story houses, 56, *57*
Fuller, Buckminster, 20
fungus, 71

garages, 205–11, *206–13*, 213
gas companies, 164
Gatewood house. *See* William C. Gatewood House, Charleston, South Carolina
George A. Nickerson House, Boston, Massachusetts, *180*
George F. Baker house, New York, dining room, *27*
George Vail House, Willow Hall, Morristown, *14*
Georgian houses, *249*, 249
geothermal systems, 170–73, *171*
German siding, 253
GI Bill, 18
Gibson House, Boston, Massachusetts, 182
Gilmartin, Greg, 216
Glassie, Henry, 43
Gold, Stephen, 160
Goldsmith-Spencer house, Madison, New Jersey, 132, *133–35*, 134–36

Gothic House, Glen Ridge, New Jersey, *111–14*, 111, 113–15
Gothic Revival houses, 246, 253
Gowans, Alan, 176
Gracie, Archibald, 122
Gracie Mansion, New York City, *122–24*, 122–24
grading, 67
graduated slate roofs, *235*, 235
grammar, of roofs, 46–49
gravity hot-water heating, 161
Great Britain, house facades in, 176, 187
Great Dixter, England, 127
Greek Revival cottage, Old Chatham, New York, *13*
Greek Revival house, Camden, Maine, *13*
Greek Revival houses, 12, 13, 56, *57*, 91, 93, 251, 252
green building. *See* sustainability
Greenberg, Allan, 33
    Guilford, Connecticut house, *100*, 101
Greenfields, 37
greenhouse-gas reduction treaty, 271
Grenfell, Milton, 141–42, 144
growth. *See* organic growth

Hale, Jonathan, *The Old Way of Seeing*, 52
half-baths, 96–97
Hall-Wister houses, Philadelphia, *182*
Handlin, David, 175
Harrison, Robert
Haviland, John, 178
Hayden, Dolores, *Field Guide to Sprawl*, 37
Head, Peter, 276
heat exchange, 157
heat-load calculation, 156
heating systems, 155–65
    calculating need for, 156
    development of, 160–61
    geothermal alternative, 170–73
    hot water heater accessory, 162–63
    hot-water zones, 157
    issues in adding to, 156–57
    kickspace heaters, 163
    outdoor reset controls, 163–65
    parlor heaters, 164–65

radiant heating zones, 162
radiators, 158–61
thermostatic radiator valves, 165
Hegel, G.W.F., 267, 268
Heinle, Edwin, 115, 117
heritage conservation, 272–73
Herman Nelson Invisible Radiator, 161
Heun, Arthur, 207
hexagonal tab asphalt shingles, 242
hierarchy, architectural, 188
high-tank toilets, 96
high-velocity air conditioning systems, 167, *168*, 169–70
Hiland Hall Turner Associates, 115
Hirshorn, Paul, 178
Historic American Buildings Survey, 65
historic districts, 59, 273
Historic New England, 182
historic preservation, 16
and change, 28–31, 119
and disjunctive additions/renovations, 120, 123, 269
history of, 20–21
requirements concerning, 28, 268
sustainability and, 23–24, 270
and theory of history, 268
U.S. vs. European concepts of, 19, 22
Historical Directory of American Architects (American Institute of Architects), 73
historical value, 22
historicism, 268
historiography, 267–68
Hodgson, 206
home improvement, 11. *See also* renovation; restoration
home offices, 76
hot water heater accessory, 162–63
hot-water zones, 157
house forms/types, 56–57, *57*
housing
mass, 35
Modernist, 35
psychology of, 50
Hubka, Thomas, 37
humidity, 172
Hunter, Christine, 176–77

Hussey, Christopher, 124
hydronic systems, 156–65

I-houses, 45, 56–57, *57*
ice and water underlayments, 245
identity, of houses, 49–53, 175–204
incandescent heaters, 164
Industrial Revolution, 35, 251
inspections, 67–72
doors, 71–72
foundation, 67
grading, slope, and drainage, 67
interiors, 72
masonry, 68–70
roof, 67–68
site, 67
vegetation, 67
windows, 71–72
wood, 70–71
Institute for Classical Architecture and Classical America, 268
interior inspection, 72
interlocking asphalt shingles, 242, *243*
iron exfoliation, 70
Italian style, 262
Ives, Charles, 140

Jackson, J. B., 206
Jefferson, Thomas, 43, 128, 160, 227
Jenrette, Richard, 25–26
jerkinhead roof, 137
Johnson, Larry, 90
Johnson Partnership, 90–91
Johnson, Philip, De Menil house, Houston, Texas, 108
Joint Center for Housing Studies, Harvard University, 11

Katrina Cottage, 52
Kelly, Jim, 21
Kennedy-Grant, Philip, 149, 151, 153, 223, 226–27
kickspace heaters, *163*, 163

Klauder, Charles Z., 81, 82, 84
Kniffen, Fred, 43
Kunstler, James Howard, 119

Labine, Clem, 21
LaGuardia, Fiorello, 122
Lambay Castle, Ireland, 124, *125*, 126
Lamdin, William, 141, 144
laminated asphalt shingles, 242–43
land-use laws, 19
Landmarks Preservation Commission, New York City, 188, 191, 194
landscape, 37
Le Corbusier, 50
lead roofing, 241
lean-to additions, *58*, 58
Lee, Duncan, 123
Leschi addition renovation, Seattle, Washington, *85*, *87–89*, 90–91, *91*
Levitt Brothers, "The Rancher" model, Bowie, Maryland, *18*
Levitt, William, 99
Levittown house, Long Island, New York, *18*
Levittown, Long Island, New York, 18, 99
life cycles of houses
and fifty-year upgrades, 23, 32
organic, 31
and twenty-five year upgrades, 34
understanding, 55–56
lighting, 164
lime-sand mortars, 258
lime stucco, 264
Lindeberg, Harrie T., 207, 209–11
Seth Thomas House, Morristown, New Jersey, *77–81*, *78–79*, 81
Lindisfarne Castle, England, 127
lintels, 71
Littlepond, Bedminster, New Jersey, 149–50, *150–53*, 153–54
local historic districts, 59
log cabins, 35–36, *36*
London, terrace houses in, 176
Long House, Mattapoisett, Massachusetts, 91, *92–95*, 93–94, *97–98*, 97
Long Island, New York, 19, 132

longue durée (long view), 267, 269, 275–76
Louis XIV, 162
Louis XV, 162
low-profile toilets, 97
Lowenthal, David, 119–20
Lutyens, Edwin, 123, 124, 126–27
    Folly Farm addition, Sullingstead,
        England, *126–28*, 126–27
    Lambay Castle addition, Ireland, 124, *125*,
        126
Lycée Français, 194

Mactavish, Cameron, 137
Madison, James, 51
Magnesite stucco, 264
mail-order houses, 16, *17*
Marcus, Clare Cooper, *House as a Mirror of Self,*
    50
Mark Alan Hewitt Architects, 132, 188
Mark P. Finley Architects, 230–32
Marks, Richard "Moby," 198–99
Martin, Steve, 162
masonry construction, 41–42, *42*, 63–64, 258–
    63. *See also* brick
masonry inspection, 68–69
masons, 259
matched flush siding, 252–53
materials, 233–65
    bricks and mortar, 256–59
    connoisseurship regarding, 26, 28
    differentiation of, 254–55
    importance of, 233
    integrity of, 42
    roofing, 234–46
    stone, 258–63
    stucco, 263–65
    windows, 246–52
    wood claddings, 252–56
Matero, Frank, 192
mattress radiators, 160
May, Cliff, ranch house, West Los Angeles,
    California, *18*
McAllister, Lee, 46
McAllister, Virginia, 46
McHarg, Ian, *Design with Nature,* 277

McKim, Charles, 180
McKim, Mead & White, George A. Nickerson
    House, Boston, *180*
McMansions, 43, 138, 272
measured drawings, 65
measurement of building, 64–66
mechanical systems. *See also* building systems
    air conditioning, 165–73
    changing nature of, 24
    geothermal alternative, 170–73
    heating, 156–65
    updating, 33–34, 155–74
Mediterranean Revival houses, 236
Meigs, Arthur, 142
Mellon, Mrs. Paul (Bunny), 219
Mellon, Paul, 227
membrane roofs, 245
Merton, Zachary, 127
metal roofing, 241–42
metal shingles, 241–42
Mid-Atlantic Capes, 56, *57*
Miller, Howard, 90
Mills, Robert, 178
Milner, John, 81–82, 84–85
miners, double houses for, Ferromonte, New
    Jersey, 43–45, *44*
mini-duct air conditioning systems, 167, *168*,
    169–70
mistakes. *See* renovation errors
mixing valve, 162, 163
Modernism
    American Institute of Architects and, 268
    attitude of, toward the past, 115, 120, 267
    and honesty in construction, 37
    housing of, 50
    and planning, 274
    roof treatments in, 46
    and technology, 35, 36
modified bitumen roofing, 245
modules, 43–46
moisture detection, *66*, 66. *See also* rising damp
monolithic structural systems, 40
Montclair, New Jersey, 274
Montespan, Marquise de, 162
Monticello, 160
Montpelier, 51

Mook, Robert, 188
Moore, Charles, 186
    "You Have to Pay for the Public Life," 273
Morris, William, 64
mortar, 69, 256–59
Moses, Robert, 122
moss, *68*
Mount Fair, Albemarle County, Virginia, 227–
    32, *228–31*
Mount Vernon, *33*
mudrooms, 205
Mumford, Lewis, 29
Murcutt, Glenn, 35
Murray, John, 145, 219–20, 223

natatorium, 223–27
National Parks Service, 120
National Register historic districts, 59
National Register of Historic Places, 227, 229,
    255
National Trust for Historic Preservation, 178,
    194
Neoclassical houses, 12
Neuhaus & Taylor, 105
new construction, 276
New England Capes, 56, *57*
New England farmsteads, 37–38, *38*, *39*
New Orleans, Louisiana, 183, 275
New Urbanism, 120, 273
New York, New York, 188–97, 275
New York Times, 215
Noguchi, Isamu, 110
nonresidential spaces converted to residential,
    115–18
novelty siding, 253
nun's hat roof, 137
Nutt, Haller, 213

Oakley Farm, Upperville, Virginia, *10*, 213,
    214–19, 215–19
Old City, Philadelphia, Pennsylvania, 273, 275
Old-House Journal (magazine), 21, 29, 49
old houses, 12
Old Santa Fe, New Mexico, 274

Olmsted Brothers, 145, 223
Olmsted, Frederick Law, 145
125 Garfield, Pine Hill, Madison, New Jersey, 47, *48*
open floor plans, 161
organic growth, 31–54
    building skeletons and, 40–43
    expansion strategies in keeping with, 53–54
    facades and, 49–53
    and history, 268
    life cycles in, 31
    logic of, 31
    modules and, 43–46
    parameters of, 35–37
    process of, 31–32
    roof shapes and, 46–49
    sites and, 37–40
    understanding your house's, 55–56
    vernacular architecture and, 35–36
organic growth patterns, 16
ornamental concrete block, 64
outbuildings, 53, 115–18, 205–32
    farm renovations, 227–32
    garages, 205–11
    swimming pools and pavilions, 212–27
outdoor reset controls, 163–65

paint, 34
paint inspection, *71*, 71
Palladian windows, *248*, 248–49
Palladio, Andrea, 43
Palladio Award, 197, 219
parlor heaters, 164–65
past, concern for, 120–22, 267
patio houses, *57*, 57
patrimony, 119
pattern language, 35, 43
pebble-dash, 265
Pennoyer, Peter, 213, 215, 216, 218
Pennsylvania Station, New York, New York, 20
Period Homes (magazine), 219
Pessac, Modernist housing complex at, 50
Philadelphia, Pennsylvania, 177–80, *178*, *179*, *182*, 273, 275
piazzas, 39

picture windows, 248
Picturesque movement, 14, 223, 253
picturesque sash windows, *251*
Pierce, Butler, & Pierce Manufacturers, 158
place, 119–20, 144, 145, 154, 258, 260
planning
    in America, 38–39
    and civic values, 273–74
    environmental approach to, 271–72
plans, 32
Planting Fields, Long Island, New York, *22*
plaster, 26, 28, 72
Plater-Zyberk, Elizabeth, 273
platform-frame construction, 62–63, *63*
Pompadour, Marquise de, 162
Poolhouse, Connecticut, *6*
pools. *See* swimming pools and pavilions
Poore, Patricia, 21
porches, 39
Portland cement mortars, 258
Portland cement stucco, 264
powder rooms, 96–97
Prairie School houses, 59, 248, 252, 263
preservation. *See* historic preservation
pressed bricks, 256
profile tiles, 236
proportion
    building skeletons and, 41
    importance of, 52
    in traditional architecture, 52
psychology, of housing, 50
public realm, 273–75

Queen Anne style houses, *255*, 255–56

Radford, 16
radiant heating zones, 162
radiators, *156*, 156, *158*, 158–61, *160*
Radnor addition, Main Line Philadelphia, Pennsylvania, *136–40*, 136–40
railroad suburbs, 39, 274
Rajkovich, Thomas Norman, 207–8
ranch houses, 18
"The Rancher" model, Bowie, Maryland, *18*
Randolph, A. C., 213

Randolph, Theodora Ayer, 215
random-coursed ashlar, 262
Readi-cut bungalow, sold by Aladdin, *17*
rear el additions, *58*, 58
reflector heaters, 164
Reliance Model radiator, *158*
remuddling, 16, 29, 49
renovation. *See also* home improvement; renovation errors; restoration
    disjunctive approach to, 120, 123, 269
    do-it-yourself, 29
    government guidelines for, 255, 268
    professional, 29–30
    respectful, 29, 51, 114–15, 117, 123, 230–31
    updating building systems, 155–74
    zoning and, 50
renovation errors
    ignorance of history/tradition, 29, 52
    interior circulation, 85
    materials and craft traditions, 26
    mechanical systems, 155
    roof treatments, 49
    technology, 24
repair cycles
    fifty-year, 23, 32
    twenty-five-year, 34
replacement windows, 24
reproduction architecture, 28
research, on building history, 73–74
respect
    for craftsmanship, 82
    for materials, 42, 233
    for the past, 121
    renovation guided by, 29, 51, 114–15, 117, 123, 230–31
    for the site, 40
restoration. *See also* home improvement; renovation
    of brick and mortar, 259
    intention of, 29
Revere, Paul, 241
reverse makeovers, 104–15
ribbon coursing, 256
Richardson, Henry Hobson, 255
Richardsonian Romanesque, 236, 262
Ridder, Katie, 215, 216

Righter, Jim, 91, 93–94
rising damp, 69–70. *See also* moisture detection
River Oaks, Houston, Texas, 145
Robinson, Karin, 111
Roland Park, Baltimore, Maryland, 39, 145
romantic style, 57
roof inspection, 67–68, *68*
roof pitches, 41, 42
roof shapes, 46–49
roof types, *47*
roofing materials, 234–46
    asphalt, 240, 242–44
    clay tile, 236–38
    homeowner's changing of, 245
    membrane roofs, 245
    metal, 241–42
    slate, 234–36
    substitute, 244
    wood shingles, 238–41
rowhouses, 176–83, *177*
rubber shingles, 244
rubble stonework, 42, *43*, 260, *261*, 262
Rumford, Benjamin Thompson, Count, 160
Rumford fireplace, 160
Ruskin, John, 121
Rybczynski, Witold, 32
Rypkema, Donovan, 24

Saarinen, Eero, 110
saltbox houses, 56, *57*
salvage brick, 259
Sammons, Richard, 128
Sanborn Fire Insurance maps, 73
sandblasting, *69*, 69
sash windows, 246
Schafer, Gil, 198–99
Schmidt, Mott B., 122–24
Sears house, Rumson, New Jersey, *16*
Sears "Modern Home No. 145," *17*
Sears, Roebuck and Co., 16, 64, 206
Seaside, Florida, 273, *274*
Seasonal Energy Efficiency Ratio (SEER), 172
Seattle bungalow, *85*
Second Empire style, 234
Second Empire style house, New York, *15*
Secretary of the Interior, 244, 255, 268

seeds (glass), 247
Sellers, Paul, *276*
Semes, Steven, 268
service wings, 29, 76–85, 90
Seth Thomas House, Morristown, New Jersey, *77–81*, 78–79, 81, *266*
74 Perry Street, New York City, 188, *189–93*, 191–92, 194
Shaker Heights, Ohio, 274
shakes, 238, *239*, 239
Shaw, Howard Van Doren, 207
Shaw, Richard Norman, 255
shawl (glass), 247
shearing layers, 23, 24, *32*, 32–34
shed-roof additions, *58*, 58
sheet lead roofing, 241
Shingle Style, 251, 256
Shingled cottage, Quogue, New York, 128, *129–31*, 131–32
shingles
    asphalt, 242–44
    inspection of, 71
    metal, 241–42
    recent materials for, 244
    wood, *238–40*, 238–41, 253–56
Short Hills, New Jersey, 39
side-gabled saltbox houses, 56, *57*
side-gabled two-story houses, 56, *57*
siding, 71
Simpson, John, 195–97
single-cell Virginia farmhouse, *44*
sites, 37–40
skin-and-skeleton construction
    origins of, 40
    structural repair of, 34
slate roofing, *234–36*, 234–36, 244
Sloan, Samuel
    Longwood, Natchez, Mississippi, 213
    The Model Architect, 213
slope, 67
Smith, John Charles, 81
snout houses, 213
Soane House, London, England, 183–88, *184–87*
Soane, John, 183, 197
Sogno Mio, Philadelphia, Pennsylvania, 81–82, *82–84*, 84–85, *86*

Soleri, Paolo, 20
Spain, 273
spatial modules. *See* modules
spatter-dash, 265
speaking tubes, *65*
St. Mark's Episcopal Church, Mendham, New Jersey, *45*, 46
stairways, 88
Standards for Rehabilitation, 255
Starr, Frederick, 176
steam heat. *See* hydronic systems
Stern and Bucek, 105, 108, 110
Stern, William F., 105
stewardship, 19, 22–23
Stick Style, 255
Stickley, Gustav, 16–17
Stilgoe, John, 37
stone bearing walls, 41–42, *42*, 63–64, 258–63
stone veneer walls, 42, *43*
streetcar suburbs, 39, 274
stress gauges, *66*, 66
structure. *See* building structure
stucco, *263*, 263–65
studs, 61–62
styles, house, 58–59, 175–76, 181–82
suburban tract houses, 12, 18, 37
suburbs, planning of, 39, 274
Sunset Magazine, 18
Susan B. Wagner Wing, Gracie Mansion, New York City, *122–24*, 122–24
sustainability, 16
    of earth's resources, 271
    in the future, 276–77
    geothermal alternative and, 170–73
    growing interest in, 269–70, 276
    historic preservation and, 23–24, 270
    planning and, 271–73
    and traditional architecture, 35
swales, 67
swimming pools and pavilions, *6*, 212–27, *217*, *220–27*

Taconic Builders, 191
tax laws, 19
Taylor, Harwood, 105, 108
TCS III roofing, 241

technology
    American embrace of, 121
    Modernism and, 35
    recent, 24, 33
    traditional, 26
tell-tales, 66
termites, 71
terne metal roof, 241
terrace houses, 176, 187
textural roofs, *235*, 235
thatch-effect roofs, *240*, 240
thermostatic radiator valves, 165
thermostats, 157, 165
three-tab asphalt shingles, 242
timber-frame construction, 40–41, 59–60, *60*,
    209–10
Timber Framers Guild, 209–10
tin roofing, 241
toilets, 96–97
Tontine Crescent, Boston, Massachusetts, 180
transitions, between living areas, *86*
Trumbauer, Horace, 194, 197
Tudor house, Morristown, New Jersey, *2*
Twain, Mark, 120
Twin-Flo kickspace heater, *163*
typology of houses, 56–57, *57*

uncoursed rubble, 42, *43*, 260, 262
understanding your house, 55–74
    building skeletons, 59–64
    chronologies, 73–74
    house forms/types, 56–57
    materials and conditions assessment,
        64–72
    style, 58–59
    time factors in, 55–56
    traditional addition forms, 57–58
unit repetition additions, *58*, 58
United Kingdom, 272
United States, attitudes toward the past in, 121
updating, 33–34, 75, 155–74
Upperville Colt and Horse Show, 213
Upton, Dell, 176
urban planning. *See* planning
urban renewal, 39

useable past, 19
utopian communities, 16

values, 19, 22–23, 269–71
Van Liew-Suydam farmhouse, Middlebush, New
    Jersey, *14*
Van Sykel Inn, New Jersey, *169*
Vaughan Williams, Ralph, 124
vegetation, 67, 68
Venice Charter (1964), 268
Verity, Simon, 149
vernacular architecture
    masonry construction in, 41–42
    modern changes to, 35
    modules in, 43
    and organic growth, 35–36
    sites for, 37
    timber-frame construction in, 40–41
    in traditional societies, 35
vestigial house parts, 65
Victorian houses, 20–21, 29, 46–47, 59, 234, *255*
Victorian T-gabled farmhouses, *57*, 57
villas, 12, 14
vintage houses
    care/neglect of, 19–23, 28–30
    characteristics of, 12
    defined, 11
    future of, 275–77
    modern lifestyles and, 29, 75
    value of, 270–71, 277
Virginia, landscape of, 227
Virginia modular layouts, 43, *44*
Voith & Mactavish Architects, 136–37, 139

Wagner, Robert, 122
wallboard, 28
walls, 72
water erosion, 68
waterproofing, 99
wavy glass, 247
Welsbach mantle, 164
Western framing. *See* platform-frame
    construction
White, Stanford, 180

Whitman, Walt, 175
Wilder, Laura Ingalls, 36
William C. Gatewood House, Charleston, South
    Carolina, *198–204*, 198–99, 204
Wilson, Henry, 90
window inspection, 71–72
window units, air-conditioning, 165
windows, 246–52
    by era, 249–52
    guidelines for, 246
    homeowners' changing of, 250
    replacement, 24
    by type, 246, 248–49
    wavy glass, 247
wing and hyphen additions, *58*, 58
wings, 141–54
Winsor Farms, Richmond, Virginia, 145
wood claddings, 252–56
wood inspection, 70–71
wood shingles, *238–40*, 238–41, 244, 253–56
Wright, Frank Lloyd, 32, 246
Wright, Mark, 111

zeitgeist, 268
Zivkovic Associates Architects, 195
zoning, 39–40, 50, 191